GERMANY FR
REPUBLIC,

POLITICS, HIERA

MATTHEW S. S
RODERICK

GERMANY FROM
1918

First published 2000 by
MACMILLAN PRESS LTD
Houndmills, Basingstoke, Hampshire RG21 6XS
and London
Companies and representatives
throughout the world

ISBN 0–333–72684-7 hardcover
ISBN 0–333–72685-5 paperback

A catalogue record for this book is available
from the British Library.

This book is printed on paper suitable for recycling and
made from fully managed and sustained forest sources.

10   9   8   7   6   5   4   3   2   1
09   08   07   06   05   04   03   02   01   00

Printed in Hong Kong

Published in the United States of America by
ST. MARTIN'S PRESS, LLC.,
Scholarly and Reference Division,
175 Fifth Avenue, New York, N.Y. 10010

ISBN 0–312–23292-6 (cloth)
ISBN 0–312–23293-4 (paper)

Germany from Reich to Republic, 1871–1918

Politics, Hierarchy and Elites

Matthew S. Seligmann and Roderick R. McLean

First published 2000 by
MACMILLAN PRESS LTD
Houndmills, Basingstoke, Hampshire RG21 6XS
and London
Companies and representatives
throughout the world

ISBN 0–333–72684-7 hardcover
ISBN 0–333–72685-5 paperback

A catalogue record for this book is available from the British Library.

This book is printed on paper suitable for recycling and made from fully managed and sustained forest sources.

10 9 8 7 6 5 4 3 2 1
09 08 07 06 05 04 03 02 01 00

Printed in Hong Kong

Published in the United States of America by
ST. MARTIN'S PRESS, LLC.,
Scholarly and Reference Division,
175 Fifth Avenue, New York, N.Y. 10010

ISBN 0–312–23292-6 (cloth)
ISBN 0–312–23293-4 (paper)

CONTENTS

ACKNOWLEDGEMENTS

The authors would like to take this opportunity to thank all the many people who helped them in the production of this volume. First of all, we acknowledge the role played by our students, whose preferences concerning topics of study did much to inform the contents of this book. In addition, we would like to thank Professor John Röhl for his constant encouragement and Professor Jeremy Black for his thoughtful suggestions about the text. Mention also needs to be made of Dr Matthew Hughes, whose skill in reducing excess verbiage was much appreciated, Dr Annika Mombauer for sharing her ideas on Schlieffen and Moltke, and Dr Karina Urbach for rushing us an advance copy of her article on Bismarck biographies. To Terka Bagley at the publishers we express our appreciation of her patience and forbearance. Finally, we are very grateful to those who afforded us access to archival material. The syndics of Cambridge University Library granted permission to quote from the Hardinge papers. The Rosebery papers and the Haldane papers in the National Library of Scotland are reproduced with permission of the Keeper of the Records of Scotland. Crown copyright material in the Public Record Office is reproduced by permission of the Controller of Her Majesty's Stationery Office. Material was also found at the Politisches Archiv des Auswärtigen Amtes in Bonn and the Geheime Staatsarchiv in Berlin.

LIST OF ABBREVIATIONS

ADV	Alldeutscher Verband
BD	G. P. Gooch and Harold Temperley (eds), *British Documents on the Origins of the War* (11 vols, London, 1926–38)
BdL	Bund der Landwirte
DKG	Deutsche Kolonial Gesellschaft
EK	John C. G. Röhl (ed.), *Philipp Eulenburgs Politische Korrespondenz* (3 vols, Boppard am Rhein, 1976)
FO	Foreign Office
GP	Johannes Lepsius *et al.* (eds), *Die Große Politik der Europäische Kabinette 1871–1914: Sammlung der Diplomatischen Akten des Auswärtigen Amtes* (40 vols, Berlin, 1922–27)
GStA	Geheimes Staatsarchiv
HA	Haus Archiv
HP	Norman Rich and M. H. Fisher (eds), *The Holstein Papers* (4 vols, Cambridge, 1955–63)
OHL	Oberste Heeresleitung
PA	Politisches Archiv des Auswärtigen Amtes
PRO	Public Record Office
SPD	Sozialdemokratische Partei Deutschlands

LIST OF SIGNIFICANT DATES

1871	January	German Empire proclaimed in Versailles
	May	Treaty of Frankfurt
	July	*Kulturkampf* begins in Prussia
1872	June	Jesuits expelled from Germany
1873	October	*Dreikaiserbund*
1878	June	Congress of Berlin begins
	October	Anti-Socialist Law passed
1879	July	German Protectionist Laws introduced
	October	Austro-German Alliance
1884	April	First German protectorate in Africa proclaimed
1887	June	Reinsurance Treaty with Russia
1888	March	Death of Wilhelm I
	June	Reign of Kaiser Wilhelm II begins
1890	March	Fall of Bismarck
		Caprivi appointed Chancellor
	June	Reinsurance Treaty expires
	July	Heligoland–Zanzibar Treaty
	October	Anti-Socialist Law expires
1891	April	Foundation of the Pan-German League
	August	Franco-Russian *Entente*
1892	August	Franco-Russian Military Convention
1893	February	Foundation of the Bund der Landwirte
	July	German Army Bill
	December	Russia ratifies Dual Alliance
1894	October	Resignation of Caprivi
		Hohenlohe appointed Chancellor
1895	June	Kiel Canal opens
1896	January	Kruger Telegram
	July	German Civil Law Code passed
1897	June	Appointment of Tirpitz to the Reich Naval Office
	October	Appointment of Bülow as Foreign Secretary
1898	April	First Naval Law

1900	June	Supplementary Naval Law
	October	Bülow appointed Chancellor
1902	December	New Tariff Law
1903	June	Reichstag elections
1904	January	Herero Rising in South-West Africa
	April	*Entente Cordiale*
	September	Hottentot rising in South-West Africa
1905	March	Wilhelm II lands at Tangiers
	July	Björkö Treaty
	December	Schlieffen's Great Memorandum completed
1906	January	Moltke appointed Chief of the General Staff
	April	Dismissal of Holstein
	June	Third Naval Law
	December	Reichstag opposes spending on colonial wars
1907	January	Reichstag elections
	August	Anglo-Russian *Entente*
1908	June	Fourth Naval Law
	October	*Daily Telegraph* Affair
1909	June	Fall of Bülow
	July	Bethmann Hollweg appointed Chancellor
1911	July	SMS *Panther* arrives at Agadir
1912	January	Reichstag elections
	February	Haldane mission
	June	Army Law
	December	'War Council'
1913	January	Jagow appointed Foreign Secretary
	June	Army Law
	November	Zabern Incident
1914	June	Enlarged Kiel Canal opens
		Assassination of Franz Ferdinand in Sarajevo
	July	Austrian ultimatum to Serbia
	August	Germany declares war on Russia and France
	September	Battle of the Marne
		Bethmann Hollweg's 'September Programme' written
	November	Falkenhayn appointed Chief of the General Staff
1916	March	Resignation of Tirpitz
	August	Hindenburg appointed Chief of the General Staff
	November	Resignation of Jagow
	December	Auxiliary Service Law

MAPS

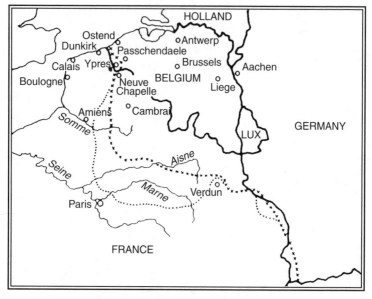

···· Limit of the German advance in 1914
▪▪▪▪▪ The trench line for most of the war

Map 1 The western front during the First World War.
Source: Taken From Norman Lowe, *Mastering Modern World History* (Macmillan, London, 1982).

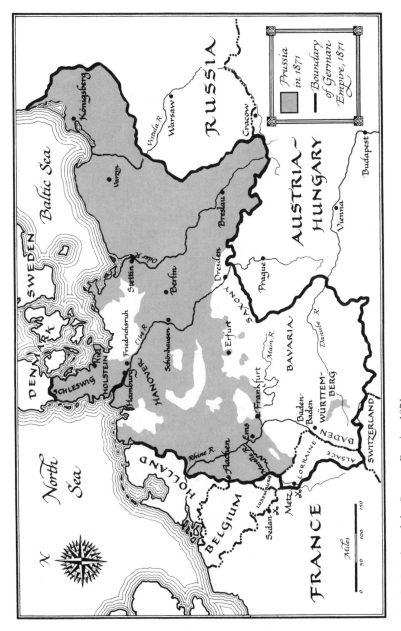

Map 2　Prussia and the German Empire, 1871.
Source: Taken from Edward Crankshaw, *Bismarck* (Macmillan, London, 1981).

INTRODUCTION

The purpose of this volume is to provide an approachable guide to the political development of Germany during the years of the Second Reich, that is to say in the period between 1871 and 1918. Since the Second World War, this topic has been the focus of considerable academic scrutiny. Ironically, the initial reason for a substantial part of this work had as much, if not more, to do with scholarly interest in a later period of German history – namely the Nazi era – than with any direct concern with the Kaiserreich itself. The desire to explain the National Socialist phenomenon and to determine whether and to what degree there was a pre-history to Hitler and the Third Reich led some scholars, in their search for the antecedents of dictatorship and aggression, inexorably back to the regimes of Bismarck and Wilhelm II.

In more recent years, the Kaiserreich has been evaluated more for its own sake. However, in a bizarre twist, while Bismarckian and Wilhelmine Germany have returned to their rightful place in the mainstream of historical scrutiny, the approach to their study has tended to depart radically from traditional methodological mores. Instead, this era of German history has served as a proving ground for all sorts of new, and often exciting, approaches to historical analysis. While in many ways very different from each other, these new historical methodologies have exhibited one consistent feature. Structural history, the social history of politics, critical social history, *Alltagsgeschichte* and the new cultural history have all been less concerned with political than with social and economic conditions. Drawn from the 'critical social sciences', they are based on the proposition that historical development, even in the realm of politics, can best be evaluated against the prevailing socio-economic circumstances. In embracing this conclusion, the proponents of these various methodologies have been motivated not only by scholarly adventurism and the desire to embroil themselves in new theories, but also, in part, by the wish to break with an old epistemology that they deemed to be discredited and unsatisfactory. The epistemology in question was the traditional approach of the German historical fraternity, which was very much centred on political history. Emphasizing the primacy of foreign policy and the autonomy of the political process, this tradition concentrated almost exclusively on the decision-making of a narrow elite. While there is nothing intrinsically wrong with such a focus, the same could not be said about the uses to which the resultant histories were regularly put. Before the Second World War, all too many German historians saw the task of their profession as the validation of the German national mission. Historians such as Treitschke, whose nationalism was so extreme that British wartime propagandists could cite him unadulterated in their campaigns to discredit the aims of their German enemy, used their writings to glorify Prussia's history of conquest and to call for the united Germany to follow these historical footsteps into an expansionist future. A hero in his lifetime, after two unimaginably destructive world wars, Treitschke's brand of historical presentation held little charm for the new generation of German historians, who deliberately sought to distance themselves from this methodological model. Unfortunately, in their ideological revulsion at the manner in which political history had been abused by past generations, they developed a disdain for political history as a genre. As a result, the desire to use methodological approaches radically different from the ones employed by their predecessors, led to a strong emphasis on economic and social history. This has proven very fruitful in all sorts of ways. Yet, it, too, can be taken too far. It is questionable, for example, whether German history is best explained, *de rigueur*, through the prism of Weber, Gramsci and Habermas, as some historians now seem to believe. In this context, it is worth asking: is it not time to revisit the political history of the Kaiserreich and to present it in an up-to-date form?

It is this setting that provides the justification for this volume. Accordingly, the analysis it will present involves a return to political history. While in no sense devaluing other methodologies, it will approach the critical evaluation of the Kaiserreich from the premise that personalities mattered, that politics was often given shape by elites and that key decisions could, and often were, made that went against the grain of socio-economic factors. As a result, the synthesis that it provides will focus unashamedly on the political process. It will take as its watchword the dictum of Derek Beales that 'when a great historian can mistake a person for a trend, when it is thought more important to analyse social background than opinions, then the time has come for a reaction'.[1]

1

THE NEW EMPIRE

Geography and People

The new German Empire which came into existence in 1871 was a sizeable entity. It covered a geographical area of over 200000 square miles, and contained almost 41 million inhabitants, a figure that would rise to nearly 65 million by 1910.[1] The Reich stretched from the French and Belgian borders in the west to the edge of the Russian Empire in the east, and encompassed extensive territories which are today located in Poland. Its geographical position in the middle of Europe made the Empire vulnerable to attack on two fronts, something which Bismarck's diplomacy in the years prior to his dismissal sought successfully to avoid, but a fact which was lost sight of by Wilhelm II and his advisers in the years leading up to the outbreak of the Great War in 1914. Given the great territorial expanse of the Reich, it is also little wonder that the climate varied considerably between western Germany, where it was temperate, and the eastern borderlands which had a continental climate reminiscent of the neighbouring Russian Empire. The landscape varied to a greater extent between the northern and southern parts of the Reich. The flat lands of the North European plain were characteristic of northern Germany, whereas the south consisted predominantly of upland regions which culminated in the Alpine landscapes of upper Bavaria.

Patterns of landownership differed between west and east. In western, and also southern Germany, small farms were common, whereas east of the River Elbe, in Brandenburg, Mecklenburg, Pomerania and the provinces of Prussia and Posen, large agricultural estates producing rye were the norm, owned by a class of landowners known as *Junkers*, and farmed by agricultural labourers, who were more often Polish than German in the eastern frontier districts. A further division was between the industrial conurbations of central and western Germany, and the small towns and rural life characteristic of the south and east of the Reich. This division was overlain by a cultural one between a Protestant core, and a Catholic periphery. One historian has gone so far as to talk of Catholic Germany as a Teutonic equivalent of Britain's 'Celtic fringe',[2] as the large Catholic minority was concentrated in the east, west and south of the new Empire, in Prussian Poland, upper Silesia, the Rhineland, Baden and Bavaria.

The new Empire was smaller than it might have been because it excluded millions of Germans in the Habsburg Empire. This was partly a result of Austrian policy, for during and after the 1848 revolution the Austrians had set themselves against German nationalism as they appreciated that a German nation state would necessitate their giving up their considerable non-German-speaking territory. However, the exclusion of German-speaking Austria from the Reich of 1871 occurred largely as a result of Austria's defeat at the hands of Prussia in the struggle for mastery in Germany of the 1860s. Prussia's victory over Austria at the Battle of Königgratz in 1866 had effectively paved the way for the division of Germany between the two powers, with the vast majority of the German-speaking lands falling within the Prussian sphere of influence. The German Empire of 1871 was thus a *Kleindeutschland* (little Germany) rather than a *Grossdeutschland* (greater Germany) as it excluded several parts of the historic German confederation, which lay on the Austrian side of the frontier.

While Great Power politics had been a major factor behind this outcome, one other pressure also played a role. Bismarck and the German liberals who together engineered national unification actually preferred the *Kleindeutschland* solution to the *Grossdeutschland* one. For the Prussian elite in general, and Bismarck in particular, an Empire which excluded Austria could be controlled more easily from Berlin. This reflected their conception of unification as the expansion of Prussia's control within Germany, encapsulated in Bismarck's declaration that 'there is nothing more German than Prussian particularism properly understood'.[3] As far as the anti-clerical liberals were concerned, and to a lesser extent the Prussians as well, a 'little Germany' was preferable as it would have a secure and permanent Protestant majority, in contrast to a 'Greater Germany', where Protestants and Catholics would have been much more evenly divided as a result of the predominance of Catholics in the German-speaking parts of the Habsburg Empire.

None the less, the divide between Catholics and Protestants was to prove one of the new Reich's major sources of weakness, particularly in the first three decades of its existence. The apparatus of the state, despite its federal character, was dominated by Prussian Protestants, and in Prussia itself, which contained 60 per cent of the Empire's population, Catholics were actively discriminated against. Indeed in the 1870s a *Kulturkampf* was directed against the Catholic Church in Prussia by the state bureaucracy, with the support of liberal politicians. Catholics came to feel like pariahs in their own homeland, as the Catholic art historian August Reichensperger indicated when he declared: 'we ultramontanes are all to some extent unclean'.[4] It is little wonder therefore that many Catholics felt little loyalty towards what they regarded as a Protestant and Prussian Empire. This was reflected in the electoral strength of the Reichstag faction which represented Catholic interests, the Centre Party, and in a fear among members of the Prussian diplomatic corps who served in south German capitals after unification, such as Munich, that the strength of anti-Prussian feeling in the Catholic regions of Germany might one day cause the Reich to break up. These persisted into the 1890s, and as late as 1896 the Prussian Minister in Munich warned against 'the strengthened tendency towards particularism among the federal states'.[5]

A further characteristic of the new Empire was that it was not a true nation state. The Reich contained 3 million Poles in Prussia's eastern provinces, together with a sizeable pro-French minority in the *Reichsland* of Alsace-Lorraine, which had been annexed by Germany in the aftermath of the Franco-Prussian War, and a small Danish minority in the northern province of Schleswig. All three of these minorities were subjected to sporadic 'Germanization' campaigns during the Imperial era. These were fairly successful in the case of the inhabitants of Alsace, who were culturally close to the Germans. However, even here, attempts at assimilation ultimately failed as a result of blunders in official policy on the eve of the First World War. The Germanization drives against the Danes and the Poles were much less successful. The authorities eventually resorted to deporting Danes from Schleswig to Denmark so intense was the anti-German feeling there. In Prussian Poland, the inhabitants responded to the efforts of the authorities to stamp out Polish culture by embracing a Polish identity ever more strongly.

Jews constituted the last of the Reich's minority communities. They represented only 1.25 per cent of the German population, a figure which fell to 0.95 per cent before the First World War.[6] During most of the nineteenth century the Jewish community had become increasingly integrated into German society. However, the years after unification were to see an upsurge in anti-Semitic prejudice in Germany as Jews were made scapegoats by those who lost out as a result of the rapid social and economic change which accompanied the Reich's transition from an agricultural to an industrial society. Jews were an easy target for such prejudice as they were prominent in many of the fields associated with economic modernization such as banking and large-scale commerce. Additionally an influx of eastern European Jews, or *Ostjuden*, into Germany in the decades after unification, who were fleeing persecution in Russia, fuelled anti-Semitism, as unlike German Jews these newcomers were alien in dress and speech, as well as in religion.

Anti-Semitism also received succour from the practices of the state itself. Jews were not allowed to join the Prussian officer corps, nor were they given prominent positions in the bureaucracy. All of this encouraged those who believed that the Jews were not really German, and who espoused anti-Semitism on racial as well as religious grounds. By the early 1880s, according to the National Liberal politician Ludwig Bamberger, anti-Semitism was prevalent across German society. He observed that 'the organs which are the lifeblood of the nation – army schools, and scholarly world – are filled to the brim with it ... it has become an obsession which does not leave one untouched'.[7] Daniel Goldhagen has recently suggested that the fusion between official and popular anti-Semitism which occurred in the decades after unification created the cultural conditions for the participation of so many Germans in the Holocaust of 1942–45. Although a controversial thesis, it draws our attention to the fact that many of the roots of the catastrophe of the Nazi era lie in the history of the Second Reich. Political and racialist anti-Semitism represents one of these roots. However, the tension between a society in the process of modernization and a governing elite drawn from a declining landowning class was another feature of the Second Reich which had implications for Germany's development in the twentieth century. For the Junker class of Prussian nobles who dominated the government and bureaucracy of the Empire resorted to anti-democratic and anti-parliamentary strategies in order to maintain power. These tactics discredited democracy and liberalism in the eyes of many Germans and made them susceptible to the appeal of Nazism later on. Additionally the Prussian governing class was imbued with a militaristic and authoritarian political outlook which also stood in the way of the emergence of a tolerant society. It is to the Reich's leaders that we now turn.

Leaders

In June 1871, on a perfect summer's day, a victory parade was held in Berlin to mark the success of German arms in the recent struggle against France. That such a celebration should take place in the aftermath of so triumphant a military enterprise can hardly be construed as surprising. None the less, the spectacle bears close scrutiny for what it reveals about the country's leaders. At the head of the parade, in full uniform, were Helmuth von Moltke, the nation's leading military strategist and Chief of the General Staff; Otto von Bismarck, Minister-President of Prussia and the first Chancellor of the new German Reich; and Albrecht von Roon, Prussian Minister of War. Behind them, riding in state, came their sovereign, Wilhelm I, King of Prussia and now, also, German Emperor. Although many other individuals held prominent positions in the political, social and economic life of the nation, it was not by accident that it was these four men who were leading the triumphant march into the Prussian capital: at that moment, they were probably the most prominent figures in Europe; they were undoubtedly so in Germany. It is with them, therefore, that this examination of the German leadership has to begin.

As a group these men had much in common. It was no coincidence, for example, that the triumvirate at the head of the procession was made up of representatives of well-established families who bore ancient names and chose to enter the capital proudly clad in the trappings of military life. This was the natural consequence of their shared background. The ruling strata of Prussia, of which they were all members, came principally from one socio-economic group: the East-Elbian rural and military nobility, the Junkers.[8] As a social class, the Junkers, although not so homogenous and unvarying as they are sometimes depicted, none the less held certain common characteristics. Foremost among these was their connection to the soil and the implications this had for their outlook and behaviour. Owing their position to the profits and status of landownership, they generally held estates (*Rittergütter*) that were large enough to provide local autonomy and influence, but were not so great as to give them total independence from the state. This circumstance had conspired over the years to create a symbiotic relationship between the Junkers and the Hohenzollern monarchy. In return for royal grants of privilege that made the Junker landowner absolute master of his domain, the members of the Prussian nobility had consented to become the mainstay of the country's administration and the basis of its officer corps. In this manner, service to the Crown, either in the army or the bureaucracy, became the Junkers' natural calling, turning the class into what one historian has termed a 'military agrarian complex'.[9]

The development of the Junkers into a militarized provincial lesser nobility – more gentry than aristocracy – that exercised power with the consent of their dynasty in return for loyalty to its interests, led to the corresponding development of a collective caste mentality. Encapsulated in the slogan 'throne and altar', fundamental to this outlook was a belief in traditional sources of authority and the importance of hierarchy and order. As a result, the Junkers became the main exponents of a legitimist political ideology that emphasized monarchy as the heart of the state and which stressed the role of the army and the bureaucracy as the natural bulwarks of this system. As the Junkers dominated both the military and civilian branches of government, the logical corollary of this presumption was that the good of the state and the Junker interest were organically and inseparably intertwined, cohesion between the two being built around mutual reliance in the defence of certain common objectives. Most important in this respect were the preservation of the legitimate order, the pre-eminence of the monarchy and the aristocracy, and the independence of the army. For the Junkers, these were all paramount issues on which no compromise could or would be entertained, a position that Moltke, Bismarck and Roon, in harmony with their class backgrounds, thoroughly understood and, in their own way, shared. So, too, did Wilhelm I.

While these four principal figures in the Prusso-German leadership were thus all influenced by the outlook of the Junker politico-social milieu, with the result that they shared certain of its mental horizons, none the less, their character, attitudes and contribution to the state reflected much more than just the collective assumptions of a distinct social caste. Rather, each of them, in his own way, transcended his background to make a major impression on the new Reich. It is as individuals, therefore, that they need to be appraised.

Leading the military parade into Berlin in June 1871 was Helmuth von Moltke. His place at the vanguard of the procession had been earned by military success. It was his strategic skills and organizational genius that had permitted Prussia to win a series of lightning victories in wars fought against Denmark in 1864, Austria in 1866 and France between 1870 and 1871. However, while responsible for Prussia's successful aggrandizement, Moltke was not a Prussian by birth. Hailing from Parchim in the Grand Duchy of Mecklenburg-Schwerin, he had been brought up in Holstein, educated in the military academy in Copenhagen and, only later, had he sought to enter the service of the Prussian army. While, therefore, not technically of Prussian Junker stock, he was, none the less, well placed to secure entry into the highest ranks of the Prussian military and to gain adoption into the kingdom's aristocracy. This was because recruitment from among the north German Protestant nobility, of which the Moltke family were members, was a

Prussian military tradition: in seeking recognition of his talents in the service of the Hohenzollerns, Helmuth von Moltke was following in the illustrious footsteps of the Saxon-born Neithardt von Gneisenau, who, notwithstanding his non-Prussian origins, had risen to become a military legend in his adopted kingdom. Moltke was to do likewise. His appointment in 1857 to head the Prussian General Staff was to have far-reaching consequences. Under his leadership and as a direct result of his skills at planning, this little known and even less respected body was to become the strategic hub of the Prussian army. At the same time, the Chief of the General Staff, from being a subordinate of the Minister of War, would be raised in status to become the main military adviser to the King. This elevated position was one that Moltke bequeathed to all of his successors in the post, at least one of whom would be encouraged to use it as a lever to gain dictatorial power. This usurpation would have appalled Moltke. Despite his famous assertion to the effect that decisions affecting the conduct of war should be left to soldiers rather than civilian politicians, Moltke was neither a narrow-minded reactionary nor a blind advocate of force. Indeed, from the perspective of someone determined to maintain his class interests in as effective a manner as possible, his political thinking was almost bold. Having experienced the revolution of 1848 at first hand, Moltke was a strong believer in order. Indeed, as a junior officer in 1848, he had been a convinced advocate of the use of military power for counter-revolutionary purposes. As he had put it to his brother at the time:

> We now have 40 000 men in and around Berlin. ... Order in Berlin and we shall have order in the country. ... [The King and government] now have power in their hands and a perfect right to use it. If they don't do it this time, then I am ready to emigrate with you to Adelaide.[10]

Despite the expression of such views, it would be wrong to assume that Moltke was against all change or that he yearned to see the restoration of absolutism. On the contrary, as he perceptively observed of the political climate of the 1860s and 1870s: 'the parliamentary form of government is a necessity in our times, to be sure, and whoever opposes this necessity will be crushed!' Consequently, in his opinion, the solution for the Junker interest was not to stand in the path of progress but to temper its effects. As he put it: 'parliament [had to be told] that it is not to touch the essential foundation of the state and the conditions of its existence'.[11] In this opinion, he was in perfect harmony with Bismarck.

Like Moltke, Bismarck possessed aspects to his character and outlook that belied the expectations of those who assessed him purely by his origins.[12] Born into an ancient family whose roots in Brandenburg pre-dated those of the Hohenzollerns, Bismarck was regarded by many as an archetypal Junker reactionary. His early career did little to dispel this notion. Selected in 1847 as the substitute delegate to represent Magdeburg in the Prussian United Diet, both his maiden speech on 17 May 1847 and his subsequent actions during the revolution of 1848 marked him out as a baiter of liberal opinion and as a champion of reaction. In this way, the 'mad Junker' image was born.

However, despite people's perceptions, Bismarck was much more than a stereotypical backwoodsman. Descended on his mother's side from a family of university professors, he had been educated not, as might have been expected, at cadet school, but at a *Gymnasium* in Berlin. This mixed background – an exposure to the twin worlds of rural Junker life as well as urban humanist values – endowed Bismarck with an extra-ordinary breadth of vision and a clear understanding of a range of diverse mentalities and aspirations. As a result, he enjoyed the rare advantage in political life of being able to comprehend the mindset of his opponents, a facility that enabled him to anticipate and counter their strategies. His method of doing this was the unusually far-sighted idea of pre-empting and even trumping their demands. Aware that standing in endless opposition to the incessant and ever more vigorous demands for change was a futile pursuit, Bismarck sought, instead, to take the lead and thereby guide such passions in directions that he found amenable. This tactic was based on a profound sense of political realism that forced him to acknowledge the utter impossibility of turn-ing back the clock. As he had clearly stated in 1848: 'The past is buried and I regret far more than most of you that it is beyond all human power to restore it to life. ... '[13] Much mistaken at the time for the lament of a reactionary, this speech was more an assertion of political conviction. It demonstrated Bismarck's willingness to rid himself of the impediment that limited the options of most traditional conservatives, namely an unquestioned reverence for the past. As he almost uniquely understood, since the past could not be re-created, it was better to build the future oneself rather than to allow this opportunity to fall into the hands of one's rivals. Consequently, Bismarck chose to be a 'white revolution-ary',[14] not opposing change, but fashioning it himself according to his own principles. He became an exponent not of blind reaction but of 'creative anti-revolution'.[15] Consequently, throughout his career, Bismarck upstaged his opponents. Aware, for example, that German liberals wanted a national parliament, but one with a restricted propertied franchise, Bismarck established an assembly, but endowed it with universal manhood suffrage, a concession as bold as it was misleading. At no stage, however, did Bismarck sacrifice any power that he held as essential to the state. Whatever else he did, he led with care.

That Bismarck ever got into a position of power from which he could demonstrate his considerable political skills was due in large part to the efforts made on behalf of his candidacy for high office by a most unlikely supporter, General Albrecht von Roon. Born at Pleushagen, near Kolberg, in the Prussian province of eastern Pomerania, a scion of an impoverished noble family of Dutch descent, Roon was in very many ways the absolute stereotype of a Junker. He was devout, extremely conservative, utterly loyal to the monarchy, and devoted to the army, a profession that gave shape to his entire life; even his appearance and bearing suggested an East-Elbian noble background. Yet, while in every respect the professional soldier, confirmed monarchist and advocate of Junker interests, Roon differed from many of his class in his respect and admiration for Bismarck. While many of the King's entourage distrusted the 'mad Junker', believing correctly that he did not share their strict legitimist principles, Roon harboured no doubts about Bismarck's political resolve and acumen. In the circumstances of the early 1860s, these were qualities that mattered. At that time Roon was engaged in a bitter political conflict with the Prussian assembly, the Landtag, over the reform of the army, which he wanted remodelled on the latest technical and professional lines. While these objectives were generally considered desirable, Roon's other aspiration, to keep the army outside of public scrutiny and to rid it of any elements not absolutely loyal to the authoritarian system, was unacceptable to informed opinion and could not find a majority. Unable to secure parliamentary consent for his proposals and unwilling to back down, Roon sought a man who could break the deadlock. In his mind that man was Bismarck. Although the King disagreed, at the height of the crisis Roon none the less telegraphed Bismarck to come to court and arranged for an audience. The result was Bismarck's appointment as Prussia's new Minister-President.

Roon's intercession on Bismarck's behalf succeeded largely because of his close association with King Wilhelm I, with whom he had once served on campaign and with whom he shared a common outlook on military matters. Like Roon, Wilhelm was a soldier by profession and dedicated to the army. Indeed, as the younger son of a reigning monarch who had originally possessed no expectation of ever becoming king, it had once been his intention to serve his life in the military. Only the childless state of his elder brother's marriage, a circumstance that marked him out unexpectedly as heir to the throne, had forced him to reconsider this decision. By then, his years of close contact with the army had left their mark, instilling in the monarch-to-be a reverence for military institutions and traditions. This outlook was to affect his behaviour as king. Reaching the throne with an acute awareness of the weakness of the Prussian army, his first priority in power was to see its fighting capacity enhanced by modernizing reforms. This did not, however, mean that he sought changes to the ethos of the service. On the contrary, as Gerhard Ritter has shown, Wilhelm was convinced that the army's strength lay in the *esprit de corps* of its officers, whom he regarded as 'paladins of the Hohenzollern throne, loyal followers of the monarch to whom they had sworn their personal fealty ... '.[16] Anything that broke this spirit, that severed the connection between monarch and officer corps and thus detracted from the Crown's ability to utilize the army to bolster its position at home and abroad, was unacceptable to Wilhelm. Herein lay the conundrum that bound Wilhelm and Roon together in their battle with the Landtag. Neither was willing to see any diminution in royal control over the military establishment. Yet, that this was the parliamentarians' long-term goal, Wilhelm had no doubt. As he had observed as early as 1832: 'The tendency of the revolutionary or liberal party in Europe is gradually to tear down all supports which provide the sovereign ruler with his power and prestige – and thus with security in moments of danger.' Given, as he went on to observe, that 'armies constitute the first and foremost of such supporting structures',[17] it was only natural, in his view, that the undermining of the army's loyalty should be the objective to which the Landtag was working. To ensure that it did not happen, Wilhelm was willing to consider such extreme measures as abdication or, worse still, entrusting the 'eruptive and eccentric' Bismarck, a man he disliked and distrusted, with the highest political office. Having once appointed him, the relationship progressively altered. As Wilhelm's confidence in his new servant grew, so he began to seek and then follow his advice, allowing him, within set limits, extensive powers of discretion over government and administration. The major exception to this was the army, where Wilhelm insisted that he have the final say.

It is evident from this brief portrait of the new Reich's four principal figures, that the leadership of the Empire was held by men sharing certain common characteristics. Foremost among these were a distinct class background, a belief in authority and state power, a desire for order, a respect for the virtues of a loyal military establishment, and a willingness to act decisively and utilize bold and unconventional methods to advance their aims. Equally, at this stage, the Reich was blessed by one other key feature: its leaders were men of great talent, whose various strengths were complementary and whose weaknesses cancelled each other out. It was to be an important determinant in Germany's future that the Reich would not always be so fortunate.

The Constitution and Political Structure

The Reich constitution of 16 April 1871 was the product of a very specific set of circumstances and conditions. In effect, it was a tactical response to two important trends in nineteenth-century European history, both of which had considerable implications for the political life of the continent.

The first of these trends relates to the field of economics. Throughout the nineteenth century developments in the European economy, spurred on by new commercial and trading opportunities, were conspiring to transform European society. New social groups, of which the industrial and financial bourgeoisie were the most important, rose in prominence as the economic transformation that was taking place enriched them to the point where they were able to challenge the old elites in terms of wealth and financial power. This in turn had political implications: the growth of the bourgeoisie's economic strength led them to seek a political position commensurate with their new financial status. As the existing political order often failed to allow for such a development, this led the bourgeoisie to adopt and advocate the ideology of liberalism, a system of political values centred upon the premise that power has to be legitimized by the consent of all 'responsible and eligible' sections of society, who should, in accordance with this principle, be included within the political process.

The impact of the rise of the bourgeoisie and the rise of liberalism upon European political life was considerable. As a consequence of these trends, for most of Europe's ruling classes the experience of the first half of the nineteenth century was an uncomfortable one, marked as it was by the turmoil of the French Revolution and the failure of the Vienna settlement. The ensuing unrest, which found expression in France in the fall of two dynasties, in Britain in Peterloo and Chartism, and elsewhere in central Europe in the maelstrom of the revolutions of 1848, convinced the continent's more far-sighted statesmen that the key challenge of the future would revolve around the conundrum of how to meet the political aspirations of those sections of society made vigorous by changes in Europe's economic and social structure, while at the same time preserving intact the conservative character of the existing political order and the dominance over it by traditional elites. The means resorted to in some countries involved the gradual broadening of the political base with a view to absorbing the new political classes into the existing system; the hope being that politics would change them, rather than they change politics. In Britain, this worked admirably: the gradual reform of the political system during the nineteenth century expanded and transformed the franchise while leaving the higher echelons of government firmly in the hands of landowning aristocrats. The premierships of the Marquis of Salisbury and the Earl of Rosebery are testimony to this situation.

This model of political evolution was, by no means, the one adopted throughout Europe. Indeed, for the continent's more conservative states such a solution would have been anathema. Politicians in these countries, some of whom recognized the challenge that they faced and others of whom did not, reacted to the changing conditions in various ways, using and adapting the structure of government to buttress their position according to a variety of different methods and principles. However, in terms of the success of their efforts to meet the challenge posed by the new social forces and to contain the pressure of political change, only one of the continental conservative regimes really stands out. That regime was to be found in Germany.

For much of the nineteenth century, German political life was characterized by two main phenomena: national disunity and governmental authoritarianism. The first of these derived from the division of Germany into 39 separate states; while the second owed its existence to the fact that 35 of these states were monarchies whose political legitimacy rested, for the most part, on traditional symbols and elites.

However, it was also the case that in Germany the challenge posed by the liberal bourgeoisie was a strong one. Germany had an advanced social and economic life and, consequently, its bourgeoisie was numerous, affluent and confident. These characteristics quickly led to political action. In 1848 and again in 1861, the German bourgeoisie attempted to assert itself. In the first instance, in the revolution of 1848, they directed their energies to the goal of establishing a national parliament at Frankfurt with powers comparable to those enjoyed by the House of Commons in Britain. This scheme was thwarted by the guns and bayonets of the Prussian army, whose soldiers put down the revolution and closed the incipient national legislature. None the less, in spite of this outcome, the efforts of that year were not totally in vain. On 5 December 1848, in response to the popular clamour for change, the Prussian monarchy granted a constitution that included provision for an elected assembly, the Landtag, with powers of veto over the budget. This assembly became the liberal bourgeoisie's next battleground. When, in 1861, the government sought to reform the army, the Liberals in the assembly made their consent conditional upon progressive constitutional change. When this was refused, the result was deadlock, political conflict and constitutional crisis.

Bismarck, who was brought into power by King Wilhelm I to resolve the crisis and who, to this end, was made Minister-President of Prussia in 1862, had not the slightest intention of allowing the Liberals to dictate the constitutional agenda. To forestall the threat of such a 'revolution from below', he decided to pre-empt it with a 'revolution from above'. Realizing that the bourgeoisie wanted a united nation state as much as, if not more than a system of parliamentary government, he decided to accommodate their nationalist desires in a manner that would force them to compromise their liberal principles. To this end, he illegally carried out the army reforms, brazenly ignoring the veto of the Landtag in the process, and then used the new and improved military forces at his disposal to unite, first northern Germany, and subsequently the remainder of Germany, under Prussian leadership. Having, in this manner, accomplished the liberal demand for a nation state, he immediately asked the Landtag for ratification of this outcome along with the unconstitutional means by which it was achieved. Faced with this Hobson's choice of upholding parliamentary rights at the cost of forgoing national integration or of accepting national unity at the price of indemnifying the arbitrary use of monarchical power, the liberals chose to capitulate to Bismarck's illegal but successful statecraft. By so doing, they obtained a united Germany, but one formulated around a constitution of Bismarck's devising, tailored to meet his particular requirements.

The fundamental purpose of Bismarck's constitution was to ensure the dominance of the Prussian government over both its own subjects and the other German states. To this end, Bismarck established a new entity – the German Empire – into which Prussia was incorporated. Though merely one of many constituents of the new Reich, this plurality created no danger of a dilution of Prussian power. Under Bismarck's system, Prussia was able to exert hegemonial influence over a German Empire, which could still continue to be governed according to traditional conservative principles. The method Bismarck employed to achieve this outcome was subtle political subterfuge. The constitution he created was a complex document, the political implications of which were often hard to determine from its individual clauses, which in isolation could seem a great deal more liberal and pluralist than when the document was taken together as a coherent working body. None the less, Bismarck was eager for his new state to attract as wide a measure of support as was possible; as David Stevenson has put it, he sought 'to base autocracy on consent'.[18] Both these influences – the desire to preserve the old order and to attract support for the new structure – were reflected in the constitution he devised.

The core provision of the constitution, the one that best illustrates Bismarck's aims and skill, was the enactment of the Reich's federal structure. In terms of maximizing popularity, this had the advantage of satisfying the nationalist desire for a German state without upsetting those with a particularist attachment to one of Germany's many distinct regions or dynasties. It also served to buttress conservative values. The Reich was declared to be a union of 25 separate states, with sovereignty residing collectively in the states themselves. As 22 of the states were monarchies, this entrenched the idea of princely sovereignty into the very heart of the new nation. It also entrenched the reality, for though, as Lothar Gall has observed, the constitution focused popular attention on the Reich and the newly created institutions at the centre,[19] these were less important than they seemed: by avoiding a unitary structure and maintaining intact Germany's existing internal divisions, the constitution ensured that in practice a substantial proportion of government was conducted at the level of the sovereign federal states, whose existing constitutions were completely unaffected by the creation of the new Reich. As a result, the Empire developed a dual constitutional structure. At one level was the Reich constitution, which governed relations between the states and which established procedures for co-operation in areas of common interest; at another level, were the individual constitutions of the various federal states. As the principle of subsidiarity was integral to the Reich with the result that the federal states held responsibility for all governmental functions not explicitly granted to the centre and were also the agencies through which Reich regulations were implemented at a local level, the nature of their constitutions was of the greatest significance in shaping most people's experience of government. Unfortunately, many of these constitutions were highly authoritarian in nature. This was particularly true for the largest and most populous state in the Reich, namely Prussia. Prussia covered two-thirds of the area of the Reich and contained two-thirds of its population. Within the borders of Prussia, absolutist principles held sway. Almost all functions of government were reserved for the King and his ministers, the sole check on whose authority was an assembly whose members were elected on a weighted 'three class' franchise that ensured a disproportionate influence to those with wealth: in some constituencies, for example, one man, as chief taxpayer, would cast a third of all votes. In the early 1860s, Prussia's constitution had been highly controversial and the focus for the bourgeoisie's political claims. Yet, as Bismarck had foreseen, though the founding of the Reich left Prussia unaltered, the new Germany was none the less able to deflect attention away from Prussian affairs towards those of the Reich.

If the Reich's federal structure served as a disguise for conservatism at the local level, it was equally effective at entrenching traditional authority at a Reich level. Again, this was despite appearances to the contrary. Outwardly the new Reich constitution contained many of the features of a liberal parliamentary regime. To begin with, the Kaiserreich was a constitutional state – a *Rechtsstaat* to use the parlance of the time – that was governed, not by arbitrary power, but according to legal conventions formally laid down and guaranteed. Furthermore, included within this framework was a legislative assembly, the Reichstag. Elected by equal, direct and secret ballot according to a system of universal adult male suffrage, it was one of the most representative popular assemblies to be found anywhere in the world. Moreover, as a result of Bismarck's desire to gain the support of the bourgeoisie for his new state, the Reichstag was accorded important legislative functions. All imperial laws, including the budget and the army estimates, required the Reichstag's consent. As the legal codes of the Empire – civil, commercial and criminal – had yet to be enacted, this placed the new assembly in a central position, one from which it could, and did, bequeath to the German state a corpus of modernizing liberal legislation. On the basis of these achievements alone, one prominent historian has described the founding of the Reich as being akin to a 'bourgeois revolution'.[20] The Reichstag's many parliamentary privileges reinforce this interpretation. Reichstag deputies, who enjoyed parliamentary immunity and freedom of speech, had the right to address questions to the Chancellor and the Reich secretaries of state. On top of this, they regulated their own procedures, chose their own officials and were responsible for their own discipline. Furthermore, Article 24 of the constitution made provision for regular elections: in the first instance, every three years; then, after modification in 1888, every five years. In effect, therefore, the Reichstag enjoyed the same legislative functions, the same formal protection from official coercion, and as close a relationship to its electorate as any parliamentary assembly in the world.

Such outward liberalism was, however, deceptive. To begin with, the constitution, the document upon which the whole legal framework rested, was not a constitution in the normal sense of the word, but rather took the form of a treaty between 25 sovereign states for the better ordering of their common affairs. Though according to the preamble an 'everlasting' arrangement, this assertion was little more than a rhetorical flourish: in both form and substance, the constitution was an agreement between monarchs which could, in theory, be abrogated at any time. The threat of such a '*coup d'état* from above', an action known in German as a *Staatsstreich*, hung like a sword of Damocles over German political life. It was no idle threat: suspending, or even abolishing, the constitution was an option that was seriously considered at times by elements in the Reich leadership.[21] That it was never carried out was not an expression of the elite's conversion to constitutionalism, but rather reflected the fact that such drastic action was never actually needed. The new constitution, by carefully distributing power in an anything but equitable manner, proved adequate to the task of safeguarding the position of those in authority. The means whereby this was achieved can be illustrated with reference to two institutions central to the new constitutional structure: the Bundesrat and the office of Kaiser.

The formal heart of the new political system – indeed, the very first of the organs of government to be defined in the articles of the constitution – was the Federal Council, the Bundesrat. Composed of the nominated representatives of the federated governments, this body possessed important legislative functions. All prospective laws, as well as constitutional changes, had first to receive its approval. As a result, the Bundesrat acted in many respects as an upper chamber to the Reichstag, with the power to frustrate its initiatives and thus act as a bastion against the excesses of the popularly elected assembly. This was particularly true when it came to constitutional amendments. On such matters, the Bundesrat's voting arrangements were carefully constructed to ensure that no changes could be enacted without Prussian consent. Thus, with only 14 of the available 58 votes needed to stop a constitutional amendment in its tracks, and with Prussia possessing 17, this was enough to ensure that Prussia could never be overruled and that change was very much the exception rather than the rule.

The Bundesrat furthered Prussian interests in other ways. As the sole constitutional structure to embody the voice of the separate member states, the Bundesrat created the impression that all the federated governments were involved in the highest reaches of Reich politics. In this respect, as in others, the appearance and reality were quite different. Theoretically, at least, the Bundesrat had the potential to serve as the Reich's executive. Not only could it originate and deliberate upon legislation, in much the same fashion as a cabinet, but, in addition, in the complete absence of any Reich ministries, none of which were ever established, its committees had the potential to act in their stead. That this never happened was in part a reflection of the constitution's status as a treaty. In accordance with this notion, the members of the Bundesrat were regarded not as ministers but as formally accredited envoys. As plenipotentiaries of the member states they naturally enjoyed diplomatic rank and privilege, a standing that gave them a respected position in the social and governmental hierarchy, but which also ensured that their official dealings were subject to diplomatic procedures and went through diplomatic channels. As no executive could possibly carry out the business of government in such a manner, the Bundesrat never achieved its potential as a policy-forming body. Power in this sphere thus fell almost exclusively on one official, the Reich Chancellor, who, although formally a 'responsible' minister, was answerable neither to the Reichstag nor the Bundesrat. Instead, his position depended exclusively upon the Kaiser.

In much the same manner as the Bundesrat demonstrated a divergence between constitutional form and practice, so the role of the Kaiser was to prove different in legal theory and real life. Formally, the Kaiser's position was a limited one, a situation indicated by the actual title he held. In place of the designation of *Kaiser Deutschlands* (Emperor of Germany), he received only the rank of *Deutscher Kaiser* (German Emperor). As such, he was head of a nation and President of a federation of German princes, but neither the sovereign of a German state nor master of his fellow monarchs. He was a regal *primus inter pares* and no more. In this respect, the Kaiser's official position corresponded with the constitutional conception of the German Reich as an agreement between sovereign rulers. It did not, however, conform to popular perceptions of his role. The Kaiser, standing at the pinnacle of the new Reich structure, was an obvious symbol of the nation and almost from the outset was viewed by the German populous as the country's sovereign head of state.[22] The Kaiser's formal powers did nothing to diminish this view. Among the Emperor's exclusive prerogatives were control over foreign policy, including the right to conclude treaties and to make war and peace; the appointment of the Chancellor, all members of the Reich bureaucracy, and all members of the diplomatic corps; and the right to declare martial law in times of civic disorder. On top of this, the Kaiser, as Supreme Commander and Warlord (*Oberster Kriegsherr*), was the holder of the absolute right of command (*Kommandogewalt*) in all military and naval matters. No civilian official or public institution had any say in these areas, which could be conducted by the Kaiser without reference to anybody else. When it is remembered that the Kaiser, who was always the reigning Prussian monarch, had a further basis of political support in his own kingdom, it is apparent that he was a central and very powerful figure in the new Reich.

Taken together, therefore, the roles of the Kaiser and Bundesrat served to circumscribe severely the effectiveness of those liberal elements in the constitution, such as the Reichstag. Excluded from any say in government appointments and unable to direct policy, the Reichstag was limited to scrutinizing legislation. Even here there were limits, for though, in theory, the Reichstag possessed unlimited control over legislation, the German practice of passing some bills, such as the army estimates, for up to seven years' duration, meant that many Reichstag sittings never had the opportunity to exercise their theoretical right of scrutiny in such matters. As in many aspects of Bismarck's system, the appearance and reality were not the same.

Historical verdicts on the Prusso-German constitutional system have reflected this discrepancy between its outward form and actual substance. Descriptions such as 'pseudo-constitutional', 'semi-constitutional' or even 'quasi-absolutist' have abounded. Also, it has been labelled as a front for a 'Bonapartist dictatorship' and as a 'fig-leaf of Prussian rule'. Probably the most balanced view comes from Wolfgang Mommsen: his appraisal of it as a 'semi-constitutional system with supplementary party-political features'[23] has a lot to recommend it. All of these interpretations have one element in common. It is generally agreed that, with its various disparate elements and conflicting authorities, even skilled hands found the political system of the Second Reich difficult to control. Consequently, if ever its management should be entrusted to those with only mediocre ability, the potential existed for polycratic chaos. Ultimately, this was to be its undoing.

2

BISMARCK'S DOMESTIC POLICIES

Negative Integration

The concept of 'negative integration', deriving from social science theory, has been used since the 1960s by historians of the German Empire as a conceptual device with which to approach Bismarck's domestic policies. Hans-Ulrich Wehler takes it to represent a manipulative strategy on the part of the Chancellor, designed to safeguard the authoritarian system in an age of rapid social and economic change by focusing the attention of ordinary Germans on a common enemy, large enough to be credible, but not serious enough to threaten the Reich's political survival.[1] The other way of defining 'negative integration' is actually a complementary one. Attacks by the regime on a particular group could act as an integrating force by creating a common identity among the victimized group which had previously been absent, or less apparent. The domestic history of Bismarckian Germany provides ample support for the second of these definitions of 'negative integration'. The model advanced by Wehler is also useful, as it helps us to understand Bismarck's political strategy. However, it has several weaknesses. It is too rigid, it ignores the fact that the Chancellor often genuinely believed that the groups which he persecuted were *Reichsfeinde*, posing a threat to national unity. Wehler also overestimates the ability of Bismarck to manipulate the German people, and neglects the fact that the impetus for campaigns against 'enemies of the Reich' often came from sections of German society as much as from the Chancellor's office. Bismarck's policies towards three groups of 'enemies of the Empire' – German Catholics, the Poles of eastern Prussia, and the Social Democratic Party (SPD) – illustrate these points.

One of the most curious episodes in Bismarckian Germany was the *Kulturkampf* (cultural struggle), which was launched by the Prussian state against its Catholic minority soon after unification in 1871, reached a peak in the mid 1870s, and diminished gradually in intensity in the late 1870s and early 1880s. During the *Kulturkampf* a whole variety of legislation was introduced which was designed to undermine the autonomy of the Catholic Church in Prussia, to reduce its financial independence, and its role in education. The May Laws of 1873 formed the centrepiece of this programme.

As far as the motives for the launching of the *Kulturkampf* are concerned, only limited support can be found for Wehler's model of 'negative integration' as a manipulative strategy on Bismarck's part. The Chancellor undoubtedly did aim to consolidate co-operation between the government and the anti-clerical forces of German liberalism, which were then politically dominant in the Reichstag, by using the power of the state against Prussia's Catholic minority. But this alone is an insufficient explanation of Bismarck's motives. The Chancellor was genuinely concerned by the potential threat which Catholicism posed to the unity of the new Empire. German Catholics had traditionally looked to Austria rather than Prussia for leadership, and thus, in seeking to weaken the hold of Catholicism, he was also aiming to consolidate the new Prussian-led Reich. The assertion by Pope Pius IX of the doctrine of papal infallibility, and the danger that Catholic powers, such as Austria, would seek to stir up trouble among German Catholics, also raised doubt in his mind as to their loyalty to the Reich. There was also a more direct political motive in the form of his desire to break the power of the Catholic Centre Party which had succeeded in winning 70 seats in the Reichstag, and a personal motive in the form of his hatred of the prominent Centre Party deputy Ludwig Windhorst. As far as the Prussian government as a whole was concerned, a determination to assert the power of the state over its citizens was undoubtedly an important motive behind the *Kulturkampf*. This would be done by undermining the rival power of the Catholic Church. The Prussian Culture Minister Adalbert Falk spearheaded this policy, based on an instruction from Bismarck: 'To re-establish the rights of the State in relation to the Church, and *with as little fuss as possible*.'[2]

However, the initiative for the *Kulturkampf* did not come solely from Bismarck and the Prussian government. It is no coincidence that it reached its height during the period in which Bismarck was co-operating extremely closely with the National Liberal Party, for German liberalism provided much of the ideological impetus behind the attack on the Catholic Church. The Liberals saw the struggle as one between progress and obscurantism, and indeed as one over two visions of what

Germany should be. For Bismarck, by contrast, the *Kulturkampf* was primarily about state power rather than the clash between liberal and Catholic ideologies.

The *Kulturkampf* resulted in certain religious orders, such as the Jesuits, being banned from Germany, and in a greater role for the Prussian state in ecclesiastical appointments, and in the education of Catholic children. However, in reality, the major consequence was that the perception of the Catholic minority as a sub-culture within Prussia and the Reich was reinforced. Greater unity among German Catholics, and a more highly developed sense of collective identity were the result. The Catholic Centre Party, rather than withering away because of the official onslaught upon it, actually gained greater longevity as a vehicle for Catholic interests as a result of the *Kulturkampf*. The majority of German Catholics voted for it at every election prior to 1914, and it registered a particularly high penetration of the Catholic vote in the 1870s and 1880s. The *Kulturkampf* was abandoned in part because of lack of success. The coercive power of the Prussian state proved inadequate to enforce the anti-Catholic legislation, something which even Bismarck conceded when he invoked the 'picture of dexterous, light-footed priests pursued through back doors and bedrooms by honest but awkward Prussian gendarmes with spurs and trailing sabres'.[3] It was also abandoned for reasons of foreign policy, as the alliance with Austria-Hungary in 1879 made it prudent to ease the restrictions on the German Catholic Church. Tactical reasons were also of some significance, for, as we shall see, at the end of the 1870s Bismarck sought to free himself from dependence on the National Liberals, and the dominant debate of the day, over the merits of protectionism, was one where the Centre Party's position was closer to the Chancellor's than that of many liberals. Finally, the accession of a new Pope, Leo XIII, in 1878, broke the impasse between the Church and the Prussian state, and created the conditions for cordial relations between Bismarck and the Vatican.

The concept of 'negative integration' can be applied equally fruitfully to Bismarck's policy towards the Polish minority in Prussia during the 1870s and 1880s. However, as with the *Kulturkampf*, Wehler's model of 'negative integration' as manipulation from above does not provide an adequate representation of the Chancellor's actions and motives. It also works less successfully than the alternative definition of 'negative integration' as a force bringing about greater unity among a minority as a result of official persecution. The Chancellor's policy towards Prussia's large Polish minority cannot be understood in terms of a desire to create an artificial 'enemy of the state' in order to bolster his own position in domestic politics, although by attacking the Poles Bismarck did win the favour of German nationalists. Instead there is every reason to believe that Bismarck genuinely believed that Polish nationalism posed a threat to the integrity of the Reich and to the future of German dominance in Prussia's eastern provinces. Security considerations were also present. The Polish minority had shown little enthusiasm for Prussia's war against France in 1870–71, and their alienation from the new Reich was of great strategic concern as they were concentrated in the Prussian provinces most vulnerable to Russian attack. Bismarck initially believed that the majority of Prussian Poles could be won over to loyalty to the Prussian Crown and the Reich. In his opinion, Polish nationalism was mainly the creed of the Polish gentry. But, by the early 1870s, he had also become concerned at the role played by the Catholic Church in Prussian Poland in promoting education in Polish and a sense of Polish identity among the peasantry. Thus measures against Polish Catholicism formed an integral part of the Prussian *Kulturkampf*. Indeed Bismarck liked to claim that such measures had been its overriding purpose.

However, attacks on the culture of Prussia's Polish minority continued long after the *Kulturkampf* had died down. They were actually stepped up in the mid 1880s. This was because much of the impetus came from German nationalists. They were concerned by demographic evidence in the early 1880s which indicated that the Polish population in Prussia's eastern province was growing much more rapidly than the German. This was the case due to higher Polish birth rates, coupled with a higher level of German emigration away from the east towards the industrial cities of central and western Germany. It raised the spectre of the Polonization of the east. It was German nationalists who created the initial pressure to reverse this through an aggressive 'Germanization' policy. However, Bismarck and the Prussian government were willing to listen. The Chancellor had come to share many of the fears of German nationalists in relation to the growth of the Polish population in the east, and the experience of the *Kulturkampf* had convinced him that the Poles could not be turned into loyal German subjects. He declared in a major speech in the Prussian House of Deputies that 'the endeavour to win over the benevolence of the Polish population ... for the Prussian state idea has been a mistake, an error ... which we consider as our duty to our country and Germany to renounce'.[4] His proposed solution to the Polish question involved mass expulsions of non-Prussian Poles from the Reich in 1886–87, and a further round of anti-Polish legislation in 1886, the centrepiece of which was the Settlement Law, which provided a fund of 100 million marks to Germans who wished to buy up Polish-owned land in the east, and facilitated such land sales. Simultaneously the Prussian Culture Minister Gossler introduced additional measures to promote education in German and to suppress the Polish language. Anti-Polish feeling came to permeate large sections of the Prussian ruling class during this period. The future Chancellor, Bernhard von Bülow, who was a diplomat in St Petersburg in the late 1880s, mused to his friend Friedrich von Holstein that one advantage of a war with Russia would be that it would allow the Reich to solve the Polish question, declaring: 'we should seize the opportunity afforded us by war to drive the Poles *en masse* from our Polish provinces'.[5]

The main legacy of the anti-Polish policies pursued by Bismarck and the Prussian government in the 1870s and 1880s was greater unity among Prussian Poles, and a stronger sense of alienation among them from the Prussian state and the Reich. Polish nationalism in the mid nineteenth century had mainly been restricted to the gentry and the intelligentsia. By contrast, in the 1880s it encompassed the Catholic Church, the emerging Polish middle class and the peasantry as well. 'Negative integration' had only worked insofar as it had created a new solidarity among Prussian Poles, based on their Polish national identity. By contrast, the Germanization drive was a failure. Economic and demographic trends were diminishing the proportion of Germans in Prussian Poland. Even the settlement of Polish lands by German farmers failed to reverse this as the agricultural labourers they were forced to employ were overwhelmingly Polish, the German equivalents having fled the rural east for better paid employment in the industrial conurbations of western Germany.

In 1878 two attempts were made to assassinate Kaiser Wilhelm I. Bismarck exploited the crisis atmosphere these created to dissolve the Reichstag, and to fight an election on an anti-revolutionary platform directed against the SPD and the Left-Liberals. As a result a majority in the Reichstag was secured for an Anti-Socialist Law, banning the SPD, and thus making it difficult for that party to operate within the Reich. Of the three examples of 'negative integration' which are being analysed here, Bismarck's policy against the Social Democrats is the one which corresponds most closely to Wehler's model of the concept as the manufacture of an artificial threat in order to impose unity where it would otherwise have been absent, notably as the SPD was still a tiny minority party in the 1870s.

However, even in relation to the Anti-Socialist Law, Wehler's definition of 'negative integration' fails to make provision for the complex nature of Bismarck's motives. The real targets of the Anti-Socialist Law were the left wing of the National Liberal Party and the Progressives, not the SPD. The law itself formed part of Bismarck's broader political strategy at the end of the 1870s of shifting the centre of German politics to the right. This involved trying to polarize German politics in order to force the National Liberal Party to disown its left wing, to embrace economic protectionism and to co-operate with the Conservative Party. The Chancellor's son Herbert admitted in 1884 that left-wing Liberals were the real target of the legislation when he stated that he 'would prefer one hundred Social Democrats to any one of those miserable creatures'.[6] This does not mean, however, that Bismarck was unconcerned by the growth of socialism in Germany. In fact he had been alarmed by this since at least the early 1870s, and he had actually been looking for an opportunity to force anti-Socialist measures through the Reichstag since the middle part of that decade. The assassination attempts against Wilhelm I in 1878 simply provided him with the pretext he had been looking for to secure Reichstag support for a strategy aimed against the SPD. Additionally, as will be seen later, the Chancellor's anti-Socialist legislation was coupled with the introduction of a social welfare programme, designed to wean the German working class away from the SPD. Therefore it should not be seen in isolation.

In one sense the Anti-Socialist Law could be characterized as a success, for during the 12 years of its operation, 1878 to 1890, the main party of left Liberals, the Progressives, saw a sharp decline in its level of support. However, it is doubtful that the Anti-Socialist Law was the main factor. It is much more likely that liberalism declined in the 1880s because the issues which had once united it had either lost their relevance, as in the case of the *Kulturkampf*, or had come to divide the different Liberal factions, in the case of the debate on the merits of free trade versus protectionism. What cannot be contested is that the Anti-Socialist Law backfired disastrously in all other respects. The same sense of unity developed among Socialists as a result of official persecution as had emerged in similar conditions among Catholics and Poles. The SPD vote was much higher at the end of the 1880s than it had been at the beginning. The party developed sophisticated and effective methods of overcoming the official ban on its electoral activities, and made a major breakthrough in the Reichstag elections of 1890, the year of Bismarck's dismissal. The Anti-Socialist Law also failed to create unity among the other political parties behind Bismarck. Some politicians saw through it, and others believed that it simply detracted attention away from more important questions of economic policy. Thus the 1880s was a decade during which Bismarck could only rely fleetingly on the support of a Reichstag majority.

As we have seen, branding entire groups as 'enemies of the Reich' proved to be a counterproductive strategy on Bismarck's part. It reinvigorated German Catholicism during the *Kulturkampf*, it turned Polish nationalism into the dominant creed among the Slavs of the Prussian east, and it worked to the advantage of the nascent SPD. By contrast, attacking these *Reichsfeinde* proved, at best, to be of only short-term benefit to Bismarck in political terms. His alliance with the Liberals broke down despite the *Kulturkampf*. His anti-Polish crusade gained him the support of German nationalists, but alienated many members of his own Junker class who were economically dependent on a supply of cheap Polish agricultural labour. His campaign against the SPD may have accelerated the decline of the Left Liberals, but it failed to secure him the backing of a reliable Reichstag majority. More importantly, his strategy of persecuting minorities polarized German politics, contributed to the atomization of society in the Reich, and set a dangerous precedent of official intolerance which, lamentably, was followed by the governments of both Wilhelm II and Adolf Hitler.

Protectionism

On 15 December 1878, in an official message to the Bundesrat that was subsequently to become known as the 'Christmas Letter', Bismarck, who had, until then, concurred in a policy of *laissez-faire*, stated in the clearest terms that he no longer accepted the argument for free trade. The ramifications of this unexpected volte-face were considerable. Shortly thereafter, a bill for the introduction of a new tariff schedule for those parts of the German Empire within the common customs area was placed before the Reichstag. In spite of some very considerable ideologically motivated opposition from the assembly's more doctrinaire liberals, the progress of legislation was nevertheless extremely rapid: the new Tariff Law secured its third reading in July of the same year; its provisions became operative on the first day of 1880.

While the import duties that it imposed were by no means high – the tariff on grain cereals, for example, amounted to a mere 1 mark per 100 kilograms – the new law, none the less, represented a sea-change in Germany's fiscal and economic policies. In effect, a country which had espoused free trade from its very creation, entered the new decade among the practitioners of protectionism. This was to be no mere transient change of attitude. Although the details of the policy and the level of the tariffs were at times subject to modification, the principle of protectionism would thereafter never be repudiated: the Second Reich would end its days firmly ensconced behind a substantial tariff wall.

Naturally enough, given the lasting nature of the resultant change in Germany's customs policy, the reason for Bismarck's imposition of new tariff legislation has been subject to careful historical enquiry. From this, two principal motives for his decision have been discerned.

The first of these concerns the weak financial position of the Reich administration, which found itself much in need of an enhanced revenue-raising capability. This situation was very much the product of Germany's governmental framework. As we have seen, Bismarck's constitutional settlement was based upon a federal structure that, in attempting to ensure that most sovereign powers were retained by the constituent states, accorded only limited authority to the centre. Under this system, one of the core powers that remained with the member governments, and over which the Reich had absolutely no authority whatsoever, was the right to raise direct taxes. As a result, funding for the activities of the central administration was restricted to two alternative sources: levies from the federal states (*Matricularbeiträge*), which were drawn proportionately according to a predetermined formula, and indirect taxes, of which import duties formed a major component. Naturally enough, with free trade in the ascendant, the revenue raised from the latter source was extremely limited, with the result that the Reich was becoming highly dependent upon the levies from the federal states for the funds necessary to meet its obligations. In Bismarck's view this reliance on contributions from the member governments had reached the point where it threatened the workings of his system. Not only was rising expenditure at the centre driving up taxation at the local level, but, in addition, the Reich's constant need to go 'begging' for funds from the federal governments made budgetary policy anarchic and was, in any case, beneath the dignity of the Empire and its chancellor. As Bismarck complained to the French ambassador: 'Every year I have to play the role of mendicant in order to ensure the necessary operation of the Empire's services: I have to beg Brunswick and Mecklenberg for charity: is that tolerable ... ?'[7] For the Chancellor, the answer to this question was not only a resounding no, but a no exacerbated by the knowledge that this already unacceptable situation was soon likely to get even worse. Foremost among the reasons for this expected deterioration was Bismarck's desire to introduce new and highly costly military and social legislation. Under the existing system, such a programme would necessitate an additional draw upon the resources of the federal states and, thus, further enhance the leverage on the central administration of petty principalities like 'Brunswick and Mecklenberg'. As a result, before embarking on any new spending programmes, it became Bismarck's goal to seek financial independence for the Reich, an outcome that could only be accomplished by changing the distribution of fiscal power between the centre and the federal governments. Bismarck's mechanism for securing this transformation was protectionism. By abandoning free trade and introducing higher tariff barriers, Bismarck could gain for the Reich government a new source of revenue. Moreover, as tariff levels were not voted annually, but were set down in perpetuity, protectionism would generate a reliable and guaranteed stream of income. This not only compared favourably with the annual 'begging' for matricular contributions, but it also had the potential advantage of making the Reich more independent from the Reichstag in financial matters. For Bismarck, therefore, as he himself put it, tariff legislation was a 'comprehensive reform ... that will make the Empire not poor, as it is now, but truly rich'.[8]

If Bismarck's objective was to use tariff legislation as a means of providing for the financial independence of the Reich, then his policy ended in failure. The parties in the Reichstag, well aware that a generous financial settlement would diminish their significance in German politics, were unwilling to give the Chancellor the monetary latitude that he was seeking. Instead, various ways of mitigating his proposals were suggested. One of these, rejected out of hand by the Chancellor, was to make the new duties on coffee and salt subject to an annual vote of renewal in the Reichstag. This idea was unacceptable to Bismarck on the grounds that it amounted to a public reaffirmation of the Reichstag's supremacy in budgetary matters. However, an alternative suggestion put forward by the Bavarian Centre Party deputy, Baron Georg von Franckenstein, did meet with his reluctant approval. The so-called 'Franckenstein clause', which allocated all revenue from customs receipts over and above the figure of 130 million marks to the federal states, was from Bismarck's point of view the least offensive compromise on offer. While it provided an inadequate level of funding and, therefore, undermined his goal of financial independence for the Reich, it did at least have the virtue of gaining for the central government a guaranteed long-term allocation of revenue. This not only injected an element of stability into budgetary matters, but also, because the tariffs were a source granted in perpetuity, ensured that a key component of the governmental process remained beyond the Reichstag's regular scrutiny. For Bismarck, this was an outcome that justified compromise. However, accepting this proposal did mean that protectionism was unable to end the Reich's need for large annual levies from the member states. In this respect, the passage of the new tariff legislation in its amended form represented a setback for Bismarck.

While it fell short of his original budgetary objective of providing the Reich with long-term financial independence, this did not mean that Bismarck regarded his new customs law as being unsuccessful. On the contrary, in many respects he perceived its enactment as an important personal political triumph. The explanation for this apparent contradiction was that redirecting fiscal policy did not provide the sole motive for his shift towards protectionism. Rather, the decision was strongly influenced by another, no less important consideration, namely Bismarck's desire to maintain his undisputed hold over the German political system. In the Chancellor's view, this was a matter of some urgency, for in his assessment, during the course of 1878, his grip on the reins of power had experienced an unhealthy and most unwelcome deterioration. The root of this decline was the nature of his relationship with the Liberal majority in the Reichstag. Since the founding of the Reich, Bismarck had governed in conjunction with the National Liberal Party, whose deputies had supplied the necessary parliamentary backing for the Chancellor's legislative proposals. While this relationship had generally proven fruitful for Bismarck, it had not been without its consequences. In particular, a decade of collaboration between the government and this one, favoured, political organization, often against the stringent opposition of other parties in the Reichstag, had led the National Liberals to consider themselves as more than just the natural supporters of Bismarck's regime; they had also come to regard themselves as being the only possible parliamentary allies for the Chancellor. Believing themselves to be indispensable to Bismarck's administration, they were, as a consequence, emboldened to raise the price of their cooperation. Towards the end of 1878, Bismarck began to wonder, firstly, if this price was not becoming too high and, secondly, if there were not alternatives to his exclusive relationship with this one particular party.

It was in this context that Bismarck began to give consideration to a new tariff policy. As the Chancellor was well aware, the raising of protectionist customs barriers, an act that would radically redefine the ideological outlook of the government, had the potential to create an entirely new situation in the fluid world of Reichstag coalition politics. Whereas Bismarck's existing policies of *laissez-faire* and national economic and political integration appealed principally to his Liberal allies, were he to convert to protectionism, this would allow him to reach out to a whole new and alternative political constituency. In particular, it would open up the possibility of collaboration with the representatives of the country's disaffected industrial manufacturers and agrarians. The reason why tariffs would facilitate such a shift was straightforward. Ever since the onset of the world economic crisis of 1873, these groups had become progressively more interested in promoting policies of economic nationalism. Especially eager in this respect were the representatives of those heavy industries, such as iron and steel production, textile manufacturing and coal mining, whose businesses were most affected by the cyclical economic downturn, sometimes accorded the overstated title 'the great depression', that was afflicting Europe at this time. In response to the dramatic drop in demand that struck their sector of the economy, these industrialists demanded state intervention on their behalf in the form of a protected home market for their goods. Accordingly, they formed a variety of pressure groups, of which the Central Association of German Industrialists was the most important, to campaign for the imposition and retention of tariffs on imported manufactured goods. That their initial efforts in this direction made little headway was largely the result of the stance taken by the representatives of Germany's agricultural sector, for whom free trade was almost an article of faith and who vigorously opposed the demands of the industrialists. For the most part, this positive attitude towards *laissez-faire* trade policies reflected the agrarians' many years of success as exporters in the global market place. Throughout the middle decades of the nineteenth century German farmers had made substantial returns by selling their products to the industrial regions of Britain and France.

However, towards the end of 1875, this profitable situation began to change owing to the emergence of overseas competition. Since the mid 1850s, new lands had been increasingly brought under cultivation in North America, Australia and the Russian steppes, leading to a considerable increase in the available supply of food products. As this rise in supply was also accompanied by a significant decline in the costs of oceanic shipping, which made it practicable to export foodstuff to Europe, the result was a sharp decline in the price of grain. With astonishing rapidity, this caused a shift in the orientation of German agriculture. Having been geared primarily towards export, German farmers suddenly found themselves dependent on their home market. However, with the price of foodstuff constantly falling, even this was not secure and many farmers feared ruin. They were not slow to act to protect themselves. On 22 February 1876 a group of influential landowners came together to form the Association of Tax and Economic Reformers, an organization dedicated to promoting tariffs on agricultural produce.

With this shift away from free trade on the part of German farmers, agrarian opposition to the protectionist demands of heavy industry came to an end. As a result, in place of the former disagreement among these two groups, the possibility of a new alignment between them – a sort of self-interested alliance of convenience – suddenly came into being. The opportunity was quickly seized, creating a powerful united front for tariffs. This was to have major political implications.

For Bismarck, the conjunction of key interest groups from both agriculture and industry, the so-called 'alliance of rye and iron', provided just the opportunity he was seeking to end his dependence on the National Liberals. In combination, the Reichstag representatives of these two economic constituencies, although not by themselves amounting to a secure majority in the chamber, were nevertheless sufficient to form the core of a new parliamentary coalition. Consequently, if he could win them over to his cause, an outcome that could be secured simply by the conceding of an end to free trade, and also gain the support of one other major grouping, then his need to rely upon the National Liberal Party would be over. Further concessions in a liberal direction would then be unnecessary for the purpose of securing the enactment of the Chancellor's forthcoming legislative programme. This calculation was to inform much of Bismarck's political strategy when it came to deciding in favour of new tariff legislation. Not only was it a major reason for his decision, but it also ensured that the new measure was devised with the key demands of the leading industrial and agricultural protectionist groups very much in mind. In this way, their long-term support was obtained.

As we have seen, Bismarck's shift away from *laissez-faire* economic policies and towards protectionist tariff legislation was influenced by two distinct considerations: firstly, the necessity of obtaining an additional source of revenue for the central administration; secondly, the need to find a way of crafting a new political coalition to back the Chancellor's political programme in the Reichstag. While both these objectives were important, many historical interpretations assert that it was the demands of coalition politics that was the principal driving force behind Bismarck's actions. According to this line of argument, the primacy of political over fiscal considerations is evident both in the nature of the legislation that Bismarck introduced and in the associated political manoeuvring that accompanied his break with his *laissez-faire* past.

Starting first with the nature of the new trade barriers, careful scrutiny shows that these were set up more with a view to attracting widespread support for the government than with the aim of maximizing revenue receipts. This can be seen most clearly from an examination of the measures relating to the protection of agriculture, which consisted of two distinct strands. Firstly, there were a series of new tariffs on the import of cereals, a measure that principally aided the large Junker estates of east Elbian Prussia. By concentrating exclusively on the grain tariffs, the most high profile element in Bismarck's system of agricultural protection, some historians have been misled into believing that Bismarck's aim was to provide aid mainly to aristocratic producers. This was not the case. In addition to the tariffs, there was passed on 23 June 1880 the less well known, but no less important, Law Concerning the Prevention and Suppression of Animal Diseases. This piece of legislation, although masquerading as a sanitary measure designed to keep Germany free of trichinosis and other serious infections, had the direct and intended effect of making it almost impossible to import meat products into the Reich. In this manner, through a non-fiscal and revenue-neutral device, both the smaller farms of the south and west of Germany and the nation's peasant livestock and dairy producers also benefited from protectionism. Consequently, the agricultural interest as a whole, not just one favoured section of it, was drawn to support the government. It is for this reason that one historian, assessing this 'dual system of protection', concluded that it was intended 'for political bargaining and for creating an agrarian bloc'.[9]

Another indication that the tariff measures were motivated more by political than fiscal considerations can be seen if one places the new excise duties within the broader context of the other initiatives pursued by the Chancellor during the years 1878–79. During this period, Bismarck not only brought a new direction to German customs policy, he also instituted a whole series of other significant political and administrative changes. These included: firstly, the undertaking of a concerted attack on the opposition Social Democratic Party through the introduction of the discriminatory Anti-Socialist Law; secondly, the dismissal of the Minister of Culture, the prominent liberal Adalbert Falk, and the consequent ending of the anti-clerical policies of the *Kulturkampf*; and finally, the appointment of the conservative Robert von Puttkamer to the Prussian ministry of state, a move, it is claimed, that led to the remodelling of both the bureaucracy and the judiciary along more reactionary lines. Taken together, these measures had one feature in common: they heralded a major governmental reorientation. Long-pursued liberal policies aimed at attacking the 'ancient superstitions' of the Catholic Church and promoting the modern doctrines of national integration were jettisoned, along with the men who had promoted them. In their place, Bismarck substituted policies and ministers acceptable to the Reichstag representatives of political Catholicism and patriarchal conservatism, former adversaries who were now courted as allies of the regime.

Not surprisingly, so radical a series of changes has attracted the attention of historians, with the result that the years 1878–79 have come to be viewed as a watershed in Germany's political development; one historian has even gone as far as to suggest that this period marks the 'conservative re-founding of the Reich'.[10] Naturally enough, this interpretation has influenced historical perceptions of the new tariff legislation, which, taking place at around the same time, is accordingly often perceived as being an additional component, albeit an important one, of this conservative political reorganization. This interpretation has some merit. To begin with, the new tariff legislation did mark a significant policy shift to the right. Furthermore, as it was a measure much favoured by the conservative political groupings that the Chancellor wished to win over to his regime, its introduction did complement Bismarck's other changes and enable him to reconstitute the basis of his political support. Yet, at the same time, it must be recognized that the concept of a 'conservative re-establishment of the Reich' can be overstated and certain elements of it, such as the notion of the 'Puttkamer purge', have been undermined by recent scholarship.[11] However, although some elements within this interpretation have been shown to be lacking substantive evidence, this does not invalidate every aspect of the theory. It is still true to say that the transition to protectionism can legitimately be viewed as part of a broader shift to the right and that, as such, tariffs were a policy largely motivated by the clear political agenda of forging a new Reichstag coalition.

If the new tariff legislation facilitated Bismarck's short-term political needs, its legacy was to be far more enduring. To start with, the relatively minor degree of protection enshrined in the law of 1879 would prove to be but the first step on a road that would lead the German Empire into further and more extreme protectionist measures. In 1885 and again in 1887, the level of German excise duties – particularly on grain – would be raised substantially. The complications that this would cause to German commercial relations with other trading nations would quickly turn out to be very considerable. In addition to this, the introduction of explicitly protectionist measures influenced German political culture. The beneficiaries of the legislation, particularly the agrarian interest, would hereafter expect to be supported by the government, irrespective of what this support might cost. Consequently, although high agricultural tariffs increased the price of food and thus became a major burden to the German worker, only one chancellor ever gave serious consideration to a re-evaluation of protectionism. The implications of this were clear: if the German worker was to be placated, this would have to come about through other means. The medium eventually chosen by Bismarck was the realm of social policy.

Social Policy

It is a striking paradox that one of Bismarck's main achievements lay in the sphere of social welfare, for he was a political conservative known for his hostility rather than the warmth of his affection towards the working class. Yet, in the 1880s, he oversaw the implementation of legislation which provided accident insurance, medical insurance, disability insurance and old age pensions for German workers. The scheme was ahead of its time and served as a model for those introduced in other countries at a later date. Yet, despite the significance of the legislation, Bismarck did not even mention his role in social policy in his memoirs. The reason for this was that in terms of the political objectives which Bismarck had set himself, his social insurance scheme was an abject failure.

The reasons for Bismarck's initial interest in social insurance were related to motives of economic and social necessity, but had much more to do with political expediency. At first glance, one might assume that the social insurance legislation of the 1880s was simply an extension of the Pan-European late nineteenth-century trend towards greater intervention by the state in social and economic policy. This was indeed the case, as *laissez-faire* liberalism, with its doctrines of self-help, proved just as inadequate as a response to the social problems thrown up by industrialization in Germany as it had elsewhere. Additionally the onset of the 'Great Depression' after 1873 gave social problems greater urgency than before, as rapid economic growth could no longer be expected to alleviate them. Finally Bismarck's own shift in economic policy, in 1879, away from free trade and towards protectionism, exacerbated the plight of the German working class as staples such as bread increased in price as a result of import duties.

The social insurance legislation is best seen as an integral part of Bismarck's political strategy towards the working class from the late 1870s onwards. According to Vice-Chancellor Stolberg it represented the 'necessary corollary'[12] to the Anti-Socialist Law of 1878. It was part of an official policy to kill off the SPD through a mixture of repression and measures designed to address the grievances of the working class. One such strategy was for the government to adopt some socialist policies. It was thus quite deliberate that the first measure of social legislation introduced by Bismarck into the Reichstag, the Accident Insurance Bill of 1881, took up a proposal made by the SPD leader August Bebel in 1879. A further aim of Bismarck's social insurance was to secure the loyalty of the working class for the existing political structure. The state would support the social insurance scheme through financial contributions, and as a consequence the workers would feel grateful for this official paternalism. The Chancellor admitted this, when he told an acquaintance years later: 'My idea was to bribe the working classes, or shall I say, to win them over, to regard the state as a social institution existing for their sake and interested in their welfare.'[13] At the time he was just as candid, remarking in December 1880 that the aim of his social insurance policy was 'to engender in the great mass of the unpropertied the conservative state of mind that springs from the feeling of entitlement to a pension'.[14] Bismarck's social insurance legislation is one of the few areas where the oft repeated assertion that the Chancellor was a 'Bonapartist' can be substantiated, because when he introduced a bill providing for old age pensions into the Reichstag, he stated specifically that he had been influenced by the example of French policy under Napoleon III, telling the assembled parliamentarians 'that the attachment of most Frenchmen to the government ... is mainly connected with the fact that most Frenchmen are state pensioners'.[15]

The final reason for Bismarck's interest in social insurance legislation was that he wished to use the measure as a populist policy against the Reichstag, and particularly the left Liberal deputies within it. Bismarck and the officials who drew up the legislation conceived of the scheme as one where the government would bypass the Reichstag by involving interest groups, such as employers, in a Prussian Economic Council, and later in a federal equivalent. The anti-parliamentary character of the measure became evident during the Reichstag election campaign in 1881 when Bismarck linked his social insurance policy to an attack on political parties, contrasting the benevolent bureaucracy of the state with the self-interest of the Reichstag factions. The policy was designed to show the Liberals in a particularly poor light by exposing the inadequacy of their ideology of self-help when faced with the gravity of the social question. This became evident in April 1881, when Bismarck first introduced the Accident Insurance Bill into the Reichstag, by telling the leader of the Progressive Party, Eugen Richter: 'I do not believe that a policy of *laissez faire, laisser aller* ... can be applied to the state, particularly to a monarchical state which is ruled paternalistically.'[16]

· If Bismarck later disowned his achievements in social policy this was because they were not accompanied by the realization of the political objectives which he had set himself when he had taken up the social insurance issue. The measures failed to wean the working class away from socialism. The SPD did well in the Reichstag elections of 1884 and made a major breakthrough in 1890. Bismarck showed himself to be a politician out of tune with the realities of politics in the industrial age by failing to appreciate that accident insurance and old age pensions were no substitute for an egalitarian society. In any case the benefits which workers received were modest and a smaller proportion of the population was covered by the legislation than one might expect. Thus in the mid 1880s only 10 per cent of the population had health insurance, and they received on average only 11 marks per annum.[17] Additionally the government showed a lack of interest in the broader welfare questions which concerned the working class. The system of factory inspections was inadequate, trade unions were discouraged in the workplace and child labour remained prevalent. Bismarck had no interest in such problems, and did not wish to undermine the right of employers to be 'masters in their own houses'.

An additional reason for Bismarck's later ambivalence towards the social insurance legislation was that many of the pieces of legislation were not carried through in accordance with his original plans. In this, as in other areas of policy, the Chancellor did not have complete freedom to determine the outcome. As we have seen, Bismarck saw the element of state subsidy as an integral part of his insurance scheme, for the working class would only be grateful to the state for the measure if it contributed to their insurance cover. However, the Centre Party, the Progressive Party and even some National Liberals in the Reichstag objected to this aspect of state subsidy and also to the centralizing tendencies which they dictated in Bismarck's original plans. Even the right-wing National Liberal Wilhelm Wehrenpfenning objected to the element of state subsidy in the Chancellor's Accident Insurance Bill of 1881 on the grounds that it seemed to amount to 'Roman grain handouts to the darling rabble in a different form'.[18] As a result of Reichstag opposition, the first Accident Insurance Bill had to be withdrawn, and many of the early measures of social insurance, such as the Health Insurance Law of 1883, contained no government subsidy at all. Instead, one-third of the contributions were to come from employers and a further two-thirds from the workers themselves. Reichstag intervention thus removed the element of state subsidy which Bismarck had seen as crucial to his political objective of securing the loyalty of the workers to the state. The workers themselves were hardly likely to feel grateful to the state for a measure which did not involve a government subsidy.

Bismarck also failed in his political aim of using the social insurance issue to discredit the Reichstag, thus allowing a new politics based on interest groups to emerge. This met with resistance from the federal states as it seemed to imply closer Prussian control over them, and understandably it also met with hostility from the Reichstag parties. The 1881 election, when Bismarck exploited the social insurance question against the Liberal parties in the Reichstag, proved to be a disaster for the Chancellor. He lamented in its aftermath that his party now consisted 'only of the King and himself'.[19] His plans for the involvement of interest groups in social policy were subsequently placed in abeyance. In any case the Reichstag elections of 1884 and 1887 produced majorities which were more favourable towards Bismarck, and he was able in 1889 to secure the passage of old age and disability insurance through the Reichstag, which both contained an element of state subsidy. However, this had come too late to secure the gratitude of the working class towards the state, as the Reichstag elections of the following year underlined.

Thus, although the social insurance legislation of the 1880s is considered to be one of Bismarck's most significant legacies in domestic politics, it was one from which he could derive no pride. This was because he was not particularly interested in social insurance as such, but rather in the political objectives which it could help him to attain. He failed to achieve these. Most notably his social insurance legislation failed to arrest the growth in support for the SPD, nor did it make the working class grateful towards the authoritarian state. This was partly because many of the government's proposals were watered down by the Reichstag, which either removed or diminished the state's contribution to the various schemes. However, the main reason was that Bismarck failed to appreciate that modest social insurance schemes could not compensate the working class for the absence of social, political and economic justice.

3

BISMARCK'S EXTERNAL POLICIES

Great Power Politics, 1871–1890

If the years of German unification between 1864 and 1871 were dominated by a succession of wars between Prussia and her adversaries, then the period which followed was one of prolonged peace. Unification had given the new German Empire a latent hegemony in Europe, which Bismarck was determined to maintain. In 1871 the Chancellor thus entered the conservative rather than the revolutionary phase of his involvement in international politics. Through a series of skilful diplomatic moves, more improvised than planned, Bismarck managed to preserve Germany's leading position among the Great Powers, and to prevent the outbreak of further large-scale wars. Indeed, the distinguished historian A. J. P. Taylor regarded it as the Chancellor's 'greatest achievement' that he 'had wanted peace for his country and helped to give Europe such peace for forty years'.[1] The alliance system which he constructed was made up of 'interconnected subsystems' and linked 'all powers, with the exception of France, ... one way or another to Berlin, ... on Bismarck's terms'.[2] As such, Bismarck's diplomacy stood in marked contrast to that of his successors, whose policies allowed a system based on opposing blocs to develop after his dismissal in 1890.

Bismarck's basic objectives did not alter over time. Firstly, he wished to ensure that the German Empire retained the dominant position in Europe which she had attained in 1871. This required that internal consolidation take precedence over further expansion. Secondly, and following on from this, the Chancellor sought to maintain the isolation of France in order to ensure that she would not be in a position to launch a war of *revanche* against Germany aimed at the recovery of Alsace-Lorraine. Thirdly, Bismarck wanted to safeguard Austria-Hungary's future as a Great Power. He had no interest in seeking to dismember the Habsburg Empire, as he was above all a Prussian conservative, rather than a German nationalist. He had never favoured a *Grossdeutschland* including German Austria as this would only have upset the religious balance in Germany, and also Prussian dominance, by replacing a Protestant majority with a Catholic one. Additionally Bismarck felt a cultural affinity on ethnic and linguistic grounds with the German rulers in Austria and an affinity based on class with the Magyar landowners who dominated Hungary and who were similar to the Prussian Junker class to which he himself belonged. Additionally the Chancellor wished to see Austria-Hungary survive because he feared a confrontation with Russia over the future of central and south-east Europe if the Habsburg monarchy were to collapse.

Two other consistent objectives can be discerned in Bismarck's diplomacy. As a true old Prussian, and a practitioner of *Realpolitik*, he was determined to maintain good, or at least correct, relations with Russia. For Bismarck, Russia was the key to everything. The Tsarist Empire was France's most likely ally against Germany, and could threaten the Reich with a war on two fronts. Russia was also the power which posed the most likely menace to Austria-Hungary's survival as a Great Power. Yet, maintaining the traditional alliance with St Petersburg proved to be Bismarck's most formidable challenge, for the ties of common adherence to the monarchical principle and political conservatism, coupled with the friendship between the Hohenzollern and Romanov dynasties, were of diminishing value, whereas new forces, such as Pan-Slav nationalism in Russia, were pointing towards confrontation between the Tsarist Empire and the Teutonic powers of central Europe, Germany and Austria. Bismarck's greatest concern was that Germany should not find herself isolated. One does not have to go as far as some historians have done, who have argued that geography dictated German foreign policy,[3] to appreciate that the Reich's position in the heart of Europe necessitated that Bismarck pursue a particularly dextrous diplomatic strategy in order to avoid what a French newspaper referred to as 'le cauchemar des coalitions'. The Chancellor admitted this in a memorandum which he wrote after reading this phrase at Bad Kissingen in the summer of 1877:

> This sort of bogey will for long – perhaps for ever – be quite rightly feared by all German Ministers. Coalitions may be formed of the Western Powers, joined by Austria, against us, or, with more danger to us, one based on the union of Russia, Austria and France. A close

rapprochement between any two of these may be taken advantage of by the third, to exercise grievous pressure upon us.[4]

There were essentially three phases to Bismarck's diplomatic activity between 1871 and 1890. Between 1871 and 1878, he sought to consolidate Germany's new dominance within Europe by maintaining the isolation of France and fostering the traditional ties between Germany, Austria-Hungary and Russia based on the Holy Alliance. During the second phase of his diplomacy as Chancellor, between 1879 and 1885, Bismarck had to abandon the *laissez-faire* approach which he had adopted in the early years of his Chancellorship. The primary reason for this was that in the late 1870s the Ottoman Empire in Europe began to disintegrate, and this seemed set to initiate a period of confrontation between Russia and Austria for supremacy in the Balkans. In order to address this new instability, Bismarck promoted the development of a more formal system of alliances with Austria in 1879, with Russia and Austria in 1881, with Italy and Austria in 1882, and with Romania and Austria in 1883. The Chancellor even sought to improve relations with France towards the end of this phase, in the hope that German support of French expansion in Africa would help France to come to terms with the loss of Alsace-Lorraine. In the third and final phase, between 1885 and his dismissal in 1890, the intricate system of alliances which Bismarck had created began to show signs of strain and the Chancellor was reduced to pursuing what one historian has described as a policy of 'stop-gaps'.[5] A protracted crisis over the future of Bulgaria placed relations between Russia and Austria beyond repair, and this, coupled with a renewed spirit of *revanche* in France, opened up the possibility of a Franco-Russian alliance. Bismarck's response was to maintain Germany's alliance with Austria, but also to enter into a separate agreement with Russia, the Reinsurance Treaty, in 1887. The time appeared to be arriving when Germany would have to choose between Austria and Russia. After Bismarck's dismissal, Wilhelm II and the new Chancellor, General von Caprivi, chose Austria.

The low-key policy which Bismarck pursued for most of the 1870s owed much to the fact that his preoccupation at the time was the internal consolidation of the new Reich. He rationalized his new conservatism in terms which illustrate this. 'When we have arrived in a good harbour', he declared, 'we should be content and cultivate and hold what we have won.'[6] A general perception in Europe that France would take a long time to recover from the defeat of 1871 also contributed to the equanimity with which Bismarck viewed the international scene.

However, two developments undermined this picture of a new international stability. Firstly, France recovered much more strongly and rapidly from her defeat than the Germans had anticipated, and had paid off her war debt to the Reich by 1873. As a result, a number of military leaders in Germany, including Field Marshal Moltke, began to urge a 'preventive war' against her. Bismarck, who was a consistent opponent of such policies, none the less permitted an anti-French campaign to occur in the German press in 1875, which culminated in the publication of a bellicose article entitled 'Is War in Sight?' in the Berlin *Post*. The campaign backfired disastrously, as the other powers made it clear that they would not allow Germany to crush France. The entire episode revealed that Germany's new-found hegemony in Europe was less complete, and more vulnerable, than many had imagined.

The second development which served to jolt Bismarck out of his complacency during the 1870s was the uprising which occurred among the Christian peoples of the Balkans against Ottoman rule between 1875 and 1877. The Chancellor refused to see the Reich drawn into the conflict, remarking, famously, on one occasion that he did not consider the Eastern Question to be 'worth the healthy bones of a single Pomeranian grenadier'.[7] However, the Russian government did consider that its vital interests were at stake in the Balkans and intervened in the conflict against Turkey. The Russian army's success against the Turks upset the balance of power in Balkans, antagonizing Austria, and Russia's intention to give its client state of Bulgaria an outlet on the Aegean Sea antagonized most of the other Great Powers, including Britain. Bismarck subsequently presided over a Congress at Berlin in 1878 which established new boundaries in south-east Europe, but this left a bitter aftertaste of Russian resentment against Germany and Austria, as the gains of Russia and Bulgaria were pruned back in the interests of international stability.

The revival of France, and the reopening of the Eastern Question, necessitated an alteration in Bismarck's diplomacy in the years after the Congress of Berlin. The Chancellor now believed that a system of formal alliances was required in order to maintain Germany's latent hegemony in Europe, and to prevent the emerging antagonism between Austria and Russia over the future of the rapidly expiring Ottoman Empire in Europe, from developing into armed confrontation. In line with his consistent objectives, a primary aim of the Chancellor's alliance system was the maintenance of the Habsburg Empire's position as a Great Power. Bismarck believed that Germany's ties with Austria were stronger than those with Russia, which were primarily dynastic. By contrast, as he informed Kaiser Wilhelm I: 'With Austria we have more in common than with Russia. German kinship, historical memories, the German language, the interest of the Hungarians for us – all that makes an alliance with Austria, more popular, perhaps also more enduring in Germany than an alliance with Russia.'[8] However, the conclusion of the Dual Alliance between Germany and Austria in the autumn of 1879 did not imply that Bismarck wished to cut the Reich's links with Russia. Indeed, as ever, he was conscious of the need for Germany to maintain ties with St Petersburg as well as Vienna. The Dual Alliance allowed him to pressurize the Russians into agreeing to the formation of the *Dreikaiserbund* in 1881, as the Tsar preferred a new accommodation with Germany and Austria to diplomatic isolation. Bismarck even sought a *rapprochement* with France in 1884/85 when he supported French imperial schemes in Africa.

However, from 1885 onwards, the Chancellor was faced with the task of trying to stabilize what appeared to be a disintegrating international system. France moved back to its traditional position of hostility towards Germany and, during the period of General Boulanger's political activity between 1886 and 1889, it looked possible that France would seek to launch a war of *revanche* against the Reich. Much more seriously, Bulgaria, under its ruler Prince Alexander of Battenberg, sought to free herself from the Russian suzerainty which had been imposed on her at the Congress of Berlin. The Bulgarian crisis revived the dormant antagonism between Austria and Russia over the future of the Balkans, for Vienna encouraged Prince Alexander to take a more independent line towards St Petersburg. The British government also gave support to Battenberg, as it feared that Russia aimed to gain control of Constantinople and the Straits linking the Black Sea to the Aegean.

The Bulgarian crisis was not just a diplomatic challenge for Bismarck, but also an issue which came to have a resonance in terms of the entire orientation of German foreign policy. The reason for this is related to dynastic politics. Wilhelm I's daughter-in-law, the English-born Crown Princess Victoria, sought to exploit the Bulgarian crisis to challenge what she had long seen as the pro-Russian course of German foreign policy under Bismarck. She promoted a marriage alliance between her daughter Princess Victoria and Battenberg, and believed that, by championing Bulgarian independence, Germany and Britain could counter Russian influence in the Balkans and eventually form an alliance between themselves. To his credit, Bismarck appreciated that Germany's vital interests depended on the preservation of good relations with Russia, and not on a *rapprochement* with Britain. The Chancellor worked tirelessly against the Crown Princess's schemes and made it clear to the Russians that as far as he was concerned Bulgaria was in their sphere of interest, while simultaneously informing the Austrians that he would support them diplomatically elsewhere.

However, the Bulgarian crisis did put an end to the *Dreikaiserbund* as there could no longer be any question of a direct link between Austria and Russia. Bismarck refused to choose between Vienna and St Petersburg. Instead Germany's alliance with Austria was maintained, and a separate agreement, the Reinsurance Treaty, was concluded between Germany and Russia in 1887. Yet by the end of the 1880s, Bismarck and Wilhelm I seemed to be the only two people in Berlin who remained committed to the Prussian tradition of friendship with Russia. By contrast the Foreign Office official Friedrich von Holstein believed that dynastic ties were no longer a sufficient guarantee of stable German–Russian relations, and accused Bismarck of standing 'in front of the Tsar, cap in hand, trying to console him with fine phrases for the fact that in the sphere of political matters we are already Russia's opponents'.[9] Military figures went even further, and urged that a 'preventive war' be launched against Russia. Thus it seemed as if Bismarck's improvised system of alliances was on the point of collapse even prior to his fall from power.

Criticisms can be made of German diplomacy under Bismarck. The annexation of Alsace-Lorraine in 1871 was a blunder for it made France Germany's permanent antagonist. This hostility reduced Bismarck's freedom of manoeuvre in negotiations with other powers as it left the Reich vulnerable on its western flank. The Chancellor can also be criticized for standing, like King Canute, against the rising tide, which in the nineteenth century took the form of nationalism. By championing the survival of the supranational Habsburg Empire, Bismarck antagonized the Slav peoples of eastern Europe, including the Russians, and made it more difficult for Tsar Alexander III to maintain Russia's traditionally friendly ties with Germany. The Tsar hesitated, for example, to conclude the Reinsurance Treaty with Berlin in 1887 because he feared that 'such an alliance would be unpopular and contrary to the national feelings of all of Russia' and would 'destroy the confidence of the country in his foreign policy'.[10]

However, on balance, the virtues in Bismarck's approach towards diplomacy are more apparent than the flaws. He appreciated that Germany's geographical position at the heart of Europe placed a particular burden on her statesmen to handle the other Great Powers with skill. The Chancellor's commitment to Austria-Hungary was not unconditional. He refused to encourage her aspirations to hegemony in the Balkans, preferring to see the region divided between Austrian and Russian spheres of interest.[11] However, Bismarck realized that the survival of the Habsburg Empire was necessary in order to prevent Russian expansion into central Europe, and in that sense later events proved his approach to have been a sensible one. Finally, and most importantly, Bismarck understood that for Germany the relationship with Russia was the key to everything else. An alliance with Russia allowed Germany to restrain Austria in the Balkans, and it also pre-empted the possibility of a Franco-Russian alliance and the danger that the Reich would face a war on two fronts. Bismarck's opponents in the late 1880s exaggerated the extent of the Russian danger, and they also played on a seeming contradiction between Germany's commitments to Austria and Russia in order to argue against the Reinsurance Treaty with St Petersburg. However, in reality, there was no contradiction between the two obligations, as Germany had made no undertaking to support Austria against Russia in the Balkans. At the very least Bismarck's successors should have made an attempt to keep his ailing system of alliances going after 1890, for by letting the Reinsurance Treaty lapse in that year they created the conditions for the formation of the combination which Bismarck had most feared – an alliance between France and Russia – and the accompanying risk that Germany would one day face a war on two fronts.

Colonial Policy

For German patriots of the first part of the nineteenth century the quest for empire had a very specific meaning. Involving neither an external focus nor any consideration of amassing colonies in distant lands or dominion over far-off peoples, it related instead to a much more precise and self-directed gaze. For such individuals, the founding of a German Empire referred specifically to the creation of a single united German state. All their interest, all their efforts and all their aspirations were bound up in this one cause, the achievement of which became the objective of a nationalist movement, whose adherents campaigned incessantly to this end.

With the foundation of the Second Reich in January 1871, the nationalist movement gained its objective but lost its *raison d'être*. It did not, however, lose its vitality. On the contrary, owing to its many years of hard, heartfelt struggle, the movement had become too dynamic simply to fade away just because its task seemed to be done. Too much energy had been devoted over too many years for the sentiments thereby generated to be dispelled so easily. Instead, following the accomplishment of German unity the nationalist movement sought a new focus for its attention. As the nationalist campaigner Heinrich von Sybel put it nine days after the founding of the Reich: 'Where at my age can a new purpose be found for the rest of my life?'[12] For many such people, the answer was to be found in the struggle for overseas empire. The pursuit of such a goal seemed to them a natural development from their initial aims. The creation of a unified Reich had transformed Prussia into a European power of the first rank. The next stage in the hierarchy of states was that of world power and Germany could only achieve such a position by acquiring a global importance of the kind possessed by the likes of Britain, France or Russia. To do that Germany required colonies.

The development of German nationalism from a movement advocating unification to one that strove for world status by the acquisition of colonies can clearly be followed in the pages of the ultranationalist academic and full-time campaigner, Heinrich von Treitschke. His works, all of which were influential and all of which showed as a common denominator a striking and vehement nationalist tone, none the less differ significantly in their emphasis according to their year of publication. While his earlier works and speeches served to advance the idea of the German nation state, after the consolidation of the Reich, he turned to the new political aim of establishing Germany at the summit of the world order by transforming the Prussian state from an instrument of great power (*Grossmacht*) to one of world power (*Weltmacht*). 'The possession of overseas lands and maritime greatness', he observed, '[are features] without which a truly great power cannot exist nowadays.'[13] Many Germans agreed with him in this assessment.

Though eloquently advocated by Treitschke, this view was not shared by Bismarck. Presented with such arguments, the Iron Chancellor was apt to dismiss them with a cursory explanation of the importance of central Europe to Germany's geopolitical position. Told by one enthusiast that the Reich needed colonies in Africa, Bismarck pointed to a map of Europe and replied: 'Your map of Africa is very fine, but my map of Africa is here in Europe. Here is Russia and here is France and here are we in the middle. That is my map of Africa.'[14] Given this outlook, there seemed no prospect that Bismarck would become an advocate of colonies. As Ernst von Weber recorded after an interview in which he had attempted to persuade Bismarck to support his scheme of African expansion: 'Prince Bismarck expressed his approbation of my patriotic sentiments but held out no prospect of these projects being entertained by the Imperial government.'[15] Such was the attitude of the authorities for the majority of Bismarck's tenure of office – 18 of his 19 years as chancellor. However, for a short period between April 1884 and May 1885, in a move that startled opinion both at home and abroad, the Chancellor transformed the nature of his attitude to overseas expansion and acquired for Germany, in a series of unexpected actions, a colonial empire, comprised of the territories of Togoland, Tanganyika, Cameroon, South West Africa and north-eastern New Guinea, that was five times the size of the Reich.

The cause of Bismarck's sudden outburst of imperialism, which lasted for precisely one year and was then never seen again, is the subject of considerable historical debate. A number of distinct hypotheses have been brought forward in explanation for his actions. Broadly speaking, these can be divided into four categories.

Firstly, there are those interpretations that stress the pre-eminent role of diplomacy and emphasize that, for Bismarck, colonial policy was grounded firmly in European considerations.[16] According to this argument, Bismarck's entry into the colonial arena was intended as a means of enhancing Germany's diplomatic position in Europe. It achieved this in a number of different ways. To begin with, it reaffirmed Germany's importance. For Bismarck marked the inauguration of his new policy in a dramatic manner. On 26 February 1884 Britain and Portugal signed a treaty delineating their holdings in west–central Africa. Germany, being exclusively a European power, was not consulted in advance, a circumstance that Bismarck used to attack the treaty, to force its retraction, and then used as a basis for summoning a conference of powers to Berlin to resolve the matter. In one fell swoop it was clearly demonstrated that German agreement was necessary for colonial as well as European diplomacy. Germany's diplomatic standing immediately grew stronger, an outcome that had a particularly dramatic effect upon the relationship between Germany and France. Long-term enemies since the German seizure of Alsace-Lorraine at the end of the Franco-Prussian War, Bismarck's colonial strategy now gave these two powers common cause against Britain. This not only proved to the British that Franco-German hostility could not be taken for granted, it proved to the French that, in spite of their differences over Alsace-Lorraine, 'there could be concrete cooperation with Imperial Germany and that it was worth looking beyond a war of revenge to areas of possible mutual understanding ... '.[17] Germany's interest in the colonial sphere thus gave the Reich greater leverage in the European diplomatic context.

Alternatively, it has been suggested that, rather than foreign policy considerations, the explanation for Bismarck's colonial acquisitions is to be found in the realm of domestic politics and, in particular, in the need for a focal point for the 1884 Reichstag election campaign.[18] This interpretation, which is strongly supported by Bismarck's record of attempting to procure extraneous issues for parliamentary purposes, draws primarily on the fact that Bismarck's colonial ventures and, in particular the high profile Berlin Africa Conference, coincided to a remarkable degree with the election campaign – beginning shortly before its commencement and ending shortly thereafter. Moreover, during that campaign, colonialism quickly developed into a major issue that divided those parties such as the Progressives, which opposed the Chancellor, from those such as the National Liberals, which were willing to give him their support. Colonialism was thus an excellent source of political capital whereby Bismarck could unify and strengthen those parties that supported him and provide them with a means of attacking the opposition as unpatriotic. Such, in any case, was to be the use to which the colonial issue would be put in the campaign of that year. Given this circumstance, it is hardly surprising that the senior Foreign Office official, Friedrich von Holstein, concluded that, for Bismarck, colonialism 'was scarcely more than an election stunt. He has in fact no interest in the colonial question.'[19]

Also stressing domestic political considerations is an explanation that focuses upon Bismarck's worries about the succession to the Prussian and German thrones.[20] After many years of mutual co-operation, Bismarck had developed a relationship with Kaiser Wilhelm I that afforded him considerable latitude and independence. Despite the fact that Wilhelm had appointed Bismarck only reluctantly and had, on many occasions, disagreed with Bismarck's policies, Wilhelm had come to rely upon his chancellor to such an extent that he rarely challenged Bismarck's views and, on the few occasions when he did, he could normally be persuaded to defer to Bismarck if the latter threatened him with resignation. The prospects of a similar relationship being forged between Bismarck and the next Kaiser were, however, exceptionally remote. Wilhelm's successor, Crown Prince Friedrich, was known to entertain liberal views and to possess constitutional ideas that were markedly at variance with those of the conservative Bismarck. Compounding this situation was the attitude of Friedrich's strong-willed British-born wife, the Princess Victoria. The eldest daughter of Queen Victoria and Prince Albert, she not only shared her parents' belief in the virtues of the British system of limited monarchy, a matter on which Bismarck had an entirely opposite opinion, but she combined this with a strong dislike for the incumbent Chancellor. These views complemented those of her husband, with the result that, in her company, Friedrich's liberal predilections were regularly fortified and strengthened.

As a consequence of this situation, it was widely expected, not least by Bismarck himself, that the death of Wilhelm I and the succession of Friedrich would quickly be followed by the Chancellor's dismissal. Given that in 1884, Wilhelm was an old man of 87 years, there was every likelihood that this change in Bismarck's political fortunes was to be expected soon. Consequently, so far as Bismarck was concerned, there existed a real and immediate need to take some form of action to forestall this eventuality and, in many respects, colonialism seemed the ideal response. The logic behind this was straightforward. By acquiring colonies, Germany entered a new diplomatic realm in which Britain was the leading player. As a colonial power, therefore, the Reich ran a good chance of developing conflicts of interest with Britain. Although there was little doubt that by careful diplomacy these conflicts could be smoothed over, it was equally true that they had the potential to be transformed into bitter open quarrels. In colonies, therefore, Bismarck had a ready-made mechanism for generating Anglo-German diplomatic incidents at any time he wished. Given that such incidents would undoubtedly create an anti-British mood in Germany, colonialism was an ideal way of making the position of a British-born empress extremely difficult. In the climate of public hostility to all things British that Bismarck could always engineer, it would be simple for Bismarck to discredit 'foreign' ideas of government and to make it patriotic to oppose them. Rather than risking such a breach between the country and his wife, Friedrich would be likely to maintain a Bismarckian course. In this way, colonies provided leverage over the future emperor. A considerable body of evidence exists to support the notion that this rationale acted as a motive for Bismarck's colonial adventure. To begin with, the idea that 'the sole aim of German colonial policy was to drive a wedge between the Crown Prince and England' was the explanation that Bismarck provided to Tsar Alexander.[21] In addition to this, it was also the explanation that was retrospectively stressed by Bismarck's son and confidant, Herbert. In 1890, he recalled:

> When we entered upon a colonial policy, we had to reckon with a long reign of the Crown Prince. During this reign English influence would have been dominant. To prevent this, we had to embark upon

a colonial policy, because it was popular and conveniently adapted to bring us into conflict with England at any given moment.[22]

Finally, there are those explanations based upon the proposition that Bismarck embarked upon expansionism as a means of mitigating against the adverse effects of industrialization and in particular against the impact of recession.[23] In the downturn of the years 1873–79, Bismarck had attempted to obtain economic and social stability through special legislation and protectionism. This had seemed reasonably successful at the time. However, with the beginning of a new period of depression in 1882, it was clear that these earlier endeavours had failed and that a new form of socio-economic manipulation was required. Under this interpretation, colonialism fulfilled that requirement. Expansion overseas, a move designed to produce a counter-cyclical effect, thus became an economic countermeasure in the struggle against depression.[24] Given that such a policy, if successfully pursued, would have had the additional benefit of helping to legitimize the status quo and thereby ensure the stabilization of both Germany's existing social hierarchy and her conservative political power structure, this expansionism has been described as 'social imperialism'.[25]

Whatever Bismarck's actual reason for embarking upon these colonial ventures – in all likelihood, it was a combination of the above factors, rather than a single motive – one possibility that can definitely be excluded is the idea, advocated by Mary Townsend, that Bismarck was genuinely converted to the virtues of imperialism.[26] All the evidence suggests that he possessed some kind of ulterior motive for his change of heart. Bismarck's behaviour after 1885 provides further evidence for this conclusion. To begin with, in the remaining five years of his chancellorship, Bismarck added no new colonies to the German collection. Such opportunities as existed, he ignored. True, he engaged in long-drawn-out negotiations over the borders of those colonies already taken, but this was designed not to increase the square mileage under German control, but to provide a bargaining tool for German diplomacy. This stance was greatly to disappoint the numerous colonial enthusiasts and pressure groups that had rallied behind the expansionist actions of the period 1884–85. Expecting bold new manoeuvres in the colonial sphere, they found Bismarck's sudden reticence both disheartening and inexplicable.

Bismarck's inherent lack of interest in colonies is further demonstrated by his policy towards them once Germany had acquired them. It had always been Bismarck's view that overseas empire was liable to be a financial burden rather than a blessing for the Reich. Particularly wor-rying was the possibility that the seizure of colonies would necessitate expensive colonial administrations as such an outcome would necessi-tate the Reich government seeking additional financial measures from the Reichstag, a body whose influence Bismarck did not want to see increased. Consequently, his intention was to hand the administration of the new colonies over to private companies that would exercise sovereign rights there under imperial charter. As he put it, in a speech to the Reichstag in November 1885: 'my goal in those regions is the governing merchant and not the governing bureaucrat – not the governing military and Prussian official'.[27] The advantage of such a policy for the German government was clear-cut: the difficulties and expense of colonialism would be transferred to those commercial organizations that benefited from it. The advantage for the companies selected to fulfil this task was much less clear and, needless to say, they proved far from willing to take on the role that Bismarck envisaged for them. Some refused outright. Some accepted only after the application of considerable governmental pressure and even then were to renounce their sovereign rights and hand back their responsibilities to the Reich authorities at the earliest opportunity. By the time that Bismarck left office, the policy of rule by chartered companies was clearly a failure and the value of the colonies, acquired for the most ulterior of reasons, was openly being questioned in government circles. Consideration was even being given to the possi-bility of their abandonment.

In spite of Bismarck's disenchantment with colonial ventures, his legacy to his country in the sphere of imperialism was not lack of inter-est in colonialism, but a Germany with imperial obligations and con-cerns. It soon transpired that once acquired these could not easily be discarded. On the contrary, Bismarck had laid foundations upon which others would subsequently feel obliged to build.

4

THE CHANGE OF REGIME

1888: The Year of the Three Emperors

The year 1888 is best regarded as a turning point in the history of the German Empire. On 9 March, Kaiser Wilhelm I finally died at the age of 91. His death brought his 56-year-old son Crown Prince Friedrich Wilhelm to the throne as Kaiser Friedrich III. The accession of the new Kaiser ought to have ushered in a volte-face in both domestic and foreign policy, in the form of a diminution in Bismarck's power, or even his dismissal, and a turning away from Russia and towards Britain, the country of Friedrich Wilhelm's wife, the Crown Princess. Instead by the time that Wilhelm I finally died, the new Emperor was himself already dying of throat cancer. His reign lasted only 99 days. During the reign, Bismarck and even Friedrich's son, Crown Prince Wilhelm, were looking towards a different future – one in which Prussian traditions and the authoritarian state would be upheld domestically, and a traditional foreign policy would be pursued externally. However, even between Prince Bismarck and Wilhelm there were differences. The Chancellor envisaged that he would continue to direct the course of German policy, whereas the 29-year-old Kaiser-in-waiting had other ideas. The senior Foreign Office official Friedrich von Holstein noted this in March 1888:

> The Chancellor is fond of telling his intimates that he feels sure of the Crown Prince. I do not believe that and I rather doubt whether the Chancellor believes it himself. The Chancellor's military opponents tell the Crown Prince that Friedrich II would never have become Frederick the Great under the political tutelage of a Minister like Bismarck.[1]

Holstein was correct. It was to prove impossible for Wilhelm to submit to Bismarck's authority in the long term. One area of contention was policy towards Russia. Bismarck wished to maintain the alliance with the Tsarist Empire at all costs, whereas Wilhelm had come to believe, under the influence of military figures, such as Count von Waldersee, that war between Germany and Russia was inevitable. Hence 1888 failed to usher in a new liberal era in the history of Prussian Germany, and ended with only superficial continuity between the regimes of Wilhelm I and Wilhelm II. Bismarck was still in office, but the new Kaiser wished to take over the reins of power himself at some point in the future, and to turn Germany in a new anti-Russian direction diplomatically. The brief reign of the liberal Friedrich III was thus followed by a continuation of reaction; but it was a different form of authoritarianism from that which had preceded. The most notable difference was that the Kaiser would not defer to Bismarck as Wilhelm I had done. The year 1888 thus represented the beginning of the end for Bismarck as well as a colossal setback for the cause of liberal reform in Prussia and Germany.

During most of the 1880s this outcome could not have been envisaged. Until Crown Prince Friedrich Wilhelm was diagnosed with throat cancer in 1887, everyone in Germany had assumed that he would enjoy a long reign as Kaiser once Wilhelm I finally passed away. There was a real possibility that Friedrich Wilhelm would have instituted significant political changes as Kaiser. The Crown Prince and his English wife, Victoria, were liberals. There is evidence that their conceptions of liberalism differed. Friedrich Wilhelm believed in liberalism from the top down. He wished to strengthen the power of the Crown at the expense of that of the Chancellor, and while wishing to turn Germany in a progressive direction, he respected Prussian traditions and had no time for political radicalism. By contrast Crown Princess Victoria's political views were much further to the left. For example, she admired Gladstone, whom her mother abhorred, and wished to see the Prussian monarchy develop into a copy of its British counterpart. She wrote to Queen Victoria on one occasion: 'I hold the British Constitution to be the best and most useful and blessed form of government in the world.'[2] Most injudiciously, she did not keep such opinions to herself while in Germany, and thus set herself against the powerful conservative forces in the Prussian establishment. Holstein noted in April 1885 that she had made the following pronouncement:

> The Crown Princess stated again recently that in the coming transformation of society there would be no more room for 'powerful'

monarchs. Power was superfluous; it was enough for the sovereign to secure personal influence – In England, for example, the Queen possessed no real power, she did nevertheless wield unusual influence and was generally loved and respected.[3]

Both she and the Crown Prince had a turbulent political and personal relationship with Prince Bismarck, and it looked likely that once they were strong enough politically, they would dispense with his services, and appoint a liberal chancellor. In foreign policy, the Crown Prince and Princess also favoured change. They were suspicious of Russia and supported the idea of an alliance between Germany and Britain. Their support for change in the Reich's domestic and foreign policy came together in the promotion of a marriage between their daughter Victoria and Prince Alexander of Battenberg. Battenberg had earned the hostility of Tsar Alexander III when as Prince of Bulgaria between 1878 and 1885 he had shown political independence, instead of acting as a Russian vassal. The Crown Princess believed that both Britain and Germany should support Battenberg, and jointly resist Russia in the Balkans. This objective had aroused the suspicion of the Bismarcks, who feared that the German-born Battenberg's actions could cause irreparable harm to German–Russian relations. The danger did not end, however, when Battenberg was deposed in a Russian-sponsored coup, for the Crown Princess began to suggest new projects for Battenberg. He might, for example, she argued, be a suitable candidate for the post of Governor of Alsace-Lorraine. This was seen as a possible prelude to Battenberg's appointment as Chancellor during the forthcoming reign. Bismarck was aware of this, and the vehemence with which he attacked Battenberg, and opposed his marriage into the Prussian royal family is only explicable against this context. Bismarck acknowledged that he feared that Battenberg 'would return to Germany and endeavour to create a position for himself here'.[4]

It would be too sweeping to argue that, but for the Crown Prince's premature death in June 1888, the Prussian monarchy would have been transformed into a copy of its British counterpart. Considerable potential for a liberal transformation of the German political structure would have been there, in the sense that as Kaiser the Crown Prince would have had the power to appoint progressive figures to high positions, and thus to influence the course of policy. However, from the evidence of the 1880s, there can be no doubt that the obstacles to the implementation of such a strategy would have been formidable. The Crown Prince himself seems to have acknowledged that any change would have to be gradual, and thus gave Bismarck an indication in the autumn of 1885 that he would retain him as Chancellor after his accession. The precariousness of the political position of the Crown Prince and Princess is attributable to several factors. It can be related in the first instance to the character of their marriage. Friedrich Wilhelm was seen as a hen-pecked husband, dominated by his headstrong and radical wife. 'The deepest popular concern', one historian has written, 'was that Friedrich and Victoria's domestic relationship would be played out upon the national stage.'[5] It would not be going too far to suggest that the Crown Prince was regarded as a pathetic figure. Holstein noted, half in regret, half in contempt: 'it is absolutely inconceivable that the Crown Prince should ever, no matter what the circumstances, assert his own will in opposition to his wife's'.[6] The Crown Princess herself was viewed with almost universal suspicion in court circles at Berlin. Even an individual as well disposed towards her as Hugo Baron von Reischach noted that her grave mistake had been that: 'She was English in Germany and German in Britain.'[7] Other observers were much less charitable. Bismarck, for example, viewed her with great suspicion because of her English sympathies. 'The only thing I reproach the lady with', he declared, 'is that she's remained an Englishwoman and exerts a pro-English influence on her husband. She's got no feeling for Germany.'[8] The hostility of Bismarck and his son Herbert, who became State Secretary at the German Foreign Office in 1885, was the second factor which would have constrained the political freedom of action of the Crown Prince and Princess. They opposed the couple's aim of detaching Germany from Russia diplomatically, and were just as unsympathetic to their political objectives within Germany. One only has to look at the trouble which Bismarck caused to Wilhelm II after he was dropped as Chancellor to realize the dangers that would have been involved had Friedrich Wilhelm dismissed Prince Bismarck on becoming Kaiser.

Of even greater significance to the Crown Prince and Princess's chances of carrying through liberal reform in Germany and the creation of an Anglo-German alliance diplomatically was the opposition which they faced from their eldest son, Prince Wilhelm, the future Kaiser Wilhelm II. Wilhelm was viewed as the coming man even in the mid 1880s, and was sometimes compared favourably to his supine and liberal father, the Crown Prince. Holstein noted that public opinion took the view that: 'The Crown Prince won't make a good ruler. We want Prince Wilhelm; he'll be a second Frederick the Great.'[9] Wilhelm's political philosophy was much closer to that of his grandfather than his father. He attached himself to the old centres of power: the Kaiser, the Kaiserin, the Chancellor, the Evangelical Church, the army and Junkerdom. His mother despaired of him. As early as 1880, she complained to Queen Victoria that, 'Willie is chauvinistic and ultra-Prussian to a degree and with a violence which is often very painful to me; I avoid all discussions – always turn off the subject and remain silent.'[10] By 1887, having been taken under the wing of the old Kaiser and the Bismarcks, and having usurped many of the functions of the Crown Prince, Wilhelm was seen in an even more negative light by the Crown Princess. 'William is used as a tool by the government and conservative party and the Emperor's court', she wrote. 'And he fancies himself consequently of immense importance, and that he is of more use to the country than his papa, who in his eyes does not keep up Prussian traditions enough.'[11]

Wilhelm's opposition to his parents was not restricted to the sphere of domestic politics. He rejected their sympathy for Britain, telling his friend Philipp zu Eulenburg-Hertfeld: 'One can never have enough hatred for England.'[12] Instead, from the mid 1880s onwards Wilhelm appeared to be a supporter of co-operation between Germany and Russia. He had first been sent to Russia on a mission to Tsar Alexander III by Wilhelm I and Bismarck in 1884. In so doing, he had earned the Chancellor's approval and the Tsar's trust. Bismarck informed Wilhelm after the visit that the Tsar had stated: 'Everything which the Prince told me pleased me enormously. He sees things as they really are and understands everything. I am very satisfied by our discussions.'[13] Two days later, Wilhelm wrote a letter to the Tsar thanking him for his kind words and warning him against his own parents, the Crown Prince and Princess, who he said saw politics through 'English spectacles'. He also gave Alexander an assurance that 'the Emperor, Prince Bismarck and myself are in agreement, and I will never cease to regard it as my highest duty to consolidate and maintain the Dreikaiserbund everywhere'.[14] The breach between Wilhelm and his parents was fuelled by the obvious favour with which he was viewed by Wilhelm I and Bismarck, but also by this disagreement over policy towards Russia.

A further issue which widened the breach between the Crown Prince and Princess and their eldest son was the Battenberg marriage project. Wilhelm was so vehement that this should not take place that he told Herbert Bismarck: 'How on earth could one prevent this unhappy marriage? If all else fails, I will club the Battenberger to death!'[15] Wilhelm's objections were probably more personal than political. He did not believe that Battenberg, as the product of a morganatic marriage, was of sufficiently high birth to marry his sister. Additionally, he was suspicious that the Crown Princess wished to give Battenberg a role in German affairs at his expense. However, Wilhelm was also made aware by Bismarck of the potentially disastrous diplomatic consequences of the match for German–Russian relations. He did his utmost to reassure the Tsar that he would use his influence against Battenberg,[16] to Alexander's evident delight.[17] The fact that Wilhelm was so disloyal to his parents as to condemn them and their plans for his sister's future marriage in letters to the ruler of a foreign power is indicative of the extent of the breach which had grown up between him and the Crown Prince and Princess by the mid 1880s. Wilhelm I had come to regard his grandson rather than his son as his true successor, speaking 'with delight of Prince Wilhelm', whom he credited with the transformation in Germany's relations with Russia and 'harshly and unfavourably of the Crown Prince'.[18] In the light of all the evidence of the political marginalization of the Crown Prince and Princess prior to 1888, it must be doubted that they could have imposed a change of political direction on Germany even during a long period of power. However, by the time that Friedrich Wilhelm succeeded as Kaiser in March 1888 all their political hopes had been dashed by his terminal illness.

The Crown Prince was first diagnosed with throat cancer in May 1887. By the time he succeeded as Kaiser, the Crown Prince was obviously a dying man. Three weeks after the Crown Prince's accession as Kaiser Friedrich III, Herbert Bismarck observed, in a letter to the British politician the Earl of Rosebery, that the new Emperor was not in a fit state to rule Germany, being terminally ill and dominated by the wishes of his wife:

> Now the present poor Emperor does not really care for politics, he is never allowed to form an opinion of his own but is only guided by the will, of whom you know. ... But even if things were otherwise he would simply not be able to transact business on account of the prostration of his whole system: ... his breathing is but a rattling, and I fear the doctors are right in anticipating that we shall see the end in May.[19]

Herbert was overly pessimistic about Friedrich III's life expectancy, but politically this did not matter greatly. Power had already slipped from the Emperor's grasp prior to his death, and Prince Bismarck felt able to ignore even minor instructions from the new Kaiser, such as his desire that honours be conferred on a number of prominent liberals. Even

Holstein, no admirer of the Emperor and his English wife, was shocked by the extent to which power had seeped away from the throne. 'It is shocking for royalists', Holstein recorded, 'to see how completely powerless the Kaiser is. It is very gratifying that he has not been able to realise his liberal fantasies. But surely he should now be deferred to in *minor* matters. But no.'[20] Prince Wilhelm, by contrast, was gaining the confidence that came from the anticipation of power. 'William fancies himself the Emperor', his mother observed, 'and an absolute and autocratic one.'[21] When he ascended the throne, Wilhelm heaped one final humiliation on his mother. He forbade the marriage which she had worked for between his sister and Battenberg; the one project which she had felt confident enough to advance during the brief reign of Friedrich III. Wilhelm's decision created a breach between him and his mother which appeared to be final. She accused him of exhibiting a 'perfectly heartless disregard' for his sister's feelings by prohibiting the marriage, and accused Wilhelm of finding 'his chief delight, in doing all he can think of to insult and wound me'. She vowed 'for the future to hold no communication' with him 'beyond what is absolutely necessary'.[22]

Wilhelm's appalling treatment of his mother had a negative impact on Germany's relations with Britain, for it was regarded as offensive by Queen Victoria and the British royal family. This, coupled with Wilhelm's continuing Anglophobia, meant that there was little chance that his parents' aim of an Anglo-German alliance would be realized in the new reign. Friedrich III's death seemed instead to promise a continuation of authoritarian policies at home and abroad. However, the accession of Wilhelm II as Kaiser shifted the balance of power subtly away from Bismarck and towards the throne. The process was a gradual one, and the final break between the new Emperor and the septuagenarian Chancellor did not come until March 1890. However, the warning signs were already there. Count Waldersee had predicted, ominously, in November 1887 that 'when Prince Wilhelm is Kaiser he will insist on appearing as the man who really rules – that is why I don't think he and the Chancellor will agree for long'.[23] It was simply impossible to expect that an Emperor who was still in his twenties would be prepared to leave the direction of government in the hands of the Chancellor, in the same way as his aged grandfather had done. The breach was made inevitable by this generational conflict, and by policy differences between the Kaiser and the Chancellor over issues as diverse as the attitude to be adopted towards the working class, south German particularism, and Russia. Holstein was the individual who predicted the disastrous consequences which would ensue during the reign of

Wilhelm II. Commenting on the rude treatment of Wilhelm's mother by Prussian courtiers, shortly before Friedrich III's death, he wrote: 'Today the Kaiserin is reaping what she formerly sowed with her ostentatious contempt of everything German. But the people who are now gratuitously insulting the Kaiserin will get their own back under Wilhelm II; he will show them what a monarch is. That is the nemesis of world history.'[24] Subsequent blunders in domestic and foreign affairs under the new Kaiser soon confirmed the accuracy of Holstein's words.

The Character of Kaiser Wilhelm II

The accession of Wilhelm II in 1888 is undoubtedly one of the key moments in the history of the Second Reich. The new Emperor was an impetuous and unstable individual of 29, who wished to rule personally, and had contempt for liberal politics, preferring absolutism to constitutionalism. He also had new ideas in the spheres of foreign, colonial and armaments policy, involving German dominance in Europe, and the building of a great navy to challenge the British Empire. Wilhelm was to set Germany on a course which led directly to world war in 1914, and the collapse of the *Kaiserreich* in 1918.

The new Emperor's personality was the subject of much comment at the time, and has been the subject of considerable historical speculation in recent decades. This is largely because it is in Wilhelm's personality and neuroses that the roots of many of the policies which he pursued as Kaiser are to be found. His character encompassed a mass of contradictions. In public, he was the supremely confident ruler and warlord, yet in private when things went wrong he was prone to self-doubt and came close to a nervous breakdown on a number of occasions, notably during the Eulenburg scandal in 1907 and during the *Daily Telegraph* affair in the autumn of 1908. He dazzled many of those who first met him, such as the British politician John Morley, the British diplomat Frank Lascelles, the future Chancellor Bernhard von Bülow, and the Prussian courtier Robert von Zedlitz-Trützschler, with the breadth of his knowledge, his quick intelligence and his charisma. Yet close acquaintance revealed an individual who was more of a dilettante than a polymath. Some of those who spent years in close proximity to Wilhelm, such as Zedlitz, eventually became very disenchanted both with the Kaiser himself and with the atmosphere of unctuous flattery which surrounded him.

The instability of the Kaiser's character, which may have amounted to mental illness, was manifested in rapid mood swings, in a love both of dressing up and of having people dress up for him, in a cruelty offset at times by kindness, and in a restlessness of mind, and even of location. Wilhelm was rarely in Berlin, and was known as the *Reisekaiser*, the travelling Emperor. It was joked that those who wished to visit Germany, but not the Kaiser, need only travel to Berlin as they would be sure to avoid meeting him. Wilhelm's erratic behaviour mattered politically, and not just because of his exalted position. Holstein observed astutely that the political danger of Wilhelm's personality lay in the fact that he was 'a sensitive character who gives vent to personal displeasure in practical affairs'.[25] This tendency to give public expression to private grievances was compounded by Wilhelm's belief that German interests and his own were synonymous. It resulted in countless embarrassments in both domestic and foreign politics.

Of crucial importance for the course of German diplomacy in the years after his accession was Wilhelm's attitude towards his mother's country, Great Britain. It can best be described as a love–hate relationship. He had a genuine admiration for his grandmother Queen Victoria and for the grandeur of the British Empire. He loved English country house life, and in exile at Doorn in Holland after 1918 he lived like an English country gentleman. The tone was set from the moment of arrival in the Netherlands at the end of the war when, seemingly without irony, he asked his Dutch host Count Bentinck for 'a cup of tea, good, hot English tea'.[26] Yet the British ruling class never really accepted him. His English was near perfect, but his accent retained as much of the Teuton as of the aristocratic Englishman, and his attempts to wear the civilian clothes favoured by British gentlemen made him appear, it was once unkindly remarked, 'more of an incongruous cad than most Bank Holiday trippers to Margate'.[27] Wilhelm's choice of English friends continued this pattern of slightly inappropriate behaviour. His closest friend in England was the debt-ridden and anti-Semitic Germanophile Hugh Lowther, Fifth Earl of Lonsdale, whom the Kaiser 'regarded as the most reliable of advisers about English things'.[28] Yet the Earl supported some of Wilhelm's most questionable diplomatic interventions, such as the Kruger Telegram, and was distrusted by both Queen Victoria and Edward VII.

Wilhelm's cultural affinity with England was not paralleled in the political sphere. Here there was more hate than love. In youth, he reacted against the liberalism of his English mother and her desire as he saw it, to turn the Prussian monarchy into a copy of its British counterpart. In a retrospective note written while in exile in Holland after 1918, Wilhelm recalled: 'Kaiserin Friedrich's programme was such, that she wanted to implement a full version of the English parliamentary system in Germany, and to turn Germany, as it were, into the land-based vassal for England's continental aspirations.'[29] Politically, even before his accession, Wilhelm had allied himself with Bismarck and Wilhelm I against his liberal parents and his opinions, according to Crown Prince Rudolf of Austria, were those of 'a dyed-in-the-wool Junker and reactionary'.[30]

Many of the disasters which befell Germany after 1888 can be attributed to the actions of Wilhelm II. The premature death of Wilhelm's father while far from destroying German liberalism, removed the prospect that German politics would be reshaped from above by a persuasive advocate of progressive ideas. The young Kaiser Wilhelm proved unable to work with Bismarck, whom he dropped as Chancellor in March 1890, and replaced with General Leo von Caprivi.

However, the real disaster of Wilhelm's reign did not lie in Bismarck's dismissal. The Iron Chancellor was 75 years old and an individual out of sympathy with modern industrial society, and thus not suited to direct Germany in the closing years of the nineteenth century. Two other factors explain the catastrophe which occurred: firstly, Wilhelm's determination to reaffirm the semi-absolutist character of the Prussian monarchy by re-establishing the practice whereby the monarch ruled personally; secondly, the fact that the new Kaiser's unstable personality made him peculiarly unsuited to fill the role of absolute ruler. The years after 1890 were characterized by the Kaiser's attempts to build up his personal power through control over policy-making and government appointments. By 1897, this process had largely been completed. However, there was a cost to this. Wilhelm was unable to tolerate talented individuals whom he feared might challenge his authority. Thus many of those promoted were mediocrities. Bernhard von Bülow, known as the 'eel' because of his talent for flattering Wilhelm, who was State Secretary at the Foreign Office from 1897 to 1900, and Chancellor from October 1900 until July 1909, showed more interest in writing florid speeches to the Reichstag than in day-to-day administration. By contrast individuals such as Marschall, the State Secretary at the Foreign Office in the mid 1890s, who showed real independence of judgement, found that their careers stalled. Marschall suffered the ignominy of being banished to Constantinople as German ambassador. In 1903 Wilhelm lamented the lack of influence which Germany had in foreign capitals, isolating Marschall at Constantinople as the exception. He noted with chilling foresight that 'if this continues we will find ourselves surprised one day by a "Global Coalition" against us'.[31] Yet it took him until 1912 to draw the logical consequence from this and promote Marschall to the key post of German ambassador to London, by which time it was too late to reverse the damage caused by 15 years of inept diplomacy.

Within Germany, Wilhelm antagonized most of the other federal rulers as a result of his vigorous assertion of his position as *primus inter pares* and his unpredictable behaviour. King Albert of Saxony summed up the view which the *Bundesfürsten* held of Kaiser Wilhelm when he remarked that the princes 'would under no circumstances follow *this* Kaiser into a fight because they would run the risk that he would change his mind in the middle of it, he is too unstable'.[32] It was little wonder therefore that within a few years of Wilhelm's accession fears that the Reich might break up had revived. Most worrying were the policy implications of the Kaiser's assertive style of kingship. In domestic politics, Wilhelm's own instability was manifested in the inconsistency of the strategies adopted. When he came to the throne, he wanted to be a worker's Kaiser, yet within a few years he was repressing them in a way which would have made even Bismarck blush. He antagonized the Reichstag deputies with his Caesaristic utterances, and belittling comments. The tone was set from the outset, when he told the Italian ambassador in 1888: 'After the French, the people I hate most are diplomats and deputies.'[33]

More disturbing, because they were more frequent and had more damaging consequences, were the Kaiser's interventions in the spheres of diplomacy and military policy, both of which were areas reserved to the Crown. In foreign policy, the initial impression is of the same inconsistency as in domestic policy. This has irritated and confused historians of German diplomacy in the Second Reich right up to the present day. Most notable seems to have been the difficulty Wilhelm experienced in choosing between Britain and the Hohenzollerns' traditional ally, Russia. The volatility of approach saw Wilhelm abandon the Reinsurance Treaty with Russia in 1890, and try to forge closer ties with Britain. During the Boer War, he sent his uncle Edward VII battle plans for the British army to use against the Boers, yet suggested to the Russians that they join with him in a coalition to destroy the British Empire. During the Russo-Japanese War, Wilhelm made strenuous efforts to bring about an alliance with Russia, yet in the last years before 1914, he sought frantically to win over the British as he knew that his hopes for a German–Russian alliance could not be realized. In addition, the Kaiser's belligerent speeches, his unattractive personality and diplomatic double-dealing, worked against Germany's international interests. By procrastinating between London and St Petersburg, and by constantly emphasizing German strength, Wilhelm created a situation in which both the British and the Russians concluded that a Germany led by him constituted a threat to world peace.

Despite the emphasis in orthodox accounts on Wilhelm II's inconsistency, two central ideas can be discerned underneath the mounds of conflicting evidence: the Kaiser's determination to turn Germany into a world power of the first rank, and a desire to place himself and Germany at the head of a United States of Europe ruled from Berlin. The latter objective first surfaced in 1892 when Wilhelm told his friend Philipp Eulenburg that his aim for Germany in Europe was 'a sort of Napoleonic supremacy ... '.[34] It reappeared in the Kaiser's utterances throughout the rest of his life. In December 1940, in the light of Nazi victories in the west, and only six months before his death, Wilhelm welcomed the formation of a 'United States of Europe' under German control, excluding British influence from the Continent.[35] These two objectives – Weltmacht and European hegemony – were bound to undermine the international balance of power. The striking lack of subtlety with which Wilhelm and the succession of mediocrities whom he appointed as Chancellors, State Secretaries and ambassadors, pursued the central policy aims ensured that German ambitions did not remain hidden for long, and provoked the antagonism of the other Great Powers before Berlin had intended.

Wilhelm turned to Britain when he felt that it would accept his plans for European dominance, and in the hope that it would assist in the acquisition of German colonies overseas. Berlin's co-operation with St Petersburg, by contrast, was pursued most vigorously when the Kaiser believed that the British had in one way or other betrayed him, most notably in the years immediately after the conclusion of the Anglo-French Entente of April 1904. The policy of playing Russia and Britain off against each other was utterly unrealistic. It depended on an overestimation of the attractiveness of Germany as an alliance partner. Bülow had set out the policy in a letter to the Kaiser in August 1898: 'The ideal for us remains the firm and independent position set out by Your Majesty between England and Russia, free on both sides, but with the possibility to go with one or other of them whenever it suits Your Majesty.'[36] The servile tone of Bülow's letter reveals much about the atmosphere at Wilhelm's court, but so too do the assumptions which he makes about German power reveal much about his and the Kaiser's false assessment of the level of diplomatic manoeuvre which Germany enjoyed. Britain could not have tolerated German dominance of Europe, as this would have placed Berlin in a position to threaten the British Empire. Similarly, Russia was not going to abandon an alliance with France, which at least had the semblance of an equal partnership, for one with Germany, which would have placed Russia in the position of a satellite state. It was more logical for London and St Petersburg to bury their mutual differences, as they did in 1907, than to enter a partnership with the unpredictable and unstable Kaiser.

However, the most disastrous manifestation of Wilhelm II's Caesaristic ambitions was undoubtedly in the sphere of naval policy. The decision to build a large fleet was a policy which could not have been better designed to antagonize the British, and the evidence makes clear that German navalism was inspired by Wilhelm and his closest advisers, and not by the pressure of public opinion. It was in the sphere of naval armaments that the link between Wilhelm's volatile personality, his love–hate relationship with his mother's country and his ambitions for Germany was most clearly exposed. The disastrous strategy in foreign policy and armaments adopted by Germany from the 1890s onwards can only be understood in the context of Wilhelm II's character. This is why the last Kaiser's accession marks such a key milestone on the road to war in 1914.

The Fall of Bismarck

If, as we have seen above, it was in the character of the new Emperor to wish to assert his independence and rule in his own right, unfettered by the constraints of over-confident and overbearing ministers, then it was undoubtedly the case that the Chancellor he inherited, who had the firmest views on his own authority and position, was not the man to accommodate him. As early as 1838, the young Bismarck had written to his father the following, highly accurate, self-assessment: 'My ambition strives more to command than to obey.'[37] For much of his life, and for all of his chancellorship, this yearning had been most effectively realized. Although Bismarck had arrived in high office as a leader of last resort, distrusted by both his king and his peers, he had quickly rectified this situation, at least insofar as the attitude of his monarch was concerned. In stemming the tide of liberalism, securing the expansion of the Prussian army, and defeating the King's enemies both at home and abroad, Bismarck had secured his sovereign's undying gratitude. This volte-face in the royal outlook was to have enormous political implications, as Wilhelm I's confidence in his chancellor conditioned their future relationship. The first Kaiser expected to be informed and to have his opinions heard, but in the last resort, he would almost always accept Bismarck's judgement on the problems of the day. Bismarck, in his turn, had become accustomed to wielding power almost without restraint. As a result the succession of Wilhelm II to the Prussian and

Imperial thrones was bound to lead to the most profound culture shock at the highest reaches of government. All of a sudden there were two men at the top, both of whom were determined to have their own way. The inevitable result of this was bound to be a power struggle in which one of the two would have to give in to the other. Such was, indeed, to occur.

If a collision between Bismarck and Wilhelm II was largely prefigured by their inherently incompatible characters and aspirations, the rapidity of their clash was far from pre-ordained. Wilhelm II, although a man brimming with self-confidence, came to the throne as an unknown quantity with limited experience of government. While he, personally, suffered no pangs of doubt as to his ability to rule with distinction, it was apparent, even to him, that it would take time for others to realize this themselves. In the interim, before his public persona was properly established, it would be useful for the new monarch to be able to bask in the prestige of the Iron Chancellor. As a result, it had always been Wilhelm's intention to begin his reign with Bismarck still at the helm. As he had unambiguously put it as early as 31 December 1887: 'Prince Bismarck would of course be needed very urgently for a few years yet; later on his functions would be divided up, and the sovereign would have to shoulder more of them himself.'[38] Such was still Wilhelm's intent when he ascended the throne a mere six months later.

This scheme of quietly easing out the Chancellor once Wilhelm had clearly established himself as Kaiser, was extremely unrealistic: it was never likely that Bismarck would co-operate with a plan to undermine his own central role. On the contrary, the Chancellor was determined not only to hold on to his office but also to continue to exercise that measure of authority to which he had become accustomed, the Kaiser's plans to reserve more power to himself notwithstanding. Consequently, once Wilhelm's objective became apparent to him, Bismarck, who had not the slightest intention of bolstering the position of the new monarch merely to facilitate his own removal, acted to counter the new Kaiser's designs. Reinforcing him in this decision was another reason for determined opposition: it had long been Bismarck's intention to establish his family at the top of the Reich hierarchy and, to that end, he had been grooming his son Herbert to be his successor. Unfortunately, a Kaiser who wished to rule himself would inevitably want to appoint a man of his own choosing – someone dependent upon him and compliant to his wishes – to the chancellorship. Herbert von Bismarck, whose reputation and position derived exclusively from the prestige of his father, would, therefore, be unacceptable to Wilhelm and almost certain not to reach the top. Consequently, only if he could constrain the Kaiser and, in some way, exert his authority over him, could Bismarck guarantee to fulfil his twin ambitions of holding on to power and passing his office to his son. Given this necessity, it is clear that Bismarck and the Kaiser were moving inexorably towards a collision. The question remained: when, and over what, would this occur?

The issue that brought matters between them to a head was the need to decide the future policy of the government towards the German working classes, the so-called social question. At first glance, it is not immediately apparent why this should have been so controversial and explosive a point of contention. The Kaiser was by no means a radical on this matter and sought no fundamental changes to the nation's class system; Bismarck, in the course of his chancellorship, had addressed this issue often, employing measures from both ends of the political spectrum, ranging from outright repression to comprehensive social insurance legislation, to deal with it. An understanding between Bismarck and the Kaiser on this point was, thus, perfectly possible. However, no agreement emerged; instead, a major political clash developed, with Wilhelm determined to see the government embark upon a programme of mild social reform, centred on labour protection measures, and Bismarck equally adamant on a new and vigorous policy of coercion. So unyielding were the two figures on their respective positions that this contest quickly escalated to the point where the fundamental question of the relationship between Kaiser and Chancellor was at stake. The severity of the argument was no coincidence. Although there were many policy areas on which the two men differed, the social question became the focal point of the power struggle between them because this was a matter that both parties to the dispute saw as politically advantageous to their cause. They both believed that a firm stand on this issue could be used to establish a position of dominance over the other.

From the Kaiser's point of view, becoming identified as a progressive force when it came to the social question seemed to offer him concrete political advantages. For one thing, it would allow him to escape from Bismarck's shadow. Any legislative measures that derived from a policy of the Kaiser's promoting would redound to his credit, not that of his famous chancellor. This would allow him to put his own personal stamp on government and thereby gain some recognition for its direction. This, in part, explains Wilhelm's considerable enthusiasm for the idea of holding an international labour conference in Berlin. A successful international event attended by foreign dignitaries in response to the Kaiser's invitation would serve the dual purpose of demonstrating Wilhelm's interest in the plight of the urban masses and, at the same time, give his solicitude in this matter an international platform for recognition, after which nobody could be in any doubt about his good intentions or his sympathetic outlook. Consequently, through the advocacy of social reform Wilhelm could hope to enhance his standing in the country. As he put it, he would become a 'roi des gueux' (king of the beggars), popular throughout the land for his championing of the people's welfare. Of course, as he was well aware, once in possession of so positive a political identity, his government's need for the sturdy image of the Iron Chancellor would naturally diminish.

From Bismarck's point of view, such an outcome was one that he clearly had the utmost interest in preventing: anything that lessened his personal authority and loosened his grip upon the reins of power had, as a matter of course, to be frustrated. On top of this, however, was another, no less pressing, reason for his promotion of his own diametrically contrary social programme. In complete contrast to Wilhelm, who sought to establish himself as Kaiser through acts of kindness designed to gain him credit for defusing social tensions, Bismarck believed that the best method of securing himself in the chancellorship was by heightening internal conflicts with a view to causing (and then, of course, solving) a domestic political crisis. For Bismarck, this was by no means a novel tactic. He had come to power during a crisis, he had held on to power because of his ability to deal with that crisis, and he had maintained his unfettered grip on power by periodically engineering crises. On each occasion, by posing as the sole bastion of order against the bugbear of chaos and revolution, he had secured the support of Germany's propertied classes, whose fear of radical upheaval made them look to him as a protector. Despite the changes created by Wilhelm II's accession to the throne, Bismarck saw no reason why the mechanism that had worked so successfully for him in 1862, 1878 and 1887 should not work for him again. Consequently, he sought to embark upon a policy of social conflict. Rather than offering the working classes the carrot of new reforms, as Wilhelm desired, Bismarck intended to present them with the stick of state repression in the hope of provoking them to outright dissent. Any overt response by the German masses would then provide the excuse for drastic measures, included among which was even the possibility of invoking martial law. Naturally, once this occurred, Wilhelm would be compelled to cling to Bismarck as the only man who possessed both the determination and the experience to steer Germany through the turmoil. For Bismarck, therefore, the social question was no less paramount than for the Kaiser: it was his means of making himself, once again, indispensable and tying the fate of yet another Hohenzollern ruler to the House of Bismarck.

With Wilhelm and Bismarck steering in opposite directions on the social question and hoping to derive very different results from their respective endeavours, it was only a matter of time before a clash occurred. The trigger that turned this underlying conflict into an open one was Bismarck's proposal that the Anti-Socialist Law, which was due to expire on 1 October 1890, be reintroduced into the Reichstag in a form that would thereafter make it permanent. Much to the Chancellor's initial delight, the bill ran into difficulties. The National Liberal Party, a key member of Bismarck's Reichstag coalition, the *Kartell*, came out against one of the bill's main stipulations. They objected to the provision that allowed the authorities to expel socialist agitators from the urban areas in which they sought to spread their ideas and send them instead to the more conservative environment of the German countryside. Accordingly, during the bill's committee stage, the National Liberal delegates voted to have the expulsion paragraph struck out from the proposed legislation. This outcome presented Bismarck with just the opportunity he was looking for. By insisting on the necessity of keeping the expulsion paragraph, Bismarck could precipitate a crisis. For one thing, such a demand on his part would drive a wedge between the Conservatives, who approved of the expulsion clauses, and their erstwhile parliamentary allies, the National Liberals, and would thus split the *Kartell*. With an election only weeks away, open disagreement between these parties was certain to lead to a devastating defeat for the forces representing the propertied classes and a corresponding enhancement of the parliamentary power of their opponents. On top of this, without Bismarck's backing, the weakened Anti-Socialist Law would not be passed by the Reichstag. No legislative measures would then exist to protect the bourgeoisie and the aristocracy from the agitation of the socialists. In such circumstances, with their political representatives decimated and their legal support removed, the propertied classes would be forced, in desperation, to turn to Bismarck for leadership: who else could be relied upon to defend the old order? Of course, once Bismarck was in possession of their backing, his position *vis-à-vis* the Kaiser would be secure. As the astute observer, Friedrich von Holstein put it: 'he would have the Kaiser in the palm of his hand'.[39]

If Bismarck was, thus, content to pursue a policy of intransigence designed to exacerbate tension and provoke social unrest, the Kaiser was not. Not only was it evident that such a *politique de pire* was guaranteed to scupper Wilhelm's hopes of gaining popular acclaim from the masses, but it was also clear that were Bismarck to succeed in engineering a major political crisis, the Chancellor would become indispensable.

Wilhelm would then be stuck with him for an indefinite period. Consequently, the Kaiser was determined to oppose Bismarck's collision-course strategy and instead place government policy on a more moderate footing. At a Crown Council – a meeting of the Prussian ministers presided over by the monarch – convened on 24 January 1890, Wilhelm demanded that the government accept the permanent Anti-Socialist Law, even in its weakened form. It was better, he argued, to have a law on the statute books and a solid parliamentary coalition than no law and no coalition. Bismarck's political strategy required him to disagree. However, in responding to the Kaiser's arguments, he made it all too clear that, behind the dispute over the Anti-Socialist Law, other issues were at stake: 'If the law is not passed,' he observed, 'we shall have to get along without it and let the waves get higher.'[40] As such a strategy risked civil disorder, it was immediately apparent that this statement represented a bid by Bismarck to assert his position and make himself less dependent on the sovereign. This was because if Wilhelm accepted Bismarck's argument, then a crisis that only Bismarck could solve would definitely occur; the Chancellor would then be able to dictate his own terms for remaining in office. As such an outcome would be tantamount to the Kaiser's surrender, this was a challenge that he had to meet. Yet, while Wilhelm steadfastly opposed Bismarck's strategy, refusing, as he put it, '[to] stain the first years of his reign with the blood of his subjects',[41] Bismarck was equally successful in blocking the Kaiser's demand that the government accept the new Anti-Socialist Law, threatening to resign if such an outcome was sanctioned. In terms of policy decisions, therefore, the result of the Crown Council was deadlock. However, with respect to the dynamics of the power struggle between the Kaiser and Chancellor, the clash that took place that day was highly significant: as one of the ministers present at the Council recorded in his diary, 'we parted with the differences unresolved and the feeling that an irreparable breach between the Chancellor and his Sovereign had occurred'.[42] This judgement was to prove accurate.

With the antagonism between them now firmly in the open, both Wilhelm and Bismarck attempted to consolidate their positions for the impending struggle. Bismarck's strategy was straightforward: it was a new 'conflict programme'. He would await the results of the Reichstag election, which he rightly assumed would be catastrophic for the *Kartell*, and then, when the new assembly convened, he would deliberately set out to provoke a confrontation with it. Accordingly, he laid plans for a huge increase in the military budget and an Anti-Socialist Law even more draconian than the one that had just lapsed. As the Reichstag was bound to reject both measures, Bismarck would be presented with a new constitutional crisis for him to exploit.

Pending this, however, Bismarck decided to make sure of his dominance over the Prussian government, whose support he would need in any further dispute with the Kaiser. To achieve this, he revived an old cabinet order from 1852, one that had long been in abeyance, that forbade ministers from being received by the monarch without the consent of the Minister-President. As it had been the Kaiser's intention to strengthen his position with respect to Bismarck by personally winning over some of the Prussian ministers to his cause, this action led to another confrontation. It also provoked Bismarck's departure from office. The Kaiser, who had no intention of being isolated from his government, demanded from Bismarck that he either revoke the old cabinet order or make way for a new chancellor who would. Unfortunately for Bismarck, having once revived the order, an act that drew attention to his need to assert his authority over the Prussian ministry, he could not withdraw it without a loss of prestige and a severe weakening of his position. Confronted with a Hobson's choice of his own making, Bismarck eventually tendered his resignation. So tempestuous and threatening had been his last months in office that few mourned his passing.

The Legacy of Bismarck – Was the Reich Manageable?

The German constitutional and political system was a structure of Bismarck's devising. He had thought out its features, presided over its birth and overseen the first 19 years of its existence. It was beyond any doubt that in 1890 he was the one man most familiar with its workings and complexities. With his departure from office, this unrivalled knowledge of the organization of the Reich was lost to the government. Although others, through the study of constitutional documents, had learnt the theoretical side of the system to the point where they knew it as thoroughly as did Bismarck, nobody else shared his practical understanding of it. His intimacy with the mechanisms of the state was, thus, unique.

That Bismarck should have been in such a position was the inevitable product of circumstance. All inventions are, initially at least, best known to their creators, a rule to which the German constitutional and political system was no exception. It does not, however, automatically follow from this that Bismarck's successors should have been unable, through experience, to gain a similar understanding and thereby develop as great a facility for managing the German Empire as Bismarck himself. Yet, none of the Second Reich's other chancellors were ever able to make more than a partial success of the business of government. Most left office under a cloud of failed objectives or, even worse, of political crisis. The question, therefore, naturally arises: why should this have been? Was the failing to be found in Bismarck's successors – the theory encapsulated in Graf Monts' damning description of them as 'a generation of Epigoni'[43] – or, alternatively, was there in the system that he devised and bequeathed to them some inherent flaw?

While historians generally agree that Bismarck's successors were less gifted than the Iron Chancellor in terms of their political skills, opinions none the less differ considerably on the question of Bismarck's legacy. Some regard the system he passed down as being fundamentally in good order. Hannsjoachim Koch, for example, the author of an important constitutional history of Germany, dismisses the notion that the Bismarckian political heritage was unsound. As he put it: 'No doubt the Imperial constitution was a very imperfect instrument. … But at the same time it was not … doomed from the start, as Germany's constitutional development up to 1918 was to demonstrate.'[44] He is not alone in this interpretation: another proponent of the view that the structure of government in Imperial Germany was both workable and capable of adapting to meet changed circumstances is David Blackbourn. In his opinion: 'The complex and contradictory nature of Bismarck's handiwork, far from suggesting some kind of historical straightjacket which confined the form of the Imperial polity, should alert us rather to its plasticity.'[45]

Although not without merit, these arguments are, none the less, in the minority; a broader strata of opinion, while not necessarily denying the positive aspects of Bismarck's system, takes the view that, examined globally, the governmental structure that he created was, from the very start, a poisoned chalice for his successors. This interpretation finds many prominent adherents. One such is Gordon Craig, who observes that 'the mistakes of Bismarck's successors might have been less disastrous if he had not contributed to the difficulties of their task by leaving them an anachronistic political system …'.[46] Others concur in this view. John Röhl, for example, characterizes Bismarck's Reich as an 'unnatural growth' that had been 'artificially forced' and always threatened to 'wither away'.[47] Preventing this was no easy task. According to Lothar Gall, even Bismarck himself, the architect of the entire structure, stumbled from one expedient to the next, like a 'sorcerer's apprentice',[48] in his efforts to maintain the system's stability. By his final years, even he had given up and was seriously considering undoing his own handiwork and starting afresh. This was a telling judgement, coming as it did from the system's own progenitor, and lends credibility to Fritz Stern's belief that 'the final months of Bismarck's rule demonstrated the essential ungovernability of the country he had created'.[49]

This negative evaluation of the Bismarckian political inheritance with its core conclusion that the system he created was inherently flawed, requires deeper analysis. In particular, the question needs to be addressed: what were the ingredients that made for so dangerous a situation? The various proponents of this interpretation have identified two factors as central to their critique.

The first of these is the suggestion that major 'structural weaknesses' were embedded in the system of government of the Second Reich. Designed to preserve the political constellation of 1871, which favoured the traditional forces that Bismarck represented, the constitutional framework that he constructed failed, even at its birth, to solve the socio-political antagonisms in German national life; instead, it merely 'concealed basic conflicts of interest'[50] that existed between the different social classes. This would not have been so problematic if the new Reich had begun life in a period of socio-economic stability. However, following unification, Germany was hit by an agricultural crisis that occurred in conjunction with the country's rapid industrialization. Both of these developments were processes that had a considerable impact on the country's economic and social systems, creating a momentum for change that progressively exacerbated the existing class differences. As a result, what Wolfgang Mommsen terms 'the partial disjunction between the political and social structures in Germany'[51] grew ever wider. By the time Bismarck fell from power, domestic politics were encumbered by significant social and economic tensions. Described by one historian as 'hopeless', it was clear that 'class conflicts had become more intense and the divisions within the nation had deepened'.[52] The impact this had on the political system was considerable. Working class dissent, when combined with the growing power produced by their increasing numbers, was leading to demands for political representation of a kind that the constitution specifically denied. Yet, such constitutional safeguards to the old order did not mean that the clamour for change could simply be ignored. While the representatives of the working class, the Social Democrats, made no headway in Prussia with its three-class franchise, they did succeed in gaining seats in the Reichstag. Governing against them at a Reich level was thus growing harder; governing with them, however, was a political and psychological impossibility for the ruling elite, whose conservative and agrarian members hoped to ride out the socio-economic tide against them. The result threatened to be an impasse, a situation in which the German Empire would become 'an almost ungovernable entity'.[53] This was a situation for which Bismarck's system made no allowance.

The second of these factors, denied by Koch,[54] but strongly attested to by among others, Golo Mann, is that Bismarck, with 'the egoism that accompanies greatness', never 'wondered seriously what would happen after him'.[55] As a result, he devised a system that, while perfectly reflecting his own needs, stood little chance of working properly for anybody else. At the heart of this interpretation lies the argument that Bismarck fashioned the Prusso-German constitution with the relationship between himself and Wilhelm I very much in mind. In support of this view, it must be acknowledged that, when Bismarck drew up his draft constitution, the interaction between him and his king had developed along particularly favourable lines. Wilhelm allowed his Minister-President almost complete freedom of action on the understanding that Bismarck kept Wilhelm informed and that he followed a conservative agenda that had as its main goals the maintenance of the power of the monarchy in Prussia and the defence of Prussia's interests in the world. As these were also Bismarck's aims, he had generally found himself undisturbed by royal interference in the practice of government. In these circumstances, a constitution that vested considerable authority in the monarchy and then made the Chancellor the monarch's sole representative in the Reich, answerable only to the monarch himself, was ideal for Bismarck's needs: it allowed him to exercise enormous power with only the most limited of scrutiny. Bismarck devised his system accordingly and the resulting constitutional arrangements worked admirably so long as Wilhelm I occupied the throne and Bismarck resided in the chancellory. However, there were always underlying dangers to a system so closely tailored to the conditions that characterized the political interaction of two men. These can be encapsulated in the following key questions: would these conditions always prevail? And, if they did not, would the constitutional structure shaped to match these conditions continue to work in other circumstances?

The answer to the first question was decidedly no. Bismarck himself clearly recognized this. Along with many others, he was aware that Wilhelm I's heir was very different from his father. Accordingly, he devoted considerable time and energy to the problem, as he saw it, of the future enthronement of Crown Prince Friedrich. In so doing, however, he failed to address the real future difficulty, namely the accession of Wilhelm II, who was to follow his father on to the throne after only 99 days and who was as different from both Wilhelm I and Friedrich III as it was possible to be. A revival of the old working relationship between Kaiser and Chancellor was thereby rendered impossible.

Under these circumstances, it is hardly surprising that the answer to the second question also transpired to be no. Wilhelm II, unlike his grandfather, had no interest in being a silent partner in government and, as we have seen, dismissed Bismarck after a mere 21 months on the throne. Having removed the Iron Chancellor, Wilhelm intended to assume more responsibility himself and devolve the rest on to more compliant and less authoritarian chancellors. In practice, however, all this achieved was the creation of ambiguities in the power structure: where there had previously been one leader, there were now two. As long as they could act in harmony this was not a problem. However, without the presence of a single determined figure to act as the co-ordinator of the various branches of government, this often failed to happen with the result that the administration of the Reich quickly degenerated into polycratic chaos. While this was in part the product of Wilhelm II's mercurial character, it also reflected the constitutional structure Bismarck devised. It was, to use the words of David Blackbourn, 'designed by and for one man'[56] and made no allowance for a monarch like Wilhelm II. This explains the judgement of the historian Arthur Rosenberg. As he observed: 'the Bismarckian Empire could not exist without a Bismarck. But in that fact lies the severest criticism. ...'[57]

Taken together, the structural problems of the Bismarckian system, when combined with its inability to cope with a monarch like Wilhelm II, suggest that Bismarck's Reich was, indeed, a problematic legacy: it does, to some extent, deserve the label of being 'unmanageable'. However, such a conclusion does not, in itself, do justice to the complex question of Bismarck's inheritance. While it was undoubtedly the case that the system's flaws caused Bismarck's successors difficulties, as we shall see, many of their problems were of their own making. Moreover, mediocre government was to be the rule after 1890. While, of course, we shall never know if inspired ideas and creative management would have fared any better, the paucity of effective leadership that was to be on offer suggests that the answer to the conundrum of whether Bismarck's legacy or Bismarck's successors were responsible for the subsequent woes of the Second Reich should follow a both/and rather than an either/or pattern.

5

DOMESTIC POLITICS UNDER WILHELM II

The New Course

The new men appointed in the wake of Bismarck's dismissal were under no illusion as to the difficult task ahead of them: in following the Iron Chancellor, they were attempting to replace a political giant. Bismarck, until then the only man ever to have been appointed to the chancellorship of the German Empire, had held the office that he personally had created for a generation. In consequence, for millions of Germans, politics under Bismarck were the only politics they had ever known. To compound this, Bismarck's reputation did not rest exclusively on his years as the towering figure in German national life; as a statesman, he had also dominated the European and global stages. He was known and respected around the world. Given these circumstances, it was probably inevitable that all of Bismarck's successors would find their actions and achievements compared to those of their illustrious predecessor. For no one, however, was this more certain than for his immediate successor, for whom there existed the ever-present danger that, through this process, he would be found wanting. Eager to encourage such an outcome was Bismarck himself. Furious at his dismissal and angry at the men who had engineered it and benefited from it, he was determined to highlight any errors by the new administration, especially if they were mistakes in areas where he was both accustomed to and known for achieving success. This wish to criticize was not merely the product of pique. In addition to any resentment he felt towards the Kaiser, Bismarck was well aware that disasters by the new government had the potential to be his route back to power. Who else could be entrusted to sort out the mess?

It was against this backdrop that the new Chancellor and his associates had to embark upon the government of Germany. Naturally enough, in these circumstances, the avoidance of any damaging or embarrassing incidents that would invite unfavourable comparison with the departed Bismarck was clearly an important, even crucial, consideration. The simplest method of warding off such an eventuality would have been to refrain both from major changes of policy and from radical innovations in government. Continuity with the actions and intentions of the previous administration would ensure, so long as the execution of such measures was reasonably competent, that Bismarck and his supporters would have little that they could legitimately criticize. Moreover, such behaviour had the added advantage, given that nobody knew how Germany would fare without Bismarck at the helm, of bringing some stability to a period otherwise marked by the uncertainty of a new and untried government. In this environment, laying stress on continuity was a natural temptation. It was one to which both the Kaiser and the new Chancellor, Leo von Caprivi, initially succumbed. 'The course remains the same', Wilhelm proclaimed openly to the readers of the *Weimarer Zeitung*; he did 'not have the intention of inaugurating a new era', Caprivi told the Prussian Landtag.[1] In such a manner did the new government make its debut.

That the emphasis on continuity would not long remain, could easily have been predicted; it had too many disadvantages. For one thing, maintaining the work of Bismarck begged the question: why replace the great man? After all, the individual best suited to implement Bismarckian policies was Bismarck himself. Anybody else attempting to fill this role was bound, sooner or later, to be shown up as a pale imitation. On top of this, the new men in power naturally enough wished to assert their own identity on the government of Germany. As such an outcome could not be achieved by anything other than a change of direction, such a transformation was ultimately inevitable. Announced to the German public in a speech delivered by Wilhelm at the port city of Bremen on 21 April 1890, this change of direction soon became known as the 'New Course'.[2]

The New Course does not lend itself easily to description. In essence, it was more an ethos of government than a coherent and predetermined set of policies. This is not to say that new policies did not exist as a goal of the new administration. On the contrary, Bismarck's dismissal from office had been precipitated by concrete differences of opinion with the Kaiser over, among other matters, social welfare reform for the working classes. It was, therefore, no surprise that the new government was committed to, and announced early on, its intention of introducing into the Reichstag a labour protection bill. Other new reform measures were designated for submission to the Prussian Landtag. However, these specific undertakings neither comprised the heart of the New Course nor, in themselves, do they explain it. Rather, at its centre, the New Course reflected the ideology of government held by the new Chancellor. To understand the New Course, therefore, it is essential to comprehend the fundamental outlook of Bismarck's successor, Leo von Caprivi.

Caprivi was by background a Prussian aristocrat and by career a soldier, in which profession he had risen to the rank of general. Yet, with the exception of a strong sense of duty, he possessed few of the stereotypical characteristics commonly associated with the holders of such a pedigree. To begin with, notwithstanding his title, Caprivi did not own, nor had ever owned, a landed estate. Nor did he aspire to such a position. Instead, he was proud to have made his way without inherited wealth and to have advanced by his own merit and self-sufficiency. This situation ensured that, unlike most titled Prussian generals, Caprivi possessed little sympathy for the common prejudices of the landed aristocracy. He did not, for instance, believe that traditional rural society was preferable to modern urban life; he did not regard it as the essential object of the government to sustain, at all costs, the political and economic power bases of the old elites; he did not hold the agricultural interest as paramount; for him, industry was not merely a necessary evil, but a useful augmentation to the strength of the nation. These social and economic views, unusual enough on their own, were partnered by an equally unusual view of the political process. Having risen on his own merit and having been driven throughout his career by a wish to advance the welfare of the nation, he expected others to be capable of comparable accomplishments when similarly motivated. Consequently, in his conception of governing, Caprivi placed great emphasis on co-operation and had limited faith in the long-term value of coercion and repression. In the polarized ideological climate of the time, these views ensured him the status of a political moderate.[3]

It is hardly surprising given Caprivi's particular outlook on the world that his core priority for the New Course was to bring a more cordial and constructive spirit to German national life. Particular emphasis was placed on transforming the country's turbulent political system from one that promoted factional strife and narrow sectional interests to one that could serve as an engine for the national good. To achieve this, Caprivi intended to adopt an essentially neutral position when it came to party politics and to appeal, not to self-interest, but to the patriotism of the country's politicians. This became clear in his first speech to the Prussian Landtag, which he used to proclaim his willingness, indeed his wish, to work with anyone interested in the common welfare of the nation. As he put it, he would 'take the good from wherever and from whomever it may come'.[4] So unpartisan a statement coming from the head of the German government represented a considerable deviation from past practice. Bismarck's attitude to party politics, far from being impartial, had been based largely upon the ancient principle of *divide et impera*, divide and rule. To get his way, he had, at various times, labelled as enemies of the Reich: Catholics, socialists, Poles, Danes and the Francophiles among the population of Alsace-Lorraine. The factional strife that he had thereby created was used to engineer parliamentary majorities and so facilitate the implementation of his policies.

Caprivi, however, deplored such methods. As his speech made clear, he intended his chancellorship to achieve success through co-operation and conciliation, not through coercion and repression. Citizens of the Empire would be encouraged to work together for the common good. At its most basic level, this meant that, under the New Course, the government would seek backing not just from the traditional supporters of the state, but also from among the ranks of its former opponents. New political constellations, especially those involving the Centre Party, would be encouraged. Naturally, such a stance had legislative consequences. Bismarck's authoritarianism had been based upon repressive measures, like the Anti-Socialist Law. Caprivi intended to muster support by a programme of conciliatory legislation. Those legitimate rights and liberties that had been removed were to be restored; laws designed to intimidate would be allowed to lapse. In short, central to the New Course was Caprivi's desire to break down the polarized political antagonisms of the Bismarckian system and govern on a more consensual and inclusive basis. This principle would be applied to party politics; it would be applied to government policy and the legislative programme; it would even be extended to the inner workings of the administration. Here, too, Caprivi believed that Bismarck had kept too tight a leash, thereby stifling the talents of those who served the state. In place of such authoritarianism, he proposed a more collegiate style of government. Ministers and state secretaries would cease to be mere functionaries taking orders from the Chancellor; they would, instead, act on their own initiative and contribute personally to the process of government. It was Caprivi's belief that with every reasonable person placated and encouraged to co-operate, a spirit of common purpose could be created. The warring factions in German political life would then unite behind the good of the nation. Such was the plan for the New Course.

Unfortunately for the new Chancellor, such high-minded goals for the New Course proved easier to formulate than they were to realize. This does not mean that Caprivi was without successes. During his time in office, a great many measures that drew life from his ideals were enacted, often with large cross-party majorities. Efforts, for instance, were made to placate Germany's national minorities. In Alsace-Lorraine compulsory passport restrictions were removed; in Prussian Poland certain limitations on the use of the Polish language in schools were rescinded. Similar efforts were made on behalf of the working classes. Among the bills passed was a law to ensure safety in the workplace, to prohibit employment on Sundays and to place limits on the legal hours of labour for women and children. In addition, new legislation was introduced to set up industrial arbitration courts. Most significant of all, the government undertook to reduce the tariff on grain, thus lowering the price of bread, an item that constituted a substantial part of every worker's budget.

The passage of these and other comparable measures made a positive impression on many sections of the German public. They did not, however, create the favourable political climate that Caprivi expected. For one thing, the traditional supporters of the government were outraged by what they saw as Caprivi's attempt to pander to their political opponents. They also viewed many of the new policies with hostility. In particular, the parties of the right, especially those associated with the agrarian interest, were implacably opposed to reductions in the grain tariff, the preservation of which they regarded as vital to their economic well-being. Consequently, the advancement by the Reich government of such a proposal struck them as little more than treachery. They reacted by withdrawing their support and beginning a vociferous campaign of opposition. If Caprivi could have relied on the backing of the other parties, this would not have been a serious problem. Unfortunately, Caprivi's non-partisan style of government was fundamentally incapable of securing him a loyal parliamentary following. To have acquired such backing, he would have been required to follow a consistent political agenda that would appeal to a particular party grouping. However, instead of attempting to cultivate a new majority by such means, Caprivi's government remained committed to the idea that support could be attracted by appealing to the common good. Consequently, they continued to put forward an eclectic series of legislative proposals on a wide variety of issues. Although these proposals contained something to please almost everybody, no one party was entirely satisfied with what was on offer. Many were highly antagonized. The result was a general political alienation that made it progressively harder for Caprivi to find majorities for his proposals.

This was not the sole problem that Caprivi would encounter. The New Course, with its emphasis on co-operation in politics and collegiality in government, took an idealized view of human behaviour and assumed standards of conduct to which real people often failed to rise. Presented with opportunities of a kind never granted in the Bismarckian era, the beneficiaries of the New Course often reacted selfishly and irresponsibly. Without strong leadership, for instance, the ministers of the Prussian government took to acting independently rather than collegially. They became less willing to accept majority decisions and undertook complicated intrigues to get their way. As a consequence, harmony inside the government quickly began to suffer. Eventually it broke down. Caprivi was soon fighting a rearguard action to regain a semblance of control over the various ministers and state secretaries. This he failed to achieve. In particular, he found himself caught in a bitter rivalry with Botho zu Eulenburg, the Minister-President of Prussia. This conflict epitomized everything that was wrong with Caprivi's conception of government collegiality. Eulenburg owed his position to Caprivi's faith in collective government. Until 1892, the post of Minister-President of Prussia had been held by Caprivi, who had relinquished it in an attempt to delegate responsibilities in which he possessed no interest to somebody with force and initiative. It never occurred to him that the force and initiative thus unleashed might work against him in that Eulenburg, once appointed, might attempt to promote a programme of government that ran contrary to Caprivi's own agenda. Such, however, was to happen. Eulenburg sought to govern on an exclusively conservative basis. So clear a partisan alignment with the parties of the right cut across Caprivi's efforts to embrace moderate opposition parties. As neither Eulenburg nor Caprivi was willing to alter his position, conflict and deadlock inevitably ensued. This stalemate would only be resolved when they both resigned.

How then can the New Course be assessed? As an experiment in government the New Course can only be counted as a failure. So discredited was the attempt to work impartially for the common good that none of Caprivi's successors would ever even contemplate a return to his methods. On the other hand, Caprivi's four years in office did prove that Bismarck was not indispensable; Germany could survive without him at the helm. Yet, notwithstanding their importance, neither of these features would be the New Course's enduring contribution to German national life. Instead, the most salient outcome of Caprivi's chancellorship was the degree, style and character of the opposition that it provoked. In these years, the Reich government was to suffer a barrage of criticism from the political right. This was not only a novelty, it was a turning point. The unleashing of the forces of the right was profoundly to shape the future conduct of German politics. This unfortunate outcome was to be the legacy bequeathed to subsequent German governments.

The Rise of the German Right

When Leo von Caprivi secured his appointment to the chancellorship in March 1890, the foremost goal of his domestic agenda was the removal of the major causes of discord from German political life. It is something of an irony, therefore, that one of the most enduring legacies of his time in office was not the much hoped-for cleansing from German politics of all the rancour and bitterness that had marked the Bismarckian years – an outcome that was never achieved – but rather the establishment of a whole new breed of organized opposition so vehement in its dissent that it was willing to employ any means, no matter how unscrupulous, to achieve its ends. These forces of protest, over whose birth Caprivi presided, would not only be one of the major factors responsible for hounding this most principled and upstanding Chancellor from office in October 1894, but would also, thereafter, act as a constant scourge to his many successors. In effect, therefore, they were to become a persistent feature of Wilhelmine politics. While this longevity was impressive, it was by no means the most striking characteristic associated with these organizations. On the contrary, what was to make this opposition phenomenon so remarkable was its ideological orientation. Against all precedent, the new opponents of Germany's conservative and authoritarian regime came, not as one might expect, from the forces of the political left, but rather from people normally considered to be the government's natural supporters, those on the political right. From this seemingly paradoxical circumstance, the question naturally emerges: how did these notional political bedfellows come to find themselves so far apart?

The mechanism by which Caprivi facilitated the development of this new style of right-wing opposition was, ironically enough, through the implementation of policies designed for the benefit of the common good. That such an approach to national leadership might have undesirable political repercussions was something that Caprivi had failed properly to anticipate. Yet, such an outcome was certainly not beyond prediction. This is particularly so given that Caprivi's policies, although conceived with a view to strengthening the well-being of the nation as a whole and although undoubtedly sensible measures for aiding the majority, were, nevertheless, by their very nature, always destined to be damaging to certain minority concerns. Not surprisingly, the affected interest groups were in no sense mindful of accepting the logic of Caprivi's actions, but rather sought means of challenging his policies instead. Finding themselves unable to sway the Chancellor by the usual means of behind-the-scenes special pleading, they decided upon new methods based upon tightly focused agitation organizations capable of wielding the machinery of mass public protest. This relationship between Caprivi's policies and the emergence of a new style of political opposition will be illustrated below through the example of two right-wing pressure groups both of which were created in direct response to key measures of the Caprivi government.

Beginning first with the realm of domestic politics, the foremost opposition organization that emerged to campaign against Caprivi's policies in this area was the *Bund der Landwirte* (or *BdL*), generally known in English as the Agrarian League. The precise origins of this rural pressure group, whose declared objective was the promotion and protection of the interests of the German farmer, is a matter of some historical debate.

One key interpretation, associated principally with the historians Alexander Gerschenkron and Hans-Jürgen Puhle, is that the BdL was created by a coterie of Prussian aristocratic landowners in direct opposition to Caprivi's decision to lower the degree of protection afforded to home-grown agricultural produce.[5] This reduction, which reflected the new Chancellor's general conception of the state's role in promoting national economic well-being, represented a considerable change in outlook on the part of the German government. Whereas Bismarck had long viewed customs policy principally as a political device for forging a block of economic interests whose parliamentary representatives firmly supported the government in the Reichstag, Caprivi regarded tariffs as a fiscal tool to be manipulated mainly for socio-economic reasons. Consequently, faced with a continued downturn in the economy during the first two years of his chancellorship, he sought to adapt German import duties in such a way as to alleviate the crisis. To this end, attempting to kick-start the German economy through a policy of promoting industrial exports, he negotiated new commercial treaties with

Germany's neighbours, whereby the Reich agreed to lower its duties on agricultural produce – the tariff on grain, for example, fell from 5 to 3.5 marks per 1000 kg – in return for a reciprocal reduction in the level of foreign protection against German manufactured goods.

Needless to say, this decision to ensure an expanding industrial sector at the expense of the interests of German agriculture, was received differently by the nation's industrial exporters and its farming community. Whereas the former group were generally favourable to the new trading arrangements, which provided them with further opportunities to secure additional and much-needed orders overseas, the latter were profoundly and universally hostile to a measure that threatened lower prices for their produce. Especially embittered by this policy were the Prussian aristocracy, the Junkers. As the owners of large grain-producing estates situated on the lighter and less easily cultivated soil of the east Elbian provinces, they were particularly dependent on tariffs to ensure a profitable return from the working of their lands. Consequently, they saw customs reductions as a threat to their economic status and, accordingly, made fighting Caprivi's trade treaties a primary concern.

Unfortunately for them, this was no easy task. Although efforts were undertaken to influence the Chancellor through such standard political means as votes and speeches in the Reichstag and articles in the press, this did not produce the desired results. As they quickly discovered, in a parliamentary setting, the Junkers and their political representatives in the German Conservative Party (DKP) simply did not possess the critical mass necessary to secure a change in government policy. According to Gerschenkron and Puhle, it was this fact that led them to form the BdL. Having become aware that they were unable to fight Caprivi either on their own or by traditional means, the more far-sighted among them realized that this made it necessary for them to adapt to these circumstances by manufacturing a mass movement that would lend their cause popular support. The Agrarian League, by claiming to represent not just the interests of Junker grain producers, but the agricultural interest as a whole, achieved this aim. As a result, it endowed the Junkers with the ability to launch a campaign against Caprivi's policies in which they could marshal at their disposal sufficiently large numbers to give weight to their demands. In this light, the founding of the BdL appears as a manipulative strategy instituted from above by pre-industrial elites in order to give their self-interested actions the populist edge so crucial in an age of mass politics.

In direct contrast to the works of Gerschenkron and Puhle, both of which depict the Junkers as the creators of a radical agrarian movement specifically engineered into being in order to give momentum to their campaign against Caprivi, are a series of more recent interpretations in which the emphasis on leadership by the elite and initiative from above is supplanted by a focus on populist pressures that arose from below, unsolicited by any aristocratic agency. The key feature of these analyses is the claim that the Junkers, far from determining the course of events by creating agrarian radicalism as a vehicle for opposing Caprivi, actually founded the BdL as a reactive measure designed to respond to unwelcome pressures from below, such as rural anti-plutocratic radicalism, that they perceived as a threat to their dominant oligarchic position in the localities.

In articulating this theory of the BdL's origins, the advocates of this view have chosen as their starting point the economic and social conditions prevalent at that time in the German countryside. From this examination, it is clear that the period after 1890 was a far from happy one for many German farmers. To begin with, this was a time when agriculture was afflicted by a series of highly destructive natural disasters, of which several major outbreaks of foot-and-mouth disease and a severe drought were the most prominent. In addition to the malaise caused by these unwelcome climatic and viral manifestations and greatly compounding their ill effects were some major difficulties caused by long-term structural problems in German agriculture. These included: a lack of cheap credit and hence a lack of available capital for introducing technical improvements in farming methods; a fall in rural incomes due to the displacement to large-scale urban producers of traditional ancillary enterprises such as brewing; rising labour wage costs due to the migration of thousands of rural workers to the cities, a form of flight (*Landflucht*) that produced a shortage of seasonal farmhands; and finally, as a result of all the preceding factors, the growing indebtedness of many of those involved in German agriculture, a situation that increasingly led to the involuntary alienation of rural property and the breaking-up of estates. Taken together, these adverse developments had a devastating effect on German farmers, creating crisis conditions in the countryside and fuelling an ever deeper sense of rural resentment. It did not take long for this emotion to bear fruit. Among the early consequences of this bitterness was the emergence of an agrarian radical movement that found institutional expression in the form of new populist organizations – in particular peasant leagues (*Bauernbünde*) – dedicated to campaigning for action to alleviate these problems.[6] Significantly, in working to this end, these organizations soon showed a marked antagonism towards the traditional leaders of the German countryside, especially the German aristocracy. This circumstance is well illustrated by the example of one Peasant League rallying cry which demanded: 'No aristocrats, no priests, no doctors and no professors, only peasants for the representation of peasant interests.'[7] Taken to its logical extreme, this campaign slogan – and all the others like it – heralded a major attack on the local influence of the aristocracy.

According to many historians, among whom Geoff Eley is prominent, this upsurge of anti-elite emotions among the rural population, with its implicit threat of undermining the dominance of the local notables (*Honoratioren*), was the factor most responsible for prompting the foundation of the BdL.[8] Terrified by the potential consequences of letting an independent peasant radical movement develop unchecked, the Junkers – or at least the more far-sighted among them – realized that it was essential to their position that they reimpose their leadership over the countryside. One means of achieving this was by setting up their own mechanism for agrarian protest and then using the institution thereby created as a vehicle for subsuming, containing and overseeing the emergent popular radicalism. Consequently, under this interpretation, rather than being an organization prompted by Junker anger over Caprivi's trade treaties and the need to set up a corporate entity to combat them, the BdL is instead perceived as a body founded out of fear of a form of populist agrarian mobilization over which the Junkers had no control.

Can these two distinct theories as to the origins of the BdL be reconciled? In assessing whether the Junkers created the Agrarian League specifically in order to campaign against Caprivi or, alternatively, whether they created it in order to suborn and redirect an existing popular radicalism, many historians have concluded that there are elements of truth in both explanations.[9] Consequently, while few would now accept uncritically Gerschenkron and Puhle's emphatic assertion of elite manipulation, it is also the case that a focus that ignored this dimension and centred exclusively on populist self-mobilization would prove equally unacceptable. A consensus exists that the BdL was moulded by forces acting both 'from the top down' and 'from the bottom up'. The synthesis that this conclusion produces provides the most compelling explanation of the BdL's foundation. It begins with the premise that, even if only a response to, rather than the creator of, rural radicalism, the Agrarian League nevertheless had a considerable, if not decisive, impact on the direction that future agrarian populist protest was to take. This, of course, was always the goal of its founders. As Baron Conrad von Wangenheim, the driving force behind the BdL, put it in a letter to his brother: 'we seek to guide the uneducated masses'.[10] Naturally, this 'guidance' led down a particular path. Like many large landowners, Wangenheim was alarmed by the growing rural populist radicalism, which

seemed to be aimed as much at destroying aristocratic authority in the
countryside as it was at seeking redress from economic grievances.
However, as a grain producer, he was also concerned at Caprivi's tariff
policies, which were having a detrimental effect on the financial return
from his estates. Forming the BdL, an action which allowed him and his
fellow Junkers to assume the leadership of the rising popular agitation
and focus it on opposition to the new trade treaties, seemed the perfect
means of killing two birds with one stone.

If, as is suggested above, the BdL was intended as a vehicle for giving
a unified voice to the agrarian interest, it was not to disappoint. Indeed,
its effectiveness was soon to become more than apparent. Almost immediately after its foundation, Caprivi found himself under attack from a
persistent agrarian lobby utterly opposed to his trade treaties and their
accompanying tariff levels. This political assault against the Chancellor
and his policies ultimately proved impossible to ignore. Led by Junkers
who were reinvigorated by the BdL's successful appropriation of the
populist idiom, the campaign they unleashed made full use of the fact
that, for the first time, they were backed by an organization that commanded unprecedented resources. In financial terms, this took the form
of a budget that by 1907 had reached almost a million marks per year;
in terms of membership, the BdL numbered 160 000 within four
months of its foundation, a figure that would rise to 200 000 by the end
of the decade and a third of a million by 1914. More importantly, this
membership would include a large cohort of supporters from parts of
Germany outside of the Junker heartland east of the river Elbe.

Naturally enough, with forces like this at its disposal, the Agrarian
League was able to exert a direct political influence. By organizing election rallies, sponsoring newspapers and attacking politicians seen as
hostile to the agricultural interest, even to the extent of putting up for
election alternative 'independent' candidates, the BdL was able to secure
the affiliation of numerous Reichstag and Landtag representatives from
both the Conservative and National Liberal parties. While it is difficult to
quantify the precise effect that this had, certain points are clear. Given the
breadth of their political coverage, the BdL was able to make the burdens
of office nigh intolerable for Caprivi. It is hardly surprising, therefore,
that when reflecting on their role in his fall from power, Caprivi would
later write critically of the agrarians. With more foresight than most, he
would pose the question:

> When our Junker starts to make his loyalty dependent on his income;
> when he demands that the state should undertake the impossible for

his sake as a precondition for his royalism ... one must ask: Is it in the state's interests to continue making sacrifices for this class?[11]

The logical answer to this question might well have been a resounding no, but it is informative to note that Caprivi was the very last Chancellor to consider a programme of agricultural tariff reductions. Thereafter, the trend in customs duties was ever upwards. Of this, the Agrarian League made absolutely certain.

In some ways analogous to the Agrarian League was the principal critic of Caprivi's overseas policies, the *Alldeutscher Verband* (or ADV), generally known in English as the Pan-German League. Founded in 1891 as the German General League (*Allgemeiner Deutscher Verband*) and refounded with a tighter organization, a more radical ideology and its new and better-known name three years later, the Pan-German League demonstrated that just as Caprivi was able to inspire vehement and determined opposition to his domestic agenda, so too could he provoke bitter dissent in respect of his management of Germany's foreign affairs. The circumstances surrounding the ADV's foundation make this more than apparent. As will be detailed in a subsequent chapter, soon after taking office in 1890 Caprivi negotiated a treaty with Great Britain in which German claims to territory in East Africa were exchanged for ownership of the strategic North Sea island of Heligoland. Whatever merits this agreement may have had, it was not well received by German colonial enthusiasts. For one thing, the transfer of large tracts of African land in return for a small sea-swept rock, even one with naval significance, was not held to be an advantageous arrangement by those fixated by the allure of colonial empire. However, even more disturbing to such people than the apparent imbalance in the terms of the treaty was what its very existence seemed to signify about the future direction of German policy. Both symbolically and in respect to substance, the arrangement made it plain that Caprivi intended to retreat from imperial expansion and institute instead a more restrained colonial policy. To those who believed in Germany's imperial mission such a shift was utterly unacceptable. Unfortunately, giving expression to this point of view was no easy task as no corporate institution existed for channelling such dissent. The most obvious body, the German Colonial Society, an organization dedicated to promoting German colonial ventures, was too *Regierungstreu*, that is to say too dominated by people close to the government, to provide an effective platform for such views. Accordingly, the opponents of the Heligoland–Zanzibar Treaty decided to set up a new organization specifically to remedy this deficit and to ensure that in the future such policy decisions would not go unchallenged. In this way the ADV was born. On the basis of the above analysis, comparisons between the Pan-German League and the Agrarian League could be drawn. It could be observed, for example, that in just the same manner as the founders of the BdL refused to accept Caprivi's conception of the national economic interest, emphasizing as it did industrial recovery over the needs of the agricultural sector, and organized accordingly, so too did the leading advocates of German colonialism decline to accept Caprivi's conception of Germany's proper overseas behaviour, linked as it was with imperial moderation and compromise with Britain, and set up their own protest movement instead. The origins of both the BdL and the ADV as highly focused, opposition pressure groups were, thus, very similar. However, it is here that the comparisons begin to end, for in many respects the Pan-German League was a very different type of organization from the Agrarian League. To begin with, the ADV was a much smaller body, whose membership of around 20 000 came mainly from the educated middle classes, especially from such professional groups as lawyers, civil servants, teachers and academics; farmers and landowners, by contrast, were not conspicuous among its ranks. On top of this, whereas the BdL represented an exclusive economic interest and could thus be said to have had forerunners in the organizations that campaigned for a reversion to protectionism prior to 1879, the ADV was an independent ideological movement tied to no single sectional interest. Instead, the focus of its activities, particularly after its refoundation in 1894, was the advocacy and promotion of a strident German nationalism based around racial notions of the *Volk*. The Pan-Germans' conception of what this meant was very broad indeed. One idea that fell within the ADV's definition of the 'patriotic cause' was the reincorporation into the German Reich of all those territories, the so-called '*membra disiecta*' or lost limbs, that had once been under German rule, a goal that made Holland, Switzerland and Austria legitimate aspirations for their activities. Another focus of their nationalist agenda was the inclusion inside the German Empire of any territories in which there were German-speaking minorities, an objective that potentially encompassed large areas of eastern Europe as well as German settlements in parts of Brazil. Yet another part of their programme, one that reflected the organization's origins as protestors against Caprivi's imperial retreat, was the acquisition of overseas lands as settlement colonies to which German migrants could travel for the purpose of establishing German communities. Most of Africa and much of Asia was considered suitable for this purpose.

If the goals of the ADV were in some respects diverse, they had two unifying features: firstly, they emphasized the primacy of the nation above all other considerations; secondly, they were unrealistic to the point of being unattainable. These two aspects of the ADV's programme were to condition its role and reception in German public life. Being a pressure group, with no official function, the ADV was under no obligation to ensure that the measures that it advocated were realistic proposals. As a result, it regularly called upon the government for modes of action that no responsible politician could seriously contemplate. This being so, it was only natural that its desires were rarely fulfilled by the state. Inevitably, this coloured the ADV's perception of the Reich leadership. Holding the government to be insufficiently committed to nationalist goals, they were heavily critical of its failure to live up to their expectations. The impact of this attitude has been aptly characterized by the principal historian of the Pan-German League, Roger Chickering. As he puts it: 'In mobilizing support for ... patriotic causes, the League displayed an evidently uncontrollable dynamism which led it, in the name of patriotism, into open conflict with the German government.'[12] In effect, therefore, by their actions, the Pan-Germans emerged as a mass opposition movement of the right.

Did the Pan-German League and the other organizations like it that were founded in its wake – collectively they are known as the *Nationale Verbände* or nationalist pressure groups – possess any influence over the direction of German politics? At one level the answer is a clear no, as Germany's unelected officials were not generally inclined to listen to the criticisms of these organizations, let alone act upon them. As Bethmann Hollweg contemptuously put it: 'With these idiots nobody can conduct a sane policy.'[13] Compounding this interpretation is the fact that on the few occasions when the views of these groups were canvassed, it is normally possible to detect an ulterior motive for this behaviour. Thus, for example, in 1897 when the government was seeking support for an expansion of the navy and again in 1911 when it sought to galvanize public opinion during the second Moroccan crisis, these organizations briefly enjoyed a direct relationship with the authorities. On both these occasions, however, the partnership was initiated by the government, who were also responsible for its subsequent termination. In effect, therefore, the pressure groups were used when it was convenient to the authorities and left out in the wilderness when it was not.

Such, at least, was the government's intention. Unfortunately for the Reich leadership, the pressure groups neither took kindly to this treatment nor did they prove willing to accept so subservient a role. Thus, while the government might attempt to use them for limited periods, requesting them to focus their efforts on particular issues relevant to government policy, there was no guarantee that these organizations, having once reorientated their activities, would then meekly agree to discontinue them when the government had achieved its objectives. On the contrary, it normally transpired that the goals of the nationalist pressure groups were much more radical and far-reaching than those of the authorities, with the result that outcomes acceptable to the latter were rarely seen in the same light by the former. The inevitable consequence of this was that these brief moments of co-operation, far from cementing relations between the government and the nationalist pressure groups, actually heightened the differences between them, for when the gulf between the government's achievements and the nationalists' expectations became apparent, the result was a sense of betrayal. This emotion led these groups to be bitterly critical of the Reich leadership and thus to continue their propaganda campaigns and their agitational activities in direct defiance of the government's claim that its objectives had been met. This behaviour would have unfortunate consequences. For one thing, it could prove genuinely embarrassing to the Reich leadership, whose main spokesmen found themselves forced into confrontation with the pressure groups in order to defend their actions. Stung by their criticism of him, for example, Chancellor Bülow scathingly referred to the Pan-Germans in a Reichstag speech as 'beer-bench politicians' (*Bierbankpolitiker*). He also had hostile articles about them planted in the press. One example, which appeared in the *Frankfurter Zeitung*, savagely depicted the Pan-Germans as having 'German strength and power so much on their lips and so little on their brains ... '.[14] Attacks such as this, however, while they made little difference to the Pan-Germans, did contribute to an increasing bitterness in the tone of public debate. It was this acerbic quality that was to prove the *nationale Verbände's* lasting contribution to German politics. Speaking to the influential journalist Theodor Wolff in 1915, Bethmann Hollweg passed his judgement on the lasting significance of these groups. As he put it: 'These Pan-Germans have brought a clamorous, overbearing, bragging, and garrulous spirit into our people.'[15] This is a judgement with which much historical opinion would tend to concur. As Geoff Eley observes: 'The nationalist pressure groups were a noisy and disruptive presence in German politics ... and played no small part in radicalizing the general tone. ...'[16] Just how much this was the case would not be truly apparent until years later.

In summary, the politics of opposition in the Caprivi era marked a crucial stage in the development of Imperial Germany. The simultaneous creation of a mass opposition movement in the countryside as well as the founding of the first of the independent patriotic societies would radically alter the pattern of behaviour in the public sphere of German political life. Thereafter, mass movements engaged in mass agitation and propaganda would be a feature that could not be ignored. The strategies adopted by the government to deal with these new phenomena as well as the successes and failures it enjoyed would help shape Germany's future.

'Personal Rule' and Bülow's Chancellorship: 1894–1905

If the rise of the German right was for ever to alter the manner in which the Reich was governed, another factor of profound importance working to the same effect was the ambition of Kaiser Wilhelm II to rule as well as reign. This ambition would develop into a practical programme following Caprivi's fall from power. Ironically, Caprivi's period in office had contributed to this development. Not only had Wilhelm become frustrated at the direction of the New Course, but, in addition, he had been irritated at Caprivi's insistence on behaving as the representative of the responsible government rather than as a pliable instrument of the Crown. As a result, the years immediately following Caprivi's dismissal were dominated by the attempt to turn monarchical rule from a fiction into a fact. By the summer of 1897, despite some opposition from the new Chancellor, Prince Hohenlohe, this had largely been achieved. The process culminated in the appointment of Bernhard von Bülow as Chancellor in October 1900; he had been chosen by the Kaiser and his closest confidant, Philipp zu Eulenburg, to be the executor of 'personal rule'.

Historians still disagree about the meaning of 'personal rule' and the extent to which it became a reality. Geoff Eley and Wolfgang Mommsen have both been critical of it as a concept and as a historical fact. However, those scholars who have examined the history of high politics in the 1890s and early 1900s in most depth – John Röhl, Isabel Hull and Katharine Lerman – have established conclusively that a political system was established during these years which depended on the personal and political predilections of Kaiser Wilhelm II, whose position at the apex of the power structure, and whose control over appointments, reduced even the Chancellor to the role of a courtier. Röhl has argued that the system of government was underpinned by a 'kingship mechanism', whereby all high officials were condemned to seek the favour of the Emperor, and where policies were introduced or vetoed on the basis of whether or not they were likely to achieve Wilhelm's support.[17]

It was always Wilhelm's intention to rule rather than to reign. This had been noted by observers as far back as the mid 1880s. However, the practical exercise of the powers of the Crown had been so eroded in the Bismarck era that the process of their restoration proved to be a lengthy one. For Wilhelm, 'personal rule' was perhaps an end in itself. He had vague notions about the need to broaden support for the monarchy among the middle classes, but the only concrete objective which a monarchical regime would allow him to achieve was the construction of a large battlefleet. The real architect of personal rule was Philipp Eulenburg. He was the Kaiser's closest friend, and claimed genuinely to 'love' Wilhelm. Eulenburg was a member of the East Prussian aristocracy, and was convinced of the necessity and desirability of restoring a system of government where the Prussian King and German Kaiser would have the final say. He was convinced that Prussia should be ruled on a Conservative basis, but saw it as essential to secure support for the regime at Reich level among the 'middle parties'. This, in turn, was motivated by his understanding of south German politics, where Conservatives tended to have particularist, pro-Habsburg and ultra-montane leanings, whereas Liberals were generally pro-Prussian. Eulenburg's political instincts proved indispensable to the Kaiser, notably during the years 1894–97, when the struggle between the court and the responsible government was at its height. Eulenburg himself preferred the political shadows to the limelight, and hence he promoted Bülow as the individual who would direct government once the objective of monarchical rule was achieved.

Several obstacles had to be overcome before the personal regime could become a reality. Many ministers still regarded themselves as representatives of the responsible government rather than servants of the Crown. The practical need to secure majorities for legislation in the Reichstag precluded certain types of government – most notably those of an overtly Conservative–reactionary stamp. If the Kaiser wished to institute a regime of this character, it could only be done by means of a *Staatsstreich* (a coup), which would have risked sparking off a civil war and necessitated the appointment of a military figure such as General von Waldersee as Chancellor. Although such a step was contemplated on a number of occasions during the 1890s, Wilhelm II and his advisers always held back. A major reason for this was that a *Staatsstreich* could well have led to the disintegration of the Empire, as there was never any possibility of the federal princes agreeing to it. Additionally Eulenburg, whose advice carried more weight with Wilhelm than anyone else's, was a consistent opponent of the coup option. Eulenburg, with his acute appreciation of south German conditions and of the fragility of the Reich, realized the danger of a *Staatsstreich* to national unity, and he also appreciated that it would remove the possibility of broadening support for the regime with Bülow as Chancellor.

Paradoxically, one of the greatest obstacles to the policies of both *coup d'état* and 'personal rule' was the personality of Wilhelm II himself. Even in the 1890s, doubts were being expressed about the Kaiser's mental stability by figures such as Holstein and Anton Count von Monts, the Prussian Minister in Munich. Both of them questioned whether an individual who was so impulsive and so injudicious in his utterances and actions was really the right person to rule Germany. Holstein referred to the Kaiser's 'glow-worm nature'[18] which he found reminiscent of Friedrich Wilhelm IV of Prussia and Ludwig II of Bavaria, both of whom had descended into madness. Similarly, after a speech in which Wilhelm II had referred to Bismarck and the elder Moltke as 'lackeys and pygmies' next to his grandfather Wilhelm I, Monts observed: 'Many are saying ... in secret that His Majesty is deranged.'[19] Even Eulenburg, despite his Old Prussian sentiments and adoration for the Kaiser, wondered at times whether Wilhelm was fit to govern. As he put it: 'When Wilhelm appears as an actual ruler, that is only his perfect right. The only question is whether the consequence can be endured in the long run.'[20] Eulenburg answered his own question in the affirmative, but by the mid 1890s he had made some extremely powerful opponents, such as Friedrich von Holstein. The latter urged Eulenburg to 'discard the false axiom that "the King can do no wrong!" This saying, consider it well, was invented in a country where the king is powerless. Power and responsibility cannot be separated.'[21]

The ministerial changes of the summer of 1897 brought the Kaiser's own men into influential positions. Admiral von Tirpitz was appointed State Secretary at the Reich Navy Office, with the remit of instituting an ambitious policy of naval expansion, and Bülow became State Secretary at the Foreign Office, charged with launching a world policy. It was also evident that the Foreign Office would simply be the platform from which Bülow would be elevated to the chancellorship when the right conditions presented themselves. Prince Hohenlohe remained Chancellor until October 1900, but from 1897 onwards he was a pathetic figure – senile and excluded from policy making. His financial dependence on secret remittances from Crown funds, and his desire not to endanger the career of his son, had long made him an ineffective champion of the government against the Crown, but in his final years he was reduced to impotence. Instead, between 1897 and 1900 Wilhelm II was his own Chancellor. Meetings of the Crown Council no longer involved genuine discussions, but simply decided how best to implement the Kaiser's preferred policies. The Kaiser also decided on major pieces of legislation during these years, such as the Navy Bills of 1898 and 1900 and the Prussian Canal Bill in 1899. A new policy of *Sammlung* (rallying together) was instituted under the auspices of Johannes von Miquel, the Prussian Finance Minister. It involved high tariffs to protect heavy industry and the still powerful agrarians, and co-operation between the Conservatives and the Liberal parties during the 1898 Reichstag elections. The policies of trying to win the support of the working class for the regime were abandoned definitively, and instead emphasis was placed on securing the support of the middle classes for the monarchy.

Paradoxically, this strategy eventually involved compromising one of Eulenburg's objectives – the political isolation of the Catholic Centre Party. Even in combination, the Conservatives and Liberals were unable to secure Reichstag majorities in 1898 and 1903. Hence, major pieces of legislation could only be passed with the Centre's support or acquiescence. The Kaiser's power was not absolute during these years. The need to secure majorities in the Prussian Landtag and in the Reichstag for legislation still limited his freedom of manoeuvre. Thus the agrarians were able to prevent the passage of the Prussian Canal Bill through the Landtag, and the Reichstag to stop the Hard Labour Bill. However, what had changed, as compared with the early years of his reign, was that his wishes were no longer thwarted by ministers in the executive. Wilhelm's control over appointments, his direct interventions in policy making, and his ability to thwart certain courses of action from being adopted by making his opposition known, had all combined to make him the dominant figure within the Prusso-German political system by the turn of the century. Contemporaries were in no doubt as to the extent of the change which had occurred since Bismarck's dismissal. Holstein, always one of the most perceptive observers of the political scene, noted in 1900: 'The Power of the monarchy, or rather the personal power of the Kaiser, has reached heights which were considered unattainable even at the height of Bismarck's rule. I consider this to be the most important phenomenon of the present day.'[22]

Bernhard von Bülow became Chancellor in October 1900 and remained in that office until July 1909. He was thus the longest serving of Wilhelm's chancellors. He was also the most significant, as he was the only one who was chosen with much prior thought and deliberation, and as the executor of a clearly defined political strategy. He had risen to prominence under the patronage of Holstein and Eulenburg, as much due to his talent for flattery and intrigue, as through innate talent or political ability. Wilhelm himself had identified Bülow as his 'Bismarck'.[23]

Eulenburg, in turn, saw Bülow as the individual best suited to act as Chancellor under the Kaiser's 'personal regime'. Questions must, however, be raised about the extent of Bülow's own enthusiasm for Wilhelm II. In his letters to Eulenburg, Bülow stressed his commitment to their common political objectives, and argued that he would be a new type of Chancellor, who would regard himself as Wilhelm II's 'political chief of staff', who would institute 'personal rule' in 'the good sense'.[24] But there was always an element of political calculation in Bülow's letters to Eulenburg, and there was a prominent degree of artifice in the gushing enthusiasm with which he heaped praise on the Kaiser. Thus in February 1898, after a meeting of the Crown Council, he wrote:

> I grow fonder and fonder of the Kaiser. He is so important!! Together with the Great King and the Great Elector he is by far the most important Hohenzollern ever to have lived. In a way I have never seen before he combines genius – the most authentic and original genius – with the clearest *bon sens*. His vivid imagination lifts me like an eagle high above every petty detail, yet he can soberly judge what is or is not attainable.[25]

Such sentiments were in conflict with Bülow's private doubts about the Kaiser's character, but he knew the political value of disingenuous sycophancy better than any other Wilhelmine statesman.

After becoming Chancellor in October 1900, Bülow's position was initially a very strong one. He seemed to enjoy considerable political autonomy. For example, he was able to secure the appointment of loyal advisers, and of ministers who would not threaten his position. During a ministerial crisis in May 1901, he was even able to secure the dismissal of his only serious political rival, Miquel, from the post of Prussian Finance Minister. He was also able to pursue policies which differed, at least in nuance, from the Kaiser's wishes. For example, he was more willing to accommodate the Junkers on the issue of agricultural tariffs than Wilhelm himself would have been, and he showed greater enthusiasm for co-operation with the Centre Party than did the Kaiser. Wilhelm's lack of interest in domestic affairs facilitated this autonomy, but so too did the fact that Bülow was the first Chancellor whom the Kaiser trusted absolutely. In July 1901 Wilhelm told Eulenburg: 'Since I have him, I can sleep peacefully. I leave things to him and know that everything will be all right.'[26] In foreign affairs, Kaiser and Chancellor were generally in agreement, but here too the strength of Bülow's position allowed him a degree of autonomy. He was, for example, not inclined to applaud Wilhelm II's sporadic outbreaks of Anglophilia, and pursued a foreign policy during the early years of his chancellorship which was consistently pro-Russian and anti-British. However, in general terms, if the first five years of Bülow's chancellorship were years of political stability, at least in terms of domestic politics, this owed much to the fact that he sought to avoid trouble. Contentious legislation was avoided in so far as possible, and Bülow's strategy appeared to be to maintain a domestic equilibrium through 'deliberate stagnation';[27] something which suited his indolent character.

However, even at this stage, Bülow's power was circumscribed by two factors: the need to ensure majorities in the Reichstag for legislation and the Chancellor's dependence on the favour of Wilhelm II. The two priorities were often in conflict. Appeasing the Reichstag could provoke the Kaiser's suspicion, whereas when the Chancellor was seen to be too loyal a defender of the Crown, he could find himself subject to criticism from Reichstag deputies. Wilhelm's concern that Bülow was becoming too accommodating towards the Centre Party in 1903 illustrates the first problem. The Chancellor's need to dispel criticism of the Kaiser's less judicious public utterances, such as a speech of 1901, in which Wilhelm warned his troops that they might have to fire on their own brothers, provides an example of the latter dilemma.

In essence, Bülow's standing with the Reichstag was not the key to his political position. The Reichstag could censure him, but it could not remove him. By contrast his 'decisive relationship' was with Wilhelm II. The Chancellor's standing within the executive, his ability to shape the course of policy, his influence over appointments, and ultimately his political survival, all rested upon his skill in preserving the Kaiser's trust and confidence. Bülow became a prisoner of the political system which he had helped to create – one where everything turned on the wishes of Wilhelm himself. In the early years of his chancellorship, however, Bülow proved adept at maintaining the Kaiser's favour. As a result of the Emperor's confidence, he was effectively given a free rein in domestic policy. Envoys of the south German states, such as Lerchenfeld, were often amazed during these years by the strength of Bülow's position with the Kaiser. But there were limits to the Chancellor's autonomy. In the autumn of 1902, for example, Bülow had to take steps to appease Wilhelm when the Kaiser, having returned from a visit to his uncle, King Edward VII, became alarmed at what he correctly perceived to be the anti-British drift of his Chancellor's foreign policy. Additionally Bülow was unable to manipulate the Kaiser beyond a certain point. As early as 1901 Albert Ballin, the Hamburg shipping magnate, drew attention to the fact that Wilhelm was aware that Bülow had a tendency to pursue independent courses of action behind his back. Although there was little serious friction between the Kaiser and Bülow prior to 1905, the Chancellor had placed himself in a precarious position. By reducing his office from that of the head of the responsible government to that of a servile courtier, Bülow had created a situation where his entire political system depended on his ability to maintain the Kaiser's support. When Wilhelm began to withdraw his trust from Bülow, as occurred from 1905 onwards, the Chancellor's political system entered a period of protracted crisis which could only end in one result: his dismissal.

Philipp Eulenburg, the chief architect of Wilhelm's *persönliches Regiment*, had been aware from the outset that the institution of a monarchical regime was a high-risk strategy, and that its failure would have disastrous consequences for the Crown. His premonition turned out to be correct. At a time of rapid social, economic and cultural advance, the Empire's political structures at the highest level appeared to be pointing towards the eighteenth rather than the twentieth century. This was appreciated by contemporaries, including Zedlitz, Wilhelm II's court chamberlain. Commenting on domestic unrest in the autumn of 1903, he observed:

> It is certain that our system of government is not adapted to the times, and has many hidden weaknesses…we are powerless to make any far-reaching social and political changes. The real reason for our social troubles is in my opinion that the culture of the lower classes and the mass of the people has progressed more rapidly than the upper classes expected. The system of government should therefore be modernised a little, and more account should be taken of the spirit of the times. Unfortunately…the reactionary forces are the ruling power.[28]

Although the crisis of the Wilhelmine political system did not occur until 1906–8, Zedlitz's testimony reveals that the flaws in the system were evident even during the relatively trouble free early years of Bülow's chancellorship. The institution of a political system which hinged on the 'kingship mechanism' had allowed Wilhelm II's volatile personality to stamp its corrupting influence on the governmental machine. All high officials, including Bülow himself, had to strive to maintain the Kaiser's favour in order to retain office. As a result they were forced to compromise their political integrity, and on occasion to pursue courses of action which they personally saw as ill advised or as politically disastrous. This political climate went hand in hand with the development of an extravagant and grotesque court culture, wholly at odds with the modern age.

The main policies initiated and pursued during these years failed. The SPD went from strength to strength in the face of official persecution, instead of withering away. The policy of *Sammlung* disguised, but did not remove, the fundamental divergence in economic interests between the industrial and commercial middle class and the agrarians. *Weltpolitik* and *Flottenpolitik* alarmed Germany's international rivals and eroded Berlin's diplomatic position. The Anglo-French *entente* of April 1904, described perceptively by Baroness Spitzemberg as the 'greatest defeat for German diplomacy since the Dual Alliance',[29] provided a foretaste of the 'encirclement' of Germany which was the response of the other Great Powers to the Kaiser and Bülow's aspirations to *Weltmacht*. Holstein's warning to Eulenburg in the mid 1890s that an 'operetta regime'[30] was not appropriate for an industrializing society at the end of the nineteenth century was thus amply borne out by subsequent events. The political system after 1897 placed too much emphasis on the power and personality of a Kaiser whose main political objectives tended to make the domestic and international situation worse rather than better, and whose unpredictable nature and unstable personality made him peculiarly unsuited to direct the affairs of the greatest power on the European continent.

The Collapse of the Personal Regime: Causes and Consequences, 1906–1914

The winter of 1905/6 saw a crisis in Bülow's chancellorship that made it evident that the attempt to construct a new-style monarchy had ended in failure. In the domestic sphere, the alliance with the Centre Party, the cornerstone of Bülow's support in the Reichstag since 1900, appeared to be breaking down as a more radical group of Centre deputies, led by Matthias Erzberger, came to prominence. Additionally, relations between the Chancellor and Wilhelm II had come under severe strain, most notably as a result of disagreements between the two men over appointments within the executive. Then there were two serious debacles in foreign policy: the failure to secure an alliance with Russia in 1905, and Germany's humiliation at the hands of France and Britain in the First Moroccan Crisis. The result of these setbacks was to discredit not only Bülow, but the government as a whole and Wilhelm personally, as the British ambassador to Berlin made clear:

> When I first came to Berlin, eleven years ago, I was told that the attitude of an ordinary German in reading a newspaper was to ask

whether the statements contained in it were official. If the answer was in the affirmative, he would read it with attention and respect.... Now, anything published by authority is received with suspicion and closely criticized, and constant attacks have been made in newspapers ... not only against the actions of the Government, but also against the person of the Emperor.[31]

However, the events of 1905/6 provided only a foretaste of what was to come. By 1909, two major crises – the Eulenburg–Moltke scandal and the *Daily Telegraph* affair – had discredited the Kaiser's closest friends and the Kaiser himself. In July 1909, Bülow finally fell from office. In the years thereafter, the Prusso-German autocracy seemed to stumble from one political disaster to the next, both in foreign and domestic affairs. Some historians go so far as to argue that these domestic problems were so severe as to compel the *Reichsleitung* to external aggression in 1914.

The first scandal to break out involved a number of Wilhelm II's closest personal friends, most notably Philipp Eulenburg, the architect of the Kaiser's personal rule in the 1890s. At first glance it seems baffling that as late as 1906 Eulenburg and his 'Liebenberg Circle' were targeted in a press campaign. After all, Eulenburg had retired from public life in 1902, when he had abandoned his post as German ambassador in Vienna. While it is true that he re-emerged from his Liebenberg estate in 1905/6 to advise the Kaiser on policy towards Russia, there is little evidence that he sought or wished for a return to the level of political influence which he had exercised ten years previously. Nevertheless, he was erroneously suspected of wanting to restore the Kaiser's personal regime as it had existed in the late 1890s, and unfortunately for him, he and his friends were vulnerable to press criticism, being both bisexual and involved in spiritualism. Additionally, Eulenburg had the misfortune that several very powerful individuals believed the rumours about his desire for an enhanced political role. Bülow suspected that Eulenburg was intriguing to have him removed as Chancellor; Friedrich von Holstein, once an influential Foreign Office official, blamed Eulenburg, erroneously, for forcing his retirement in April 1906; and Maximillian Harden, the editor of *Die Zukunft*, the journal which first drew attention to rumours of the camarilla surrounding the Kaiser, was motivated by political opposition to the old Prussianism which Eulenburg represented, and also by revulsion at the homosexuality of the Prince and many of his friends.

The attacks on Eulenburg and his friend Kuno von Moltke were, in reality, attacks at one remove on the Kaiser himself, and the political system of autocracy which he upheld. Harden himself admitted this, when he implied that he had held his fire during the controversy 'in the interests of the monarchy and the Reich'.[32] However, he was determined to destroy Eulenburg's influence once and for all. 'I cannot persuade myself to make Phili the evil genius of Germany's destiny',[33] Harden vowed in a letter to Holstein. The personal motivation of Holstein's opposition to Eulenburg was more obvious. In a letter accusing Eulenburg of having engineered his removal from the Foreign Office, he declared ominously: 'I am now free, and I need exercise no restraint, and can treat you as one treats a contemptible person with your characteristics.'[34] Bülow never admitted to a role in Eulenburg's downfall. However, it seems that he too played a concerted part in the campaign to undermine the Prince and the Liebenberg circle. The Chancellor would gain from Eulenburg's downfall, and he also had a further reason for encouraging Holstein's wrath against the Prince, for it was Bülow not Eulenburg who had in reality brought about Holstein's removal from office. Axel von Varnbüler, the envoy of Württemberg in Berlin, and a close friend of Eulenburg's, was in no doubt in relation to the Prince's fate in the scandal that 'Bülow co-operated in his downfall through Holstein.'[35]

The details of the scandal need not be rehearsed here, other than to say that Kuno von Moltke was forced by revelations which emerged in a succession of legal actions against Harden to resign his commission in the army. Eulenburg was also driven out of public life as a result of the scandal, and avoided imprisonment on charges of perjury only as a result of ill health. In Harden's articles in *Die Zukunft*, and in the evidence brought forward in court proceedings, the homoerotic nature of the attachments between the members of the Liebenberg circle was exposed, and humiliation was heaped not only on those directly implicated, but also on the Kaiser. The scandal tarnished the monarchy. When Eulenburg went on trial for perjury, Princess Radziwill observed: 'it is a good thing that the Emperor is away out of the country during such a filthy trial which does no credit to him who chose the Prince for an intimate friend'.[36] The scandal had certainly thrown the Kaiser into a depression. He learnt of the revelations about Eulenburg and Moltke from the Crown Prince, and initially demanded that both men defend themselves with the utmost vigour, which had the disastrous consequence of ensuring that the scandal would escalate. When Moltke's initial action for libel against Harden collapsed in the autumn of 1907, Wilhelm retreated from public view as a result of the humiliation.

For a time, it looked as if the political repercussions of the scandals would be favourable, in the sense that they would strengthen the authority of the Kaiser's responsible advisers, and weaken that of Wilhelm himself and his court. Bülow seemed to recover authority as Eulenburg and the Liebenbergers went into eclipse. Additionally, the outcome of the Reichstag elections in January 1907, when the SPD suffered reverses, and a Conservative–Liberal majority prepared to work with the Chancellor came into existence, seemed to indicate that the domestic crisis was drawing to a close. Hermann von Lucanus, the head of the Kaiser's Civil Cabinet, interpreted the results as evidence of the attachment of the German people to 'the national idea' and of their enthusiasm for the monarchy.[37] In reality neither Eulenburg's downfall, nor the election results had solved anything. The so-called 'Bülow Bloc' in the Reichstag was nothing like as monolithic as its name suggests: Bülow only held it together by avoiding contentious legislation during 1907 and 1908, notably on the pressing, but divisive, issue of the Reich financial reform. Similarly the destruction of the power of the camarilla was, in reality, a pyrrhic victory. Eulenburg had long ceased to be a major political figure, yet the scandal had left the real problem of government – the irresponsible exercise of power by the Kaiser – unaddressed. As Zedlitz noted, it would take another scandal to prove to the Kaiser 'that nothing could be more ruinous both to himself and the development of the people than his delusion that it is still possible nowadays to coquet with absolutism'.[38] This lesson was to be brought home to Wilhelm during the *Daily Telegraph* affair of November 1908.

A few months after his arrival in Germany as British ambassador to Berlin, Sir Edward Goschen expressed frustration at the fractured system of authority in Germany:

> I must say that on coming to Berlin I expected to find order in affairs developed to the highest point. What I *do* find is more muddle, more confusion than I have found in any country during my 35 years experience.[39]

Goschen was not always the most perceptive of observers, but in this instance he did touch on the truth. Effective government was compromised by the tangled lines of authority. The *Daily Telegraph* crisis of November 1908 resulted to a large extent from this very problem. On 28 October 1908 the *Daily Telegraph* published an 'interview' with Wilhelm II, which was in reality constructed from remarks which the Kaiser had made to Colonel Stuart-Wortley, his host in England after his state visit to Windsor in the autumn of 1907. The 'interview' was approved by Wilhelm, who told Stuart-Wortley: 'I firmly hope that it may have the effect of bringing about a change in the tone of some of the English newspapers.'[40] His comments, designed to improve Anglo-German relations, created more amusement than anything else in Britain. However, his claims to have dreamt up the battle plan which allowed the British to defeat the Boers in the South African War, his assertion that the French and Russians had wished to attack Britain during that war, his insistence that he was alone in Germany in being a friend of England, and his remark that the German navy was being built 'for any eventualities in the Far East'[41] were greeted with outrage in Germany, where the population had finally tired of being humiliated on the international stage by the indiscretions of their own Emperor.

There was one great irony in relation to the publication of the 'interview'. The Kaiser had gone through the correct constitutional procedures when first sent a transcript of it by Stuart-Wortley. He had submitted it to Bülow with instructions to read it. The Chancellor had failed to do so, and had instead sent it to the Foreign Office to be vetted. The official who read it, Baron von Jenisch, the Chancellor's nephew, suggested only minor changes, and implied that Bülow had examined the text.[42] When the crisis broke, Bülow moved quickly to shift the blame on to the officials of the Foreign Office, claiming that he had been too busy to read the 'interview' and would have advised against its publication had he done so. He offered his resignation to the Kaiser, but this was rejected. However, as the days passed Bülow scrambled to save his own position, even at Wilhelm's expense. In a speech in the Reichstag on 10 November, he made very little attempt to defend the Kaiser and noted that he trusted that Wilhelm would act with greater restraint in the future. The result of this was to shift the blame for the fiasco from the Chancellor to the Emperor, as a report from the British Minister in Dresden on the day after Bülow's speech indicated:

> No-one can speak of the Emperor and his indiscretions without getting purple in the face. I am very distinctly under the impression that the patience of the German people has strained to breaking point, & that any more indiscretions would cause a universal demand for abdication.[43]

The Chancellor was further able to outmanoeuvre the Kaiser by advising him to proceed with a hunting trip to Donaueschingen on 3 November, just when the crisis was reaching its height, thus creating the impression that Wilhelm was indifferent to the popular indignation about the 'interview'. In reality, during his trip, Wilhelm underwent a nervous collapse. He criticized the Chancellor for failing to shield him from criticism, and asserted that he was the victim of 'a judicial murder'. Wilhelm was 'seized with the deepest depression, alternating with fits of fury, or hysterical weeping', and his host Prince Fürstenberg noted: 'Something has snapped in the Emperor which will never be mended.'[44] On his return to Berlin, Wilhelm did indeed consider abdication, and it was also suggested by his sister Princess Charlotte of Saxony-Meiningen that the Reich could be placed under a collective regency.

Bülow took advantage of the situation in order to extract an assurance from the Kaiser at an audience at Potsdam on 17 November 1908 that Wilhelm would act in accordance with the constitution. However, it was only a verbal one, and the Kaiser's intentions of adhering to it were doubtful from the first. Wilhelm insinuated angrily that Bülow had leaked details of their discussions to the press in order to embarrass him,[45] an allegation which the Chancellor strenuously denied.[46] Contrary to the views advanced by some historians, it seems that Bülow was intent during the crisis on making the Kaiser behave in accordance with the existing constitution, rather than on bringing in constitutional innovations such as responsible Reich ministers. He simply believed that the most effective guarantee against personal rule was 'a Reich Chancellor who has the confidence of the federal governments and the Reichstag and supported by that confidence, can stand up to HM'.[47] The Chancellor also told the British ambassador 'that in judging recent events people should not forget that Germany continues to be intensely monarchical. ... All they wish for & *will* have – is that the rule of their monarch should be less personal.'[48] The essential weakness of Bülow's position after the November crisis was precisely that he did not recognize the need for more profound change, such as the introduction of a parliamentary monarchy. He remained a courtier to the last, and hence dependent on the very Kaiser whom he had criticized and antagonized. The signs were that his days in office were numbered. Zedlitz recorded of the Kaiser's attitude towards his Chancellor at the end of November: 'He is keeping Bülow for the present, but cherishes a deep resentment against him.'[49]

In fact, Wilhelm only retained Bülow as Chancellor until the summer of 1909 and then only because he needed him to ensure the passage of a reform of the Reich's finance through the Reichstag. Bülow proved unable to manage even this. The Conservative–Liberal bloc on which he based his power fell apart over the issue as the Conservatives would under no circumstances support a proposed inheritance tax, and the Liberals believed that further reliance on indirect taxation would be inequitable. Thus the political association between Bülow and Wilhelm II, which had begun with such great hopes in the 1890s, ended in mutual bitterness. The Kaiser declared subsequently in relation to his former Chancellor 'that the world had not seen such a hypocrite or liar since Cesare Borgia',[50] whereas Bülow lamented that ministers were in an 'impossible position in Germany' because they had 'to serve two masters (monarch and parliament) whereas elsewhere they are only dependent on one'.[51]

The *Daily Telegraph* affair and Bülow's fall from power mark the effective end of the era of the Kaiser's personal regime. Wilhelm never established the same rapport with Bülow's successor, the gloomy Prussian bureaucrat, Theobald von Bethmann Hollweg. Additionally the Kaiser retreated into a life of lethargy, and seemed constitutionally averse to hard work, which reduced his involvement in the governmental process. However, the opportunity to bring about a change in the constitution by limiting the Kaiser's power had been missed in November 1908, and no other one would present itself before the Great War. Instead of leadership at the top, there seemed to be a vacuum. In domestic politics, the conflicts between labour and capital, and between the political parties in the Reichstag seemed only to intensify in the last years of peace. Political polarization left the well-meaning Bethmann in an impossible position. He attempted to cobble together Reichstag majorities on an *ad hoc* basis for legislation. He proposed modest domestic reforms, such as a broadening of the electoral franchise in Prussia, which still used the discriminatory three-class franchise which favoured the parties of the right. Yet, this satisfied neither the Conservatives nor the SPD. It was difficult for the Chancellor to seek the middle ground, when that had so obviously given way.

Nor should one interpret the outcome of the Eulenburg–Moltke scandals and the *Daily Telegraph* affair as having transformed Wilhelm into a 'shadow Emperor'. It is true that in domestic politics he interfered less than in the years of Bülow's chancellorship. Yet he was still more than capable of rendering Bethmann's task more difficult by making speeches in favour of divine right monarchy, pronouncements condemning the disloyalty of the Conservative Party, and nonsensical comments on Reich finance reform. The Kaiser was himself an obstacle to domestic reform, for he guarded his prerogative powers jealously, and viewed Bethmann's willingness to consider co-operation in the Reichstag with the SPD with distaste. In foreign affairs, the Kaiser was even more of an obstacle to the Chancellor's policy than he was in the domestic sphere. The single most important effect of the scandals of

1906–9 seems to have been to cause Wilhelm to retreat politically into the areas where his power was least restricted: foreign and military policy. He was still capable of dramatic personal interventions in both areas. He accepted an invitation to visit London in the spring of 1911 without consulting his advisers first, he imposed his choice of ambassador to London in November 1912 against the Chancellor's wishes, and his intransigence on the issue of naval armaments, and support for Admiral Tirpitz, was a decisive factor in preventing the achievement of Bethmann's major aim in the military–diplomatic arena: a naval and political agreement with Britain. This, in turn, had a knock-on effect in domestic policy, for the Kaiser's insistence on the completion of the naval building programme worsened the Reich's finances, and played into the hands of the SPD, because the strategy was funded primarily by indirect taxation.

The growth in support for the SPD was the most striking development on the domestic scene in the last years of peace. In the Reichstag elections of January 1912, the Social Democrats gained 34 per cent of the vote and 110 seats, a result which seemed to underline the rejection of the class-based regime among a large segment of the population, and also an aversion to the jingoistic nationalism which the government had whipped up in the months before the election during the Second Moroccan Crisis. The consensus among historians used to be that the SPD victory in 1912 proved that the constitutional status quo in Germany was becoming untenable, and particularly the class-based electoral franchise in Prussia. The rise of socialism coupled with labour unrest created a siege mentality among the ruling elite, who, driven into a cul-de-sac of their own making, reacted by launching a war in 1914, which had as one of its major aims the isolation of the old order's domestic opponents. This is a thesis which requires some modification. It is evident that the SPD was a reformist rather than a revolutionary party. They made fewer difficulties for the Chancellor than has often been supposed, voting, for example, in favour of the Reich Property Value Increase Levy in 1913, which served to fund the Army Bill of the same year. They were unable to prevent the passage of the army increase itself. They were also reluctant to use direct strike action against the government, for example on the question of the Prussian suffrage, and they voted the government the credits which it needed to go to war in 1914. In this context, the Social Democrat threat to Bethmann's chancellorship begins to look like a 'paper tiger'.

The immediate threat to domestic stability before 1914 came from the right not from the left. It originated among pressure groups such as the

Pan-German League, who believed that the Chancellor and the government were insufficiently strong in standing up for German interests. One of the leaders of the League, Heinrich Class, actually published a pamphlet on the eve of the war entitled *If I were Emperor* in which he argued for a dictatorship. Secondly, the threat to stability came from the Conservative Party, the political representatives of Old Prussia, which opposed all concessions in the domestic sphere, such as reform of the Prussian suffrage and a move from indirect to direct taxation. Bethmann saw Heydebrand, the Conservative leader, as his most dangerous opponent in domestic politics, lamenting that through his intransigence Heydebrand 'advances the parliamentary system as no-one else'.[52] However, the opposition of the Kaiser and his court to any opening to the centre-left, and Bethmann's own hostility to a parliamentary system meant that he was condemned to seek a *modus vivendi* with the Conservatives, giving Heydebrand a virtual veto over domestic reform.

Thirdly, and most importantly, the threat to domestic stability lay in the growing power and influence of the military leadership within the political structure. This was symbolized in the Zabern affair of the autumn of 1913 when an army officer who had insulted the inhabitants of a town in Alsace by calling them by the offensive term *Wackes*, and then arresting those who protested, was acquitted by a court martial. The incident seemed to indicate that the army was above the law. Bethmann was forced to defend the army's conduct in the Reichstag, and suffered the humiliation of a crushing vote of no confidence. This had no effect on his position, as he was dependent on the Emperor, not the Reichstag deputies, and Wilhelm supported the army. The attitude of the ruling elite towards the Zabern affair was summed up by Heinrich von Tschirschky und Bögendorff, the German ambassador to Vienna, in conversation with his British counterpart, who subsequently recorded:

> He says ... Germany is compelled to back up her army through thick and thin. Its task is to keep the principle of authority above water. A 'wave' of democratic and even anarchic sentiment is for ever pressing on Germany from East and West, and even from the interior. This Germany will resist at all costs.[53]

This sense of domestic and external encirclement extended into military circles, who were obsessed with the idea of a 'preventive war' against the Social Democrats at home and the Russians abroad. Significantly the military leaders had considerable influence over Wilhelm II himself in the last years of peace, and also a steadfast ally in the Imperial family in the form of the Crown Prince, who wrote to his father in January 1912 advocating a war. 'The German *Volk* has arrived at a turning point', he wrote, 'it is either going forward or backwards. The well known place in the sun will not be cleared for us and so we must grasp it for ourselves.'[54] When the Crown Prince repeated similar pro-war remarks to a member of the staff of the British embassy two years later, the British ambassador remarked ominously: 'I have heard … some of these opinions expressed in still higher quarters.'[55]

The influence of the militarists around the throne was the gravest threat to peace, for in a state where the military leaders are not subject to effective civilian control, the ruling group is more likely to resort to war than in one where the military are the subordinates. This was the position in Germany in 1912–14, symbolized by the 'military–political conference' of December 1912 when the Kaiser convened with the military leaders to debate on war or peace, and did not even invite his Chancellor. The years of scandal in 1906–9 had caused Wilhelm to retreat from domestic politics, but to concentrate to a greater extent than ever on questions of foreign and military policy. The scandals had, in turn, led to a severing of links between the monarchy and the civilian leadership, for no civilian after 1909 attained the political influence with the Kaiser which Bülow and Eulenburg had once enjoyed. Axel von Varnbüler who knew the Kaiser well in both eras regretted in 1913 that Wilhelm now surrounded himself only with 'courtiers and adjutants', rather than with the 'better elements' with whom he had been brought into contact by Eulenburg.[56] Most worrying of all were the political opinions of the military men who now formed the Kaiser's entourage. They opposed all domestic reform, thus exacerbating demands for it, while simultaneously exaggerating the threat from the SPD, and became obsessed that the international balance of power was shifting against Germany. It was this siege mentality among the ruling elite which constituted the greatest threat to peace at home and abroad. Unfortunately it was individuals such as Helmuth von Moltke, the Chief of the Prussian General Staff, who had the Kaiser's ear and Moltke was famous for stating: 'I believe a war is unavoidable and the sooner the better.'[57]

6

EXTERNAL POLICIES UNDER WILHELM II

The New Course in German Foreign Policy

When, in March 1890, Otto von Bismarck was dismissed from the chancellorship, his son Herbert, indignant at the peremptory treatment accorded to his father, responded promptly by tendering his own resignation as State Secretary at the Foreign Office. This development was most unwelcome to the Kaiser. Wilhelm, even though he found Herbert von Bismarck overbearing as an individual and extremely difficult to deal with, had nevertheless hoped to retain him in his post. Naturally, this desire was not motivated by altruism, but reflected the strong political advantages that were to be gained from such a course of action. Firstly, in terms of the domestic situation, Wilhelm was very conscious that the former Chancellor, who was bound to be bitter about his enforced retirement, could be very dangerous as a member of the opposition. By persuading Herbert to stay in office, he hoped to retain an institutional link with the Bismarck family and, thereby, forestall the unwelcome eventuality of Otto von Bismarck attacking the government from the sidelines. In addition to this, and of especial relevance to the question of foreign affairs, maintaining Herbert's presence in the government would have been an act of enormous symbolic significance. In particular, it would have served as a powerful signal, both to the German public and to governments overseas, that the change of chancellor did not mean a total break with the diplomacy of the past. Rather, by retaining an experienced figure at the helm of foreign policy, especially one with the name of Bismarck, the impression of continuity in Germany's external relations could have been maintained. Unfortunately,

Herbert's emphatic resignation upset all these calculations. As a result, contrary to the desire of those involved, March 1890 did, indeed, mark a significant break in the course of German foreign policy. At the end of that month, control of the Reich's external relations passed out of the grasp of the experienced Bismarck family and into the hands of two newcomers: Leo von Caprivi and the new State Secretary, Adolf Freiherr Marschall von Bieberstein.

In making an assessment of the characters of Caprivi and Marschall, it is possible to advance any number of positive attributes. Both, for example, were conscientious and upstanding men of great honesty and integrity, who intended in their public careers to be of service to their nation and people. Both, moreover, had some experience of domestic politics, Caprivi having held the position of State Secretary at the Reich Naval Office and Marschall having been Baden's representative in Berlin. Yet, when it came to international diplomacy, neither could claim to be anything other than a novice. So notorious was this inexperience that both figures became the subject of pointed witticisms among the officials of the Foreign Office. Marschall, for example, was regularly referred to, not by his official title, *Ministre aux Affaires étranges* (Minister for Foreign Affairs), but rather as *Ministre étranger aux affaires* (Minister ignorant of affairs). In a similar fashion, it was said of Caprivi: 'The Chancellor will not become a diplomat in the course of the next century. I do not wish to make prophesies beyond that date.'[1]

Despite the jokes, however, there was a serious side to this unfamiliarity with foreign relations. As a result, both Caprivi and Marschall came to high office lacking the depth of knowledge and intimate grasp of detail that was so vital a prerequisite in those charged with the direction of the Reich's complicated external relations. Compounding this ignorance of overseas policy was the even more serious problem that in place of the hard lessons of experience, they brought instead a number of preconceptions about the management of diplomatic affairs that were to prove less than successful when put into practice. In particular, Caprivi believed – and Marschall did not demur over this – that German diplomacy as it stood was too complex and needed to be simplified. As he is reported to have said when first being briefed about the system he was to inherit: 'He could not juggle with five balls at once, ... but would do well to manage with only two.'[2] Just what such a scaling down would mean in practice would become apparent almost immediately with the first two foreign policy initiatives associated with the new administration.

The first of these was in the area of German relations with Russia. In 1887 Bismarck had signed a secret agreement with the Tsar's government which, in addition to looking to the future of the Balkans, had regulated the behaviour of the two countries in the event of war. Should a conflict arrive in which one of the signatories were involved, the other promised to maintain a benevolent neutrality. The only exceptions were if Germany were to attack France or if Russia were to turn on Austria. As these eventualities happened to be the only likely scenarios leading to war, it was clear to all concerned that the stipulations of the Reinsurance Treaty, as it was called, bordered on the irrelevant. But then, it was not for its written guarantees that Bismarck had actually signed it. Its real purpose, so far as the Chancellor was concerned, was to forge a link between Russia and Germany and thus provide the Tsar with no incentive for looking elsewhere for treaty arrangements. In this respect, it had worked. In the years after 1887 Russia remained tied to Germany alone, a situation that had not altered in 1890 when the treaty came up for renewal. Had Bismarck still been in office at this point, there is no doubt that an extension to the treaty would have been signed. Unfortunately, Bismarck was dismissed just as the negotiations were beginning and, as a result, the decision as to the future of the link with Russia passed to the new regime. Sadly, its leading members failed to understand the real purpose of the treaty. Far from seeing the tie to Russia as an asset, Caprivi was persuaded by the officials at the Foreign Office – most notably by Friedrich von Holstein, the head of the Political Division – that the treaty was an unnecessary complication that was potentially damaging to Germany. As they explained it, its terms were incompatible with the existing alliance with Austria and could, therefore, cause the Reich great embarrassment if they were made public. Being, in any event, naturally inclined towards a simplification of German foreign relations, Caprivi accepted this advice. Accordingly, the Reinsurance Treaty was not renewed.

Given the many disastrous foreign policy decisions that were to be made by Germany's leaders in the following 25 years, it is far from easy to decide which should be categorized as the worst ever taken. However, there can be no doubt that the non-renewal of the Reinsurance Treaty must rate as a candidate for this rather dubious distinction. While it did, as intended, simplify German diplomacy, it did so in a highly disadvantageous manner that prejudiced Germany's geopolitical position in a way that was only too predictable. Cut off abruptly and unexpectedly from its former ties with Germany and, thereby, left entirely isolated in the international arena, Russia was literally driven by this action into the arms of an only too delighted France. Events moved quickly thereafter. In July 1891 a French naval squadron made a courtesy visit to the Russian port of Kronstadt. Then, in 1892 Russian and French negotiators agreed the terms of a military convention, which was ratified as the Dual Alliance in January 1894. In one fell swoop, the nightmare that Bismarck had always striven hard to avoid – that of Germany being surrounded on two sides by a hostile coalition – was not only allowed, but actually encouraged, to come into existence.

Following hot on the heels of the breach with Russia was an initiative designed to improve relations with Great Britain. This took the form of a colonial agreement between the two powers. In return for the strategic North Sea island of Heligoland as well as a wedge of territory linking German South-West Africa with the Zambezi river – this land was known hereafter as 'the Caprivi strip' – Germany surrendered to Britain most of her outstanding territorial claims in East Africa. From Caprivi's point of view, the purpose of the Anglo-German colonial agreement of 1 July 1890 – or the Heligoland–Zanzibar Treaty, as it soon came to be called – was twofold. Firstly, it was designed to extricate Germany from the messy and expensive world of African imperialism. This desire to limit Germany's extra-European activities reflected the fact that Caprivi, even more than Bismarck, was not only unconvinced by the argument for colonies, but was actually hostile to the whole imperial idea. Far from seeing overseas territories as positive augmentations to the geopolitical position of the Reich, he believed that they were strategic liabilities that could only be maintained at great cost. On top of this, he also held that involvement in imperial politics was an unnecessary distraction that diverted German attention to the global periphery rather than facilitating a concentration on the one part of the world that really mattered to her security, namely central Europe. Consequently, it was his belief that 'the less Africa [that Germany has], so much the better for us',[3] a point of view that renders it unsurprising that he proved only too willing to surrender German claims to African territory when Britain was prepared to offer in return a European island, possession of which could enhance Germany's coastal defence.

If one of Caprivi's motives for signing the Anglo-German agreement of 1890 was that the acquisition of the island of Heligoland contributed directly to German security in Europe, then a second reason behind Caprivi's enthusiasm for the treaty was the thought that it might further augment Germany's strategic position by providing diplomatic benefits as well. In particular, Caprivi hoped that this agreement would be the prelude to a new and closer relationship with Britain. As the Chancellor and his advisers saw it, whereas secret ties with Russia were a factor complicating German diplomacy and rendering the nation open to embarrassment should they be revealed, a link with Britain suffered no such disadvantage. On the contrary, it was their judgement that German and British foreign policy objectives were broadly in line. Both nations wanted peace and stability in Europe; both were suspicious of Russian intentions in the Balkans and the Straits. By removing the only possible source of friction between the two powers – namely competing colonial claims – they hoped to establish an *entente coloniale* between Germany and Britain that would provide the basis for a diplomatic alignment between the two countries. In particular, it was hoped that this *rapprochement* might even lead to Britain becoming a committed partner of Germany's by joining the Triple Alliance.

If this was the expectation, then Germany's leaders were to be sorely disappointed. The British government, while pleased to resolve their differences with Germany, still lived in the era of 'splendid isolation'; they had no interest in a formal alliance with Germany or, indeed, for that matter, with anybody else. Mutually beneficial co-operation was certainly welcomed in London, but no signed and sealed guarantees would be given. Had Germany's leaders proved willing to accept this limitation to the expression of British support and had they possessed the imagination to realize that an informal link forged in good faith was as useful as an official alliance, then Anglo-German relations might have developed, in all essentials, along the lines they hoped. However, unlike their French counterparts, who, when placed in a similar situation after 1904, would recognize that the *Entente Cordiale* had all the substance if not the form of an alliance, Germany's leaders either would not or could not make this leap of faith. Disappointed by British reticence, they sought continually for some means to make Britain's relationship to them more concrete. This was unnecessary. As the German ambassador in London, Paul Graf von Hatzfeldt, rather colourfully put it: 'If people in Germany will only sit still, then the time will come when suckling-pigs will run ready-roasted into our mouth.'[4] Patience, however, was a virtue that was in short supply in Berlin. When neither waiting nor cajoling brought British adherence to Germany, then disenchantment set in. This was to colour perceptions of Caprivi's foreign policy.

As a consequence of the inability to achieve the expected results, many observers in Germany quickly came to regard the foreign policy of the Caprivi government as a failure. This was, in some respects, a harsh judgement. Caprivi had several achievements to his name, including numerous new trade treaties with Germany's neighbours. However, it cannot be denied that there were grounds for this view. During his tenure of office, Germany's potential enemies had become more united. Yet, at the same time as a hostile coalition had been formed against the Reich, the sacrifice of substantial German territorial claims in Africa had produced no further enhancement in Germany's own alliance system. Despite the best endeavours of the Reich's diplomats, Britain remained, as before, friendly but aloof. As a result, so far as his critics were concerned, the only tangible outcome of Caprivi's actions was the need for a costly new army bill to enhance Germany's military capacity to protect against a war on two fronts. Needless to say, this did not compare favourably with the achievements of Bismarck, a fact that the old Chancellor did not let go unnoticed. Others rallied to this theme. Agrarians criticized Caprivi's trade treaties and demanded a return to the overseas trade policy – in other words, high tariffs – of the later Bismarck years. In a similar fashion, nationalist pressure groups, incensed by the Heliogoland–Zanzibar Treaty and bitterly critical of Caprivi's hostile stand on colonialism, demanded that Caprivi's Eurocentric foreign policy be abandoned and that the colonial expansion endorsed by Bismarck in 1884 (but not, of course, thereafter) be reinstituted. So great was this clamour that by the time Caprivi was forced from office, it had built up such a head of steam that the new government, even had it wanted to, would have been unable to ignore it. Persevering with Caprivian foreign policy was, however, the very last thing that the new administration had in mind.

The Origins and Onset of German Expansionism

With the fall of Caprivi from the chancellorship in October 1894, the approach to foreign affairs that had been associated with the policy of the New Course came to an end. That the resignation of Caprivi should result in a change of direction in the management of German foreign affairs came as no surprise to observers of the Reich leadership. Both in Germany and abroad it was generally recognized that the new government had every incentive to distance itself from the former Chancellor's political failures. As international relations was one of the many areas in which Caprivi was felt to have been unsuccessful, diplomacy naturally fell within the sphere of policies where new initiatives were expected. Accordingly, speculation was rife as to the diplomatic posture that the new government would take. Illustrative of this sense of anticipation was a memorandum written by Martin Gosselin, the chargé d'affaires at the British embassy in Berlin. As he noted, a mere month after Caprivi's resignation:

> the new Government have as yet not had time to show their hand, but they are universally believed to be in favour of a more 'forward' policy than that adopted by Count v[on] Caprivi. ... [5]

At this stage, it was by no means clear just what this 'more "forward" policy' would mean when put into practice. Answers on this point, however, would soon be forthcoming. When they arrived, Martin Gosselin would be one of many British diplomats who would wish that the question had never arisen.

There can be no doubt that when Prince Chlodwig zu Hohenlohe-Schillingsfürst accepted the office of chancellor and, with it, responsibility for the conduct of Germany's external relations, he had not the slightest intention of instituting a foreign policy designed to alienate the British. On the contrary, both by character and inclination, Prince Hohenlohe was a man who eschewed controversy and abhorred confrontation and, as a result, the very last thing that he would have wanted was to preside over a diplomatic strategy likely to provoke a clash with an otherwise friendly power. Equally, however, Prince Hohenlohe entered high office conscious that the attitude towards international relations that had been adopted and fostered by his predecessor had ended up arousing considerable opposition to the government from some very vocal groups inside Germany. Possessing absolutely no desire to suffer the same fate that had befallen Caprivi at the hands of this opposition, he made reducing the temperature of German politics his most vital goal. Reorientating government policies in a more popular direction, an action capable of achieving this end, thus appealed to Hohenlohe. Accordingly, he took the significant decision to move away from Caprivi's highly criticized moderation in matters of empire and his, by now, much berated Eurocentrism in the identification of Germany's key interests, in favour of an approach to foreign affairs that was more acceptable to public opinion. Unfortunately, this would involve changes in German overseas policy that would severely complicate relations with Britain.

The principal change and the one most responsible for this undesirable outcome was the re-evaluation of the German attitude towards colonial empire. If it had been axiomatic of the New Course that Germany should be cautious in imperial matters – Sir Edward Malet, the British ambassador in Berlin, had once observed that 'there will be no *politique d'aventure* so long as Caprivi is in office'[6] – this was not the attitude taken by the new Chancellor. Rather, given the opposition that his predecessor's overt hostility to colonies had engendered from nationalist organizations and pressure groups, his instinct was to break completely with Caprivi's policy. Consequently, upon taking office, Hohenlohe, whose cousin, Prince Hermann zu Hohenlohe-Langenburg, had been the first president of the German Colonial Society (*Deutsche Kolonial Gesellschaft* or DKG), decided to make an overture to the colonial movement with a view to reducing the mutual mistrust and antagonism that had built up during Caprivi's chancellorship. Accordingly, in a speech to the Reichstag made just two months after his appointment, Hohenlohe observed:

> The colonial movement is also a national movement. It has grown out of the strengthened national feeling, which after the founding of the Empire sought a field of endeavour for the expansion of national activity; it is a valuable prop for the feeling of unity and no government will be able or will wish to do without this new and strong bond which unites the individual branches of the nation and the various classes of the population.[7]

As a guide to future policy, this speech was significant both for the message it contained as well as for what it left unsaid. On the one hand, in making public the termination of the government's former hostility to imperialism, it was an unambiguous olive branch to the colonial movement. On the other hand, it was entirely devoid of any concrete measures and thus left opaque the substance of the government's new-found enthusiasm for imperial development. As a result, the question remained unanswered: how would this new amity to colonial expansionism be manifested? It is not difficult to divine why this should be: when Hohenlohe made his speech to the Reichstag he probably had no clear idea himself of where it would lead. For one thing, it was a mere two months into his administration; too early for any new policies to have been properly formulated. On top of this, and much to character, it had always been the Chancellor's intention to let his subordinates frame the policy for him. As a result, although it was Hohenlohe himself who presented the change of direction to the Reichstag, the substance of this transformation was not an issue that he let disturb him. As was his want, he devolved the matter down to the appropriate official, in this case the State Secretary at the Foreign Office, Adolf Freiherr Marschall von Bieberstein.

In Hohenlohe's view Marschall's suitability for this task was never in doubt. In one respect, this is surprising: Marschall, after all, had served under Caprivi throughout the period of the New Course and was thus intimately and directly associated with the former Chancellor's anti-imperial ideas. Nevertheless, it was well known that Marschall had long been interested in colonialism. Indeed, prior to his elevation to high office, he had been a member of the Colonial Society. As a result, he not only possessed the right connections to build bridges between the government and Germany's colonial enthusiasts, he also happened to be personally familiar with the precepts behind their movement. As he understood the key principles by which their demands for colonial expansion were given an ideological foundation, he was in the perfect position to develop an overseas strategy that would be popular with them. All he needed to do was to make sure that his policy corresponded to their ideology, which, broadly speaking, emphasized four core arguments.

Firstly, there was an economic argument based upon the idea of trade and investments following the national flag. According to the proponents of this view, colonies would provide Germany with access to new markets, raw materials for industry and opportunities for the profitable use of surplus capital. Consequently, Germany ought to acquire more colonial territory, especially in areas with economic potential.

Secondly, there was an argument based upon population movement. Between 1830 and 1880 over a million Germans had emigrated to the United States. Tens of thousands more had left for other parts of the world. So far as German nationalists were concerned, these migrants represented an undesirable diminution in national demographic strength. If this haemorrhaging of manpower were to be prevented in the future, it was essential that Germany acquire overseas territory to which Germans could migrate while at the same time retaining their nationality and identity. In effect, this meant acquiring colonial territory with settlement potential.

Thirdly, there was an argument based upon a broad definition of German ethnicity. German nationalists regarded Germany not as a geographically delineated entity, but rather as an ethnic unit composed of all those who were 'Teutonic' by language and culture. This meant that there were large parts of the globe, including both areas to which Germans had migrated, as well as areas settled by such 'Germanic' peoples as the Dutch or Danes, that ought, according to this conception, to be 'reincorporated' into the Second Reich.

Finally, there was the issue of proximity and contiguity. A principal motivating force of governmental action throughout human history has been the desire to build territorial possessions into contiguous blocks. For German colonial enthusiasts this was also true. They had seen German territory united on the continent of Europe; they wanted the same done overseas. Accordingly, they emphasized the importance of acquiring new colonial lands to bring together the nation's existing but scattered overseas possessions into one cohesive territorial mass.

All of these arguments, being the stock responses of the colonial movement, would have been familiar to Marschall and it is, therefore, notable that the focus he was to provide to German colonial policy in the aftermath of Hohenlohe's Reichstag speech was to be centred upon a part of the world to which, be it by accident or design, all of these principles could be applied. The region in question was southern Africa, at the heart of which lay the Boer republic of the Transvaal.[8] This state was an area of considerable German commerce and capital investment; it was an area to which large numbers of Germans had migrated and in which they felt reasonably at home due to the linguistic similarities between German and the Afrikaans language spoken by the ruling Boer people; it was an area that mixed pastoral land with cities, making it ideal for migrants of all sorts; and it was an area situated in the middle of southern Africa, close to the German colony of South-West Africa and adjacent to the Portuguese possessions of Mozambique and Angola, both of which were lands that it was widely expected would soon have to be put up for sale to pay off Portugal's huge national debt. Consequently, if the Reich could acquire these Portuguese possessions and if the Transvaal could be brought under German protection, the possibility seemed to exist of forging a large block of territory under German ownership, with a German population, containing German investments and trading extensively with Germany.

Under any circumstances, these factors would have made the Transvaal a desirable focus for the Reich's new colonial aspirations. There was, however, an additional factor that seemed to make it a suitable target for German colonial endeavours and that was the ambiguous nature of the country's political status. Closely tied to Britain by virtue of treaties that made its foreign relations subject to the approval of the government in London, the Republic was regarded by the British as something akin to a vassal. Needless to say, this was not the view of the Boers whose external outlook, shaped in opposition to the British perception, was dominated by the desire to abrogate those agreements that imposed this limitation upon their independence. Unfortunately, the Republic, endowed as it was with great mineral wealth, was so situated as to ensure that its commerce was vital to the economic well-being of the neighbouring British territories of Cape Colony and Natal. Naturally enough this situation affected British colonial thinking with the result that plans were drawn up in Cape Town and London for a British-led South African economic federation. The success of this scheme depended upon the Transvaal's participation and consequently, the colonial authorities in Whitehall, far from being willing to loosen their ties with the Republic, as was wished by the government in Pretoria, not only jealously guarded such powers as they already held but, in addition, sought to acquire further leverage over the unwilling Boers. As these objectives were in essence mutually incompatible, antagonism between the two parties was bound to arise and for this conflict the Boers sought allies. The problem for the Transvaal government and the opportunity for Germany was that, while undoubtedly requiring assistance, it was the case that, by accepting aid and allowing another country to speak for her in the conflict with Britain, the Transvaal opened herself up to the risk of becoming reliant upon her benefactor and thus, in effect, exchanging one suzerain for another. For to be free of Britain solely by the grace of another power was to be dependent upon that other power. Consequently, the struggle between Great Britain and the Transvaal over the Boer Republic's international status represented a unique opportunity for any country seeking to expand her interests in the area. Such a country was Germany.

Consequently, over the course of the years 1894 and 1895 Marschall made sure that Germany involved herself constantly in the affairs of the region. Time after time, in an effort to become by her actions the Transvaal's natural protector, Germany blocked British diplomatic initiatives designed to gain additional leverage over the Boers. This was to culminate in January 1896, after numerous smaller incidents, in the major crisis of the Kruger Telegram. In late December 1895, troops of the British South Africa Company under Dr Leander Starr Jameson made an unauthorized attempt to overthrow the government of the Transvaal. The raid was repudiated by Britain and defeated by the Boers. Nevertheless, it served as the pretext for the German government to send a public message to the Transvaal that, in effect, challenged the British position in the region and implied that Germany was prepared to deploy military force in aid of the Transvaal. As if to prove the latter point, an attempt was made to force Portugal to allow the passage of German troops through Portuguese colonial territory to reach the Boers.

The Kruger Telegram would act as a watershed in German diplomacy. To begin with, it would have a devastating impact on Anglo-German relations. As the career diplomat, Johann von Bernstorff, would remark retrospectively in the 1930s:

> the Kruger Telegram played essentially the same role in Anglo-German relations that the sinking of the Lusitania would later play in German–American relations, namely it would never be forgotten in England because it was felt to reveal the true inner disposition of Germans.[9]

Partly as a result of this, the Kruger Telegram would mark the bankruptcy of Marschall's efforts at colonial expansion in southern Africa.

Abandoning this policy did not, however, mean a return to Caprivian concepts of a limited German role in global affairs. Rather, the retreat from Marschall's South African policy would lead to the inauguration of two new initiatives in international relations, both of which would have a major impact on Germany's future. These were *Weltpolitik* and *Flottenpolitik*.

Weltpolitik

In 1897 the Reich government embarked upon a new policy of social control designed to cement its authority over the existing socio-economic order. The levers of this policy, which is generally known as *Sammlungspolitik*, were an ostentatious and expansionist foreign policy (*Weltpolitik*), designed to secure for Germany new territorial possessions and spheres of influence in every corner of the globe, and an extensive and highly visible naval building programme (*Flottenpolitik*), based around the construction of a large fleet of modern battleships capable of projecting German power into both the Baltic and the North seas.

In almost every conceivable way, the colonial and naval components of this new governmental agenda represented considerable departures from existing policy directions. Until the enunciation of *Weltpolitik*, for example, German foreign and colonial policy, although no longer exclusively Eurocentric in the Caprivian sense, had nevertheless been focused mainly on Europe, the only significant extra-European objective being the securing of a German advance in the Boer Republics of southern Africa. Likewise, prior to 1897, Germany's naval development plans had extended no further than the maintenance of a minor force of cruisers and coastal defence craft designed to indulge in small-scale commerce raiding and the protection of the German seaboard. *Weltpolitik* and *Flottenpolitik*, with their much more ambitious targets, thus represented a considerable expansion in German aspirations in respect to both colonial and naval policy. The question, therefore, naturally arises: from where did the impetus for these new and ground-breaking initiatives arise?

Two factors were of particular influence in this process. Firstly, there was the German government's own analysis of the success or otherwise of its early attempts, made during the years from 1894 to 1896, to move away from the exclusively Eurocentric foreign policy associated with the New Course. The results of the Reich's first tentative steps on to the world stage in the aftermath of Caprivi's fall seemed to provide instructive guidance as to how German foreign and defence policy should be managed in the future. As will be outlined below, the lessons from this experience appeared to many of Germany's leaders to point in the direction of a more ambitious and far-reaching foreign and fleet policy. On top of this, and greatly reinforcing the conclusions drawn from the analysis of recent diplomatic experience, was the growing acceptance by large sections of the German government and public of new ideological perspectives on the place of nations within the global power system. These theoretical and intellectual devices for understanding global developments all pointed to the necessity for enhancing German national power and prestige. Taken together, therefore, the ongoing evaluation of past diplomatic experiences alongside the adoption of new theories of international affairs would provide a powerful driving force for the emergent policy initiatives of *Weltpolitik* and *Flottenpolitik*.

Beginning first with the role of recent experience, it is clear that, for many of those situated in the upper echelons of the German leadership, the re-evaluation of the Reich's then existing diplomatic strategy was the decisive factor in promoting the desire for an immediate and radical change of direction in respect to the management of the nation's foreign affairs. For the most part, this reflected a burgeoning awareness that existing German policy had not only been ill-advised, but had, moreover, ended in complete failure. Particularly significant in promoting this view was the experience of Germany's involvement in the imperial politics of southern Africa. The Reich's attempt to compete with Britain for influence over the Transvaal had culminated on 3 January 1896 in the debacle of the Kruger Telegram. This diplomatic disaster would provide Germany's leaders with several salutary lessons.

To begin with, the British reaction to the Kruger Telegram demonstrated unambiguously how easy it was for a European land power like Germany to overextend itself when entering the colonial arena. By challenging a strong and established imperial power like Britain in an area that was beyond the operational reach of the German army but where, conversely, Britain could deploy considerable military and political assets and was, moreover, willing to do so, the German government simply exposed itself to the risk of a confrontation in unfavourable circumstances. Being the weaker power in colonial terms, Germany was ill-equipped to face this eventuality. In essence, therefore, as the German ambassador in London, Paul Graf von Hatzfeldt, reported, this left Germany with no choice but to back down. The only other alternative was war. As he observed:

> [In Britain] we have to deal with an entirely altered situation. ... It is not a question of annoyance on the part of the government, but of a

deep-seated bitterness of feeling among the public, which has shown itself in every way.... I have no doubt that the general feeling was such that if the government had lost its head or had for any reason wished for war, it would have had the whole of public opinion behind it.[10]

Such overwhelming hostility towards Germany was not the outcome to the Kruger Telegram that the Reich government had either desired or anticipated. On the contrary, the extremity of the British reaction came as something of a shock to Germany's leaders who, far from seeking war, had expected their actions to do no more than intimidate the British into conceding easy gains for the Reich. However, once faced with the genuine prospect of the outbreak of war with England – and Britain's insular position meant that this would be a conflict fought only in distant colonial lands – it instantly became apparent that this was a confrontation that Germany could ill afford. As Hatzfeldt noted, 'without a strong fleet, which unfortunately we still lack, it would not be materially possible for us to give the Transvaal Republic decisive assistance...'.[11] Therefore, as he observed in a second letter:

> If...[Britain] decided on aggressive action, no protest on our part and no dispatch of auxiliary troops...could prevent it from being carried out. The sole result of such steps would be a conflict between England and ourselves, in which we could do absolutely nothing against the English; whereas they could take Heligoland away from us again and perhaps bombard Hamburg.[12]

In the face of so unfavourable an analysis – one which, however, all the experts agreed was essentially correct – the lessons of the situation were clear. In existing circumstances, sticking to a confrontational colonial policy that antagonized Britain to the point of war was not only counterproductive, it was suicidal. Consequently, if the calamatous experience brought about by the Kruger Telegram were not to be repeated again, German policy would have to change. The direction of change was no less obvious than the necessity for it. In place of their existing approach of challenging Britain for colonial spoils in southern Africa, an area that the British considered of vital national interest, Germany had to show more circumspection in its imperial endeavours by limiting itself to seeking territorial gains in less sensitive areas of the globe. To any diplomat with an opportunist frame of mind, this meant eschewing specific, long-term territorial objectives in favour of pursuing only those gains that were readily attainable.

If the violence of the British reaction to the Kruger Telegram forced the key members of the German government to the realization that their country was ill-equipped to undertake a policy of overseas expansion that led to serious confrontation, this was not the only aspect of the experience that was of instructive value to the German leadership. From their point of view, no less revealing than the explosive response from the British public was the equally unambiguous reaction to the incident from the people of Germany. Ironically enough, even though the Kaiser's missive to Kruger had been highly detrimental to the Reich's international position, producing a considerable worsening in Anglo-German relations, it had nevertheless proved extremely popular with the German public. Indeed, as the government were quick to observe, the German newspapers were almost universally ecstatic about the Emperor's action. This was as true in the Reich capital, Berlin, where Marschall observed that 'Our press is wonderful. All the parties are of one mind ... ',[13] as it was in the rest of the country. In Saxony, for instance, the Prussian consul was able to report that 'seldom has there been such a great degree of unanimity in public opinion and the pronouncements of the bourgeois party press as in this case'.[14] The lesson of this situation was clear: ostentatious and visible actions in defence of Reich interests overseas were very popular with the German public. Clearly, therefore, there was political capital to be exploited from an ambitious foreign policy.

On the face of it, the contrasting reactions elicited by the Kruger Telegram in Britain and in Germany – the one implacably hostile, the other unambiguously favourable – seemed to provide the Reich leadership with very different lessons. On the one hand, it was now clear that there were real and considerable diplomatic and military dangers to ill-advised overseas intervention. On the other hand, German action in the colonial sphere had considerable domestic appeal. Taken together, these facts were capable of providing the rationale for a single cohesive overseas policy. Simply stated, it was apparent as a result of reactions to the Kruger Telegram that the Reich government could use diplomacy as a means of bolstering its position at home but, if it were to do this without incurring the risk of undesirable complications abroad, it would have to focus its efforts only on the less diplomatically sensitive parts of the globe. Such reasoning would provide a major justification for *Weltpolitik* in government circles.

The second factor responsible for the shift towards *Weltpolitik* was the development, dissemination and popularization within Germany of new theoretical perspectives on the conduct of international affairs. An especially significant component of this new outlook was the growing acceptance of Social Darwinist notions of the role played by struggle in forging a nation's position in the global arena of international politics. Broadly speaking, according to this belief system, relations between states were dominated by the existence of constant competition between them. In these circumstances countries were faced with only two choices: successful competition leading to expansion or unsuccessful competition and its attendant consequence, decline. Illustrative of the inner logic of this theory are the views of the director of the Imperial Shipyards at Kiel, who in 1898 observed:

> The 'struggle for survival' exists between individuals, provinces, parties, states. The latter conduct the struggle either with arms or by economic means. We cannot do anything about this; hence, we join in; whoever refuses to join in will go under. ... [15]

He was not alone in this view. As the 1890s wore on, this opinion grew ever more widespread, particularly in the ranks of the German middle classes. Among the many effects of this process was a growing sense that Germany had to demonstrate its competitive spirit in some tangible form and, of all the possible ways of achieving this, the acquisition of new lands overseas seemed the most visible and convincing. Colonial expansion, it was felt, demonstrated territorial vigour in the international arena at the same time as it provided new economic opportunities for German industry and commerce. New colonies were simultaneously seen as prestige symbols and the focus of growing national energy. It is, therefore, hardly surprising that the clamour for their acquisition on Social Darwinist grounds grew ever louder. Strongly epitomizing this trend is a famous passage from Max Weber's inaugural lecture at the University of Freiburg. Commenting on the need for Germans to understand 'the meaning of the great questions of political power', he observed:

> We must grasp that the unification of Germany was a youthful spree, indulged in by the nation in its old age; it would have been better if it had never taken place, since it would have been a costly extravagance, if it was the conclusion rather than the starting point for German power-politics on a global scale [*Weltmachtpolitik*]. [16]

Comparable public statements were made by other middle-class public figures of the 'liberal imperialist school', the most notable of whom were

Friedrich Naumann, Paul Rohrbach, Ernst Jäckh, Theodor Barth and Ernst Francke. Naturally, they were also made by more extreme nationalists, the influential historian Heinrich von Treitschke being the most famous example. More significantly, however, and indicative of the reach that these opinions obtained, was the fact that such ideas also began to be expressed by key figures in the German leadership. One example of this was Admiral von Müller. Writing in 1896 to the Kaiser's brother, Prince Heinrich, he noted that the German people believed it to be 'their ability and duty to expand...' and, thus, urged decisive action. As he observed:

> ...our policy must be all or nothing. Either we harness the total strength of the nation, ruthlessly, even if it means accepting the risk of war, or we limit ourselves to continental power alone.[17]

Equally clear as to the need for Germany to compete for new colonial lands was Bernhard von Bülow, who was appointed State Secretary at the Foreign Office in 1897. As he put it: 'The question is not whether we want to colonize or not, but that we *must* colonize whether we want to or not.'[18]

As the views of Müller and Bülow make clear, by 1897 there were a number of figures in the German government convinced on ideological grounds of the need for Germany to expand. Equally, however, and this was especially true of Bülow, they were well aware of the fiasco that had befallen Marschall's attempt to further German interests in southern Africa. This realization would be an important factor conditioning the practical application of this expansionist ideology when it was adopted as government policy under the slogan of *Weltpolitik*. As a result, *Weltpolitik* must be understood as the outcome of two distinct processes: it was both the product of a didactic approach to recent foreign policy failures and a response to current dogmas of power politics. The former laid stress on the value of cautious diplomacy, the latter on the vigorous assertion of German rights. How would these impulses be reconciled in practice?

In the years after 1897, the German government talked a lot about its world role and attempted to act dramatically on the world stage, but it never made its overarching goals clear. This was deliberate. *Weltpolitik* was a nebulous and inchoate policy that reflected the political dexterity of its originator Bernhard von Bülow. As a result, those historians who have laboured to discover *Weltpolitik*'s territorial scope and its precise geographical aims have always failed. The main reason for this is neither a lack of documentary evidence concerning German foreign policy nor a shortage of public statements about it, rather it reflects the fact that *Weltpolitik* did not have precise territorial aims. The objective of the policy was to achieve popularity. To that end, expansion anywhere at any time was always welcome to the German government, whose members kept their eye on every corner of the globe seeking favourable opportunities to obtain territorial trophies that they could present as successes to the German public.

Contrary to expectations, however, such blatant opportunism proved to be politically expensive. The fact that German diplomats were always to be found hovering near the world's trouble spots looking to gain territorial compensation out of any unfortunate incident quickly alienated the other powers, who were disconcerted by German claims. Similarly, Germany's aspirations to global reach and her unwillingness to confine her efforts to particular spheres of interest made everyone feel threatened. In the end, this would provoke a reaction from the other powers that would lead to major changes to the international system that were far from favourable to Germany.

Flottenpolitik

As we have seen above, in the late 1890s the German government embarked upon an ambitious and ultimately disastrous world policy. That policy went hand in hand with the development of a large fleet of battleships, concentrated in the North Sea, drawn up under the auspices of Admiral Alfred von Tirpitz, who became head of the Reich Naval Office in 1897. The Tirpitz plan did not bring the colonial gains which had been hoped for; nor did it bring about the long anticipated breakthrough to world power. Instead the policy, like *Weltpolitik*, was based on flawed geopolitical calculations, which were compounded by strategic blunders. Within Germany, navalism had been conceived as a strategy which would bolster support for the Kaiser's regime. Ultimately, the failure of *Flottenpolitik* played a major role in discrediting Wilhelm II, Tirpitz and the entire Prusso-German political structure. Yet even in the last years before the outbreak of war in 1914, the Tirpitz plan was not officially abandoned, nor its failure acknowleged publicly by either the Kaiser or his naval chief, for it had become a symbol of the Wilhelmine system, and to admit to the plan's failure would have been to accept the bankruptcy of the political order which had implemented it.

The reasons behind the decision to build a battlefleet are very similar to those which led to the institution of *Weltpolitik*. There is some evidence that merchants and shipping interests in coastal towns, together with those involved in export industries, favoured the construction of a navy to secure colonies for Germany and to defend German commercial interests overseas. This was also the reason given for navalism by official circles in Germany, not least when explaining the policy to foreign governments. Additionally Social Darwinist assumptions about the need to expand or face decline had an impact on *Flottenpolitik* as well as on colonial policy. Finally a book published in 1890 by the American Admiral Mahan entitled *The Influence of Sea Power on History* convinced many in Germany, notably in official circles, that to gain admission to the ranks of world powers at the end of the nineteenth century a large fleet was required.

However, it is unclear that these pressures alone would have been sufficient to cause the *Reichsleitung* to make the fateful decision in 1897 to construct a large battlefleet, given that such a policy was at odds with the continental traditions of German foreign policy and anathema to many in the Junker class which had such influence in Prussia. Two further factors were required in order to make *Flottenpolitik* a reality: the keen sense of humiliation in Germany in the aftermath of the Kruger Telegram fiasco, and the decisive support of Kaiser Wilhelm II for the construction of a battlefleet. As we have seen, Hatzfeldt's reports from London during the Kruger Telegram crisis emphasized that Germany was not in a position to act to secure her own colonial ambitions against those of Britain. The main reason for this was that she lacked a navy which could challenge the Royal Navy. This was also a factor in Marschall's decision to counsel Wilhelm II against his original plan when the crisis broke out in the Transvaal, of landing a German expeditionary force in Mozambique which could then assist the Boers against British encroachments on their territory. The crisis proved that *Weltpolitik* would remain mere rhetoric if it was not backed up by naval force. This in turn played into the hands of those such as Tirpitz and Admiral von Müller who had long cherished ambitions to mastermind the expansion of the navy.

The Kaiser himself felt Germany's humiliation by Britain over the Kruger Telegram extremely keenly. Initially he read many of the letters which he received from British correspondents about the telegram himself, which reportedly contained 'the coarsest swear-words and insults'.[19] Even two years later his outrage at his treatment by British public opinion still rankled, as he made clear in a letter to his mother, who had expressed her enthusiasm for an Anglo-German alliance as 'the *most blessed* thing that could happen *not only* for the 2 Countries but for the *world* and civilization!!'[20] Expressing objections, Wilhelm contrasted his friendly feeling for Britain in the early years of his reign with the British government's behaviour towards Germany: 'instead of thanks or help in our colonising enterprises I got nothing whatever, and for the last 3 years have been abused, ill-treated and a butt to any bad joke any musikhall [*sic*] singer or fishmonger sought fit to let fly at me'.[21]

Wilhelm had been greatly frustrated at Germany's impotence in the Kruger Telegram affair and had proved quite unable to keep the vow which he had made in a letter to the Tsar: 'I shall never allow the British to stamp out the Transvaal.'[22] Yet, the Kaiser's interest in naval matters dated back to his childhood and was ironically a legacy of his English ancestry. He had favoured naval expansion prior to the Kruger Telegram affair, but the impact of the crisis on German public opinion and on Germany's relations with Britain created a potential constituency for navalism which had not existed before. Within three weeks of the despatch of the telegram to Kruger, Friedrich von Holstein reported to his friend Hatzfeldt that 'H.M. has only one interest at the moment, to use the political clash with England as a pretext to carry through a giant expansion of the fleet.'[23] A year later, nothing had changed. 'With the Kaiser, the navy question now takes precedence over everything', Holstein observed. He blamed the head of Wilhelm's naval cabinet Admiral von Senden-Bibran for this, noting that the Kaiser wanted a fleet like that of England 'and wants to direct his entire domestic policy to that end i.e. to a fight'.[24] Wilhelm II remained a steadfast supporter of naval expansion throughout the years down to the outbreak of the First World War. Tirpitz himself admitted that the Kaiser had been an invaluable ally when he recalled in his memoirs: 'Without the Emperor, Germany's estrangement from the sea and the tasks of civilization bound up with it, would never have been overcome.'[25]

Historians such as Eckhart Kehr and Volker Berghahn have stressed that *Flottenpolitik* has to be examined in the context of its domestic political aims as well as in terms of *Weltpolitik*. Berghahn has argued that the construction of a battlefleet was linked to a bargain between the Prussian agrarians and the leaders of heavy industry, and their political representatives, in 1897, designed to protect the economic interests of both through the maintenance of high tariffs.[26] The policy in turn was designed to ensure co-operation between Conservatives and Liberals against the Social Democrats in the 1898 Reichstag election. This theory, while an attractive one, has been criticized. The link between the *Sammlung* of 1897 and the decision to construct a battlefleet was at best a tenuous one. The agrarians were never great enthusiasts of naval expansion for they associated it with the industrial and commercial future which filled them with dread. One of their representatives lamented that the passage of the first Navy Bill through the Reichstag would 'lead us further along the path of development towards a state of industrialists and wholesale traders'.[27] Similarly many members of the middle class supported naval expansion because they believed it would accelerate the processes of domestic economic and political change, not because they believed it would uphold the *ancien régime*. Thus, Max Weber stated on one occasion:

> Not a policy of '*Sammlung*' with its anti-capitalist slogans, but only a decisive pursuit of the consequences of our powerful bourgeois-industrial development can lend sense for the bourgeois class to the demand for sea-power. For the protection of ground-rents we need no fleet.[28]

Tirpitz himself seems to have had some sympathy with the commercial aspect of such views, although as an ardent monarchist he certainly did not wish to use the fleet as a vehicle for domestic reform. His main aim seems to have been the implementation of his naval programme. There is little evidence that he conceived of the fleet in terms of a 'crisis strategy in domestic politics'.

Nevertheless, there was a link between *Flottenpolitik* and the domestic political context. It was certainly hoped that building a fleet would bolster support for the monarchy. Additionally the navy, being a truly German institution, unlike the various armies of the Reich, served as a symbol of the Empire's unity and brought men from different parts of Germany together. Wilhelm II himself described it on one occasion as 'a living embodiment of the unity of the Empire'.[29] Thirdly, the navy became an organization in which the middle classes could take particular pride because they formed a high percentage of its officer corps, and were not excluded from its upper ranks as was still often the case in the elite regiments of the Prussian army.

However, it is also evident that popular enthusiasm had to be orchestrated from above. The Navy League, the pressure group which agitated for increases in the fleet, was not formed until the end of April 1898, three weeks after the passage of the first Navy Law, and the Imperial Naval Office saw it mainly as an organization which should do its bidding. Tirpitz acknowledged that the German people had to be educated into accepting the importance of naval expansion. It was a slow process.

In reply to a letter from the Grand Duke of Baden, in the spring of 1903, Tirpitz agreed that a programme of public education was still needed to convince the German people of the value of the fleet:

> Real enthusiasm for the forceful promotion of our military strength at sea is absent among our people and their parliamentary representatives. This enthusiasm can however only come from a deep understanding that just as up to now the army has been an absolute condition for Germany's existence as a great power, so in the future will be the navy for the German Empire's as a world power.[30]

The Kaiser himself supported these efforts to make the German people aware of the significance of the fleet building programme. Sometimes this could take a cynical form. In August 1905, for example, he commanded that free rail tickets be provided for members of the public who wished to go and see the British Home Fleet on a visit to the Baltic port of Swinemünde. 'Such an inspection would be very revealing with regard to certain naval matters and politically very useful',[31] he declared. Thus a goodwill visit by the Royal Navy was exploited by Wilhelm as an excuse to increase German enthusiasm for naval expansion.

The letters by Tirpitz and the Kaiser quoted above provide an insight into the political and strategic aims of *Flottenpolitik*. The fleet was being built to ensure that Germany achieved a colonial empire alongside the other powers, but it was also being built against the greatest of the imperial powers, Britain. Tirpitz made no secret of the fact that the fleet was designed for war against England. Bernhard von Bülow, the Chancellor during most of the period of naval expansion, set out the purpose clearly in a letter addressed to the Kaiser in August 1900, in which he implied that the glories of the Hohenzollern dynasty lay in the future as well as the past:

> in Your Majesty's reign the British play the same role as the French under the Great Elector and the Austrians under the Great King. Dealing with the English is infinitely troublesome, infinitely difficult, requires infinite patience and skill. However, just as the Hohenzollern griffin defeated the double-headed Austrian eagle on the battlefield and clipped the wings of the Gallic cock, so too with God's help and through Your Majesty's power and wisdom will it cope with the English leopard.[32]

Such sentiments chimed with the Kaiser's own enthusiasm for *Flottenpolitik*. Baroness Spitzemberg recorded in May 1903 that

Wilhelm's 'first and fundamental idea is to break England's position in the world to Germany's advantage; it needs a fleet for that purpose'.[33]

The naval strategy put in place by Tirpitz underlines the anti-British orientation of the policy. Wilhelm II had initially favoured a fleet of cruisers which could defend German trade and secure colonies for the Reich. However, Tirpitz had objected on the pretext that Germany did not have enough coaling stations overseas to make such a strategy viable. Instead the fleet which he proposed, and the one which was built, consisted of battleships, with only a short range, based in the ports of Kiel and Wilhelmshaven, and clearly intended for use in a confrontation with the Royal Navy in the North Sea. Tirpitz's aim was to construct a fleet of sufficient size to deter an attack upon Germany by the Royal Navy. The German fleet was to be used as a bargaining tool to force concessions from Britain in the colonial arena. However, as it became obvious that this strategy had failed, the main aim began subtly to shift towards the deterrence of any British attempt to prevent Germany from seeking hegemony on the European continent. Tirpitz's strategy required cautious diplomacy on the part of Germany's political leaders, for the construction of the navy was conceived to be the work of a whole generation, and it was imperative not to provoke the British into making a pre-emptive strike against German ports – a so-called 'Copenhagening' – before the fleet was ready. Tirpitz's desire to mask the purpose of the navy building programme also explains why measures to expand the fleet were often accompanied by disingenuous attempts to improve Anglo-German relations. This was most noticeably the case on two occasions – in November 1899 and November 1907 – when visits by the Kaiser to Britain were followed closely by new Navy Bills. Holstein commented perceptively in relation to the second visit that naval armaments increases made Wilhelm II's protestations of friendship for Britain on such occasions 'useless and meaningless' and gave them 'an air of fraud'.[34] For Tirpitz such visits were smokescreens for naval expansion, and nothing more.

Tirpitz's assumptions as to the political context in which he would be able to enact his plan rapidly proved to have been erroneous. German diplomacy was too inept, and the nationalist sections of German public opinion too vociferous in their condemnation of Britain, to hide the purpose of *Flottenpolitik* from the British government for long. As early as the autumn of 1902, long before the German navy would be completed, the Kaiser was shocked to learn on a visit to England that British politicians already suspected that the German fleet was being built against them. 'Therefore caution!', he advised Bülow, 'They have thirty-five cruisers in service here and we have only eight!!'[35] The strategic assumptions of Tirpitz's risk theory proved to be equally flawed. The Admiral failed to appreciate that the Royal Navy would not necessarily need to attack the German High Seas Fleet in a war, and thus place Britain's maritime supremacy in jeopardy. It could equally undermine the German war effort through a long-range blockade of German ports. This is precisely what occurred in the Great War. The final weakness of the Tirpitz Plan lay in the sphere of finance. The German Empire, unlike Britain, required a large army in addition to a navy, yet was still a poorer country than Britain. Political factors, such as the opposition of the Social Democrats to *Flottenpolitik*, and the complicated revenue-raising structure of the Reich, also led Tirpitz to favour a cautious, long-term programme of expansion. However, when political conditions allowed him to get a Navy Bill through the Reichstag in the winter of 1907/8 which accelerated the pace of German naval construction, the British were able to respond quickly and to maintain a substantial lead in the number of battleships. By 1909 it was evident to many observers that *Flottenpolitik* had failed, and in 1912/13 this was tacitly accepted in official circles when the decision was made to divert resources from the navy to the army.

Wilhelm II and Tirpitz were not prepared to admit that *Flottenpolitik* had failed both as a power political instrument and as a mechanism of national integration. Instead they held fast to the policy until almost the end. When the German ambassador to London pleaded for a naval agreement with Britain in the spring of 1909, the Kaiser wrote half in despair, half in pity: 'Poor Metternich! He can neither understand nor tolerate the fleet.'[36] The Kaiser's intransigence frustrated diplomats other than Metternich. Alfred von Kiderlen-Wächter, the State Secretary to the Foreign Office, commented with irritation in January 1911: 'His Majesty is sincere: he wants to have ships, ships, ships, and then not to use them, but rather to keep them all in Kiel like a plaything.'[37] It was Wilhelm II's continuing support for his 'evil genius'[38] Tirpitz which prevented the abandonment of the navy building strategy. The Kaiser's support gave Tirpitz an effective veto over any naval agreement with Britain, as the British statesman Lord Haldane recognized, after his own attempt to negotiate a deal with Berlin disintegrated in the winter of 1912: 'The Germans have sent us rather an ungenerous memorandum, in real Prussian style. It is not written by Bethmann Hollweg – of him I am pretty sure. The Admirals have beaten him and they are wrapping up their refusal.'[39]

Tirpitz's career would have been brought to an end by such an agreement. For Wilhelm the reasons for opposing a naval agreement had as much to do with psychology as politics. It was the symbol of his reign and manifested his own and Germany's claim to be treated as the equal of the British Empire. Yet the territorial gains achieved by Germany in the era of *Flottenpolitik* – Kiaochow, the Samoan Islands, and a strip of jungle in equatorial Africa – were paltry, and the attempts to present them as major triumphs had a hollow ring. Bülow claimed, for example, to have brought the British Prime Minister, Lord Salisbury, 'to his knees'[40] in the negotations over Samoa in 1899. Yet the territory acquired was small and virtually worthless. *Flottenpolitik* thus served to discredit the Kaiser's regime because it was such a conspicuous failure. It antagonized the British without securing an empire for Germany. It also exacerbated domestic tensions within Germany for two reasons. Firstly, the failure of *Weltpolitik* and *Flottenpolitik* caused some of the radical nationalist pressure groups which had emerged in the 1890s to become disenchanted with the government and to move into opposition, a process which was complete by the time of the final failure of navalist *Weltpolitik* in the Agadir crisis of 1911. Secondly, the fact that naval expansion was funded through the inequitable method of indirect taxation increased the resentment of the working class against the regime and drove them into the arms of the Social Democrats. Hence *Flottenpolitik* must be judged as a failure not just in terms of Great Power politics, but in those of domestic politics as well. It would be the effects of the former, however, that would be most noticeable, especially in the area of Anglo-German relations.

The Breakdown of Anglo-German Relations

On 11 August 1914, one week after Britain declared war on Germany, Prince Lichnowsky, the former German ambassador to London, sent a letter to Kaiser Wilhelm II. In it he claimed that he had never hidden the fact that he expected Britain to support France in a war against Germany, and had never sought to delude Wilhelm into believing that the British would remain neutral.[41] Lichnowsky's motive for sending this letter was the desire to avoid becoming the scapegoat for Britain's hostile action. Nevertheless, ulterior reasons notwithstanding, his analysis was accurate. Despite some improvement between 1912 and the summer of 1914, Anglo-German relations were such that British intervention in the Great War, against Germany, was to be expected. How had this come to pass?

In the early 1890s, relations between Britain and Germany were relatively cordial. The two countries were bound together by cultural, religious and dynastic ties. In both Prussia and Britain, the main religion was Protestantism. The Germans and British regarded themselves as racial cousins, and Kaiser Wilhelm II was half-British, being the grandson of Queen Victoria. In addition to these ties, the British and the Germans could look back upon shared historical experiences. Britain and Prussia had both played a leading role in the defeat of Napoleon in 1815, and throughout most of the nineteenth century, Britain and Germany had shared the common objective of preventing the resurgence of France. Between 1890 and 1894, Wilhelm II and Chancellor Caprivi pursued a policy of co-operation with Britain in world affairs; a tendency encouraged by the *rapprochement* between France and Russia. The Kaiser's frequent visits to Britain in the early 1890s also indicated that the bilateral relationship between Berlin and London was a close one, although these occasions were not without an element of family tension.[42]

However, beneath the surface, there were warning signs that Anglo-German relations were unlikely to remain friendly. Three developments in particular indicated that the future would see greater turbulence between the two powers: the emergence of commercial rivalry, imperial competition, and a growing ideological distaste in certain circles in Germany for Britain. The era between 1890 and 1914 saw Germany race ahead of Britain in many of the most important indices of industrial production. Germany's economic dynamism had important implications for the way in which both Germans and Britons perceived the global geopolitical order. Many in Germany came to believe that the distribution of the world's territory no longer reflected economic realities, and in particular that Germany deserved greater recognition as a world power. Such feelings were coupled with resentment of British condescension. On the British side, there was alarm at economic competition from Germany, which found its expression in campaigns against the import of German goods in newspapers such as the *Daily Mail*. The era was also that of the 'New Imperialism'. An increasing body of opinion in Germany believed that as a Great Power, Germany deserved a large colonial empire. Initially Wilhelm II had hoped to gain colonies through co-operation with Britain. However, such efforts failed to find a response from London. Radical pressure groups such as the Pan-German League grew in size and influence, and agitated in favour of a more confrontational policy towards Britain in international affairs.[43]

The third development which contributed to anti-British feeling in Germany in the 1890s was ideological. Those who lost out as a result of Germany's transformation from an agricultural to an industrial economy, such as small shopkeepers, and East Elbian landowners, came to equate Britain with the harsh capitalism which was undermining their livelihoods, and which was associated in their minds with the influence of the Jews. As a consequence, anti-English feeling came to be infused with disdain for those who placed profit above all else, and with anti-Semitism. Anti-English feeling was also manifested in the disdain of the Prussian aristocracy for the parliamentary system, and in a concomitant tendency to emphasize the virtues of the Prusso-German constitution. Also of crucial importance to the ideological development of Anglophobia in the 1890s was Social Darwinism: the belief that Charles Darwin's theories about the survival of the fittest in the animal kingdom could be applied to the relations between states. In particular the theories of the historian Heinrich von Treitschke came to influence many figures in the German elite. Treitschke was convinced that it was Germany's mission to obtain global supremacy, and this could only occur by challenging the British Empire at sea. The two individuals appointed by the Kaiser to implement a navalist 'world policy' in 1897 – Tirpitz and Bülow – knew and admired Treitschke's work.[44]

It was a conscious decision by the German government, in 1897, to pursue *Weltpolitik* and to build a navy to rival that of Britain which turned the latent antagonism between Britain and Germany into active confrontation and accelerated the pace of estrangement between London and Berlin. It was the type of navy envisaged by the Kaiser and Tirpitz which alarmed the British. The decision to concentrate battleships in the North Sea gave the lie to German claims that the fleet was being built for colonizing enterprises. This in turn led the British to the correct assumption that the German fleet was being constructed for a future war against the Royal Navy. There were two subsidiary factors for British alarm. Firstly, the pace of German naval increase was disconcerting. In the mid 1890s, the German fleet had been of negligible significance as compared with those of France and Russia, yet by 1906 it was projected to be the next largest after the Royal Navy. Secondly, a combination of incompetent diplomacy on the part of Wilhelm II and his leading advisers, and the bombastic utterances of sections of the German press, drew attention to Germany's global ambitions, and to the anti-British character of these objectives. Consequently, as Tirpitz bemoaned in his memoirs, the German fleet was not constructed in the conditions of international calm which he had regarded as essential if Germany were to become a maritime power of the first rank.[45] A combination of strategic miscalculations on his part, together with forces beyond his control, led the British to appreciate the true character of German navalism, long before the fleet-building programme had passed through what Tirpitz termed the 'danger zone'.

There were several other reasons as to why *Weltpolitik* altered the British perception of Germany. The German challenge emerged at a time when Britain's global pre-eminence appeared to be under threat from all sides. Her economy was in decline relative to the USA as well as Germany, and the South African War of 1899–1902 had exposed the weakness of the British army and the Empire's potential vulnerability. This gave rise to a mood of defensiveness in which the British public and government were determined to respond vigorously to German naval-ism.[46] Secondly, *Weltpolitik* altered British perceptions of what had previously been seen as German virtues. Germany's military efficiency and technical brilliance were still regarded as models to be copied. Yet, para-doxically, many of those who admired Germany also came to see her as a threat. Such attitudes were prevalent among right-wingers in Britain, who feared the *Kaiserreich* precisely because they believed it was stronger politically, economically and militarily than Britain. Thirdly, Social Darwinist attitudes also extended to the British elite, and provided an ideological basis for resistance to *Weltpolitik*. Many prominent Britons came to believe that Britain and Germany were locked into a Darwinian struggle for supremacy, and hence that there was little room for compro-mise. Edward VII's close friend Lord Esher depicted the contest between London and Berlin in such terms in 1906: '*L'Allemagne c'est l'Ennemi* – and there is no doubt on the subject. They mean to have a powerful fleet, and commercially to beat us out of the field before ten years are over our heads.'[47]

However, it should be borne in mind that German navalism and *Weltpolitik* were not the initial causes of the reorientation of British for-eign policy after 1900. British policy-makers were still inclined to think in imperial terms, and hence it was the perceived danger of imperial over-stretch which initially caused them to seek understandings with France and Russia. Paradoxically, no colonial agreement with Germany could be reached because it was not clear what form such an accord would take. The very vagueness of *Weltpolitik* led the British to read into it an all-pervasive German threat to the British Empire, whereas the lack of concrete Anglo-German territorial disputes overseas meant that there was little opportunity for a lasting understanding between London and Berlin. It was only in 1905, when the German government tried to destroy the Anglo-French *Entente* by challenging the agreement's assumption that France would be allowed a pre-eminent position in Morocco, that Britain's policy switched from being one based upon imperial concerns to one which aimed to contain German power in Europe in order to prevent the destruction of the 'balance of power' on the Continent. There were many reasons why no understanding could be arrived at between Britain and Germany before 1914. 'Patriotic' pressure groups in both countries became increasingly influential after 1900, and opposed concessions in the colonial and naval spheres. German fears that the Royal Navy would attack the High Seas Fleet in its ports, and British ones of German spies and of a German invasion also complicated the picture and reduced the room for compromise between the two governments. Secondly, cultural ties were of diminishing value. Wilhelm II often made reference in conversation with British diplomats and naval attachés to the 'spirit of Waterloo' and to the natural racial compatibility between the German and their Anglo-Saxon cousins. There were organizations in Britain, such as the Anglo-German Friendship Society, which sang from the same hymn sheet. However, more often than not, such similarities were used to explain why the two peoples could not be reconciled. Many Germans who knew England well were among the most prominent Anglophobes, and a German diplomat lamented on one occasion that Britons who were most familiar with Germany were often those who were most suspicious of Germany politically.[48] The French ambassador to London concluded correctly in 1912 that the British would not return to the tradition of friendship with Germany, dating back to the mid-Victorian period, because circumstances had changed. Germany had been transformed from a collection of small and medium-sized states into a power which aimed at dominance in Europe. This was an objective to which Britain could never be reconciled.

There were two further factors which rendered it extremely difficult for the two powers to co-operate: the deterioration in the dynastic relationship between the Kaiser and the British royal family, and the reluctance of the two governments to seek an accommodation with one another. During the last years of Queen Victoria's reign, relations between the British and Prussian courts had not been without friction. However, the Queen showed remarkable restraint in her dealings with the Kaiser, despite provocations such as the Kruger Telegram. Additionally, Wilhelm's inherent respect for the Queen acted as a partial antidote to the Anglophobia of his entourage and a large section of public opinion. Wilhelm II remained popular in Britain long after the emergence of anti-German feeling. In 1902, the German ambassador went so far as to state that the 'only thing which to some extent still preserves the much loosened bond between Germany and England is the person of H.M. the Kaiser'.[49] However, this complacency about the Kaiser's popularity disguised what was actually happening. Wilhelm and Queen Victoria's successor, the Kaiser's uncle, King Edward VII, loathed one another. Over time the rivalry between the two monarchs became itself a complicating factor in Anglo-German relations. The Kaiser came to believe that the King was working towards the encirclement of Germany. Wilhelm's intransigence on the naval question was connected to this paranoia. The King, while by no means a Germanophobe, did gradually become extremely suspicious of his nephew's intentions, and used his influence, notably over diplomatic appointments, to ensure that most of the British ambassadors in key posts were alive to the danger posed by German navalism and *Weltpolitik*.[50]

Of greater importance was the attitude adopted by the British and German governments. British policy-makers were convinced that the Germans aimed to dominate Europe. This was the theme of the Crowe memorandum of 1907, and it was also the conviction of the Foreign Secretary in the Liberal government of 1905–14, Sir Edward Grey. Grey operated a 'balance of power' policy, aimed at Germany's containment. He and his officials placed strict limits on co-operation with Berlin. Ambassadors who had doubts about the malevolence of German policy were pensioned off, and replaced with diplomats whose views better reflected the official line. Grey simply did not believe that a lasting understanding was possible with the Germans until the naval armaments question was resolved. As a consequence he adopted a relentlessly negative attitude towards Germany, particularly in the early years of his tenure as Foreign Secretary. On the surface, the attitude of the German government towards Britain was more accommodating. Wilhelm II and Bülow emphasized their desire to see friendly relations restored. However, words were not matched by deeds. In 1906 and 1908 further Navy Bills were passed into law by the Reichstag, manifesting clearly, in British eyes at least, that Germany was not prepared to accept the Royal Navy's maritime supremacy.

Despite such evidence of Anglo-German estrangement, relations between the two powers appeared to improve markedly in the last years of peace. Negotiations on the future of the Portuguese colonies made substantial progress, and the two sides had reached agreement on the Berlin–Baghdad railway project by July 1914. Co-operation between London and Berlin was most conspicuous in the Balkans. Grey, and Bülow's successor as German Chancellor, Bethmann Hollweg, jointly sponsored the peace agreement at the end of the first Balkan war in 1912/13. It has even been suggested that during the July crisis of 1914,

Bethmann and the Kaiser acted more boldly than they would otherwise have done, because they were convinced that Britain would remain neutral in a war between the continental powers. Certainly Wilhelm's own condemnation of British treachery when such hopes proved misplaced, bears this out.[51]

The extent of the improvement in Anglo-German relations should not be overemphasized. It was concentrated in areas of minor importance. The Portuguese colonies were not Britain's to give, and London's discussions with Berlin on the matter thus had a somewhat academic character. Similarly, Britain's agreement to participate in the Baghdad railway was hardly an unprecedented step, particularly given that her *Entente* partner Russia had reached an accommodation with Berlin on the project in 1910. When one broadens the focus, it is clear that the *rapprochement* between London and Berlin was largely cosmetic. From 1911 onwards the military and naval ties between Britain and France were extended, and by 1914 the British government was coming under pressure from Russia to conclude an alliance. German aspirations to detach Britain from her *Entente* partners had failed to bear fruit. Simultaneously, the Anglo-German *détente* in the Balkans broke up in 1913/14, as Berlin was dragged ever deeper into disputes in the region between her ally, Austria, on the one hand, and Russia and Serbia on the other. The increasingly partisan stance by the Germans led to the collapse of Anglo-German co-operation in the Balkans, as this had been predicated on the assumption that London and Berlin would both act as honest brokers in regional disputes.

More significant still was the failure of the two governments to reach an agreement on the issue of naval armaments. There were two main reasons for this. Both governments believed that their national interests would be compromised if an agreement were to be reached in unfavourable circumstances. Secondly, any pretence that the conflict of interest was purely about battleships had been lost. Considerations of European power politics now carried equal if not greater weight in the bilateral dispute. By 1911, the German leadership had given up on *Weltpolitik* as an immediate objective. There was an emerging consensus that the Reich would have to gain a position of hegemony in Europe before expanding overseas. Resources were diverted from the navy to the army, yet the navy was still to be used as a bargaining tool in Germany's relations with Britain. The Germans were only prepared to enter into a naval agreement with Britain in return for a political agreement guaranteeing British neutrality in a future European war. The British, by contrast, opposed the idea of linkage between a naval and a political agreement, because they appreciated that the guarantee of British neutrality would simply allow Germany to overrun France, and then potentially to attack the British Isles. The conflict between Britain and Germany had thus gone beyond naval armaments. It had become an open confrontation over the future of Europe. The last major attempt to find a solution to the naval arms race – the Haldane mission of February 1912 – foundered as a result of this conflict between British insistence on the maintenance of a European balance of power and the German leadership's thinly veiled aspiration towards a European hegemony.

Economic change and the alteration in the relative weight of Germany and Britain within the international system, coupled with commercial, colonial and ideological rivalry, all contributed to the sharp deterioration in Anglo-German relations after 1890. However, it was German *Weltpolitik* and more particularly the *Reichsleitung*'s decision to build a fleet of battleships, concentrated in the North Sea, which turned tension into confrontation. The German leadership, at the behest of Kaiser Wilhelm II and his entourage, tried to assert German power in a most precipitous and inept manner. Even when it became evident that the strategy of buying colonial concessions and a guarantee of neutrality in a future war from the British had failed – by 1911/12 at the latest – the Kaiser and Tirpitz continued to resist a naval agreement. The motives for the intransigence of Wilhelm II and Tirpitz are complex. It is evident that patriotic pressure groups, and the representatives of the steel and shipbuilding industries would have condemned a naval arms limitation agreement with Britain. It is equally obvious, however, that the Kaiser and Tirpitz mistook considerations of prestige and honour for vital interests in opposing a compromise with London on naval armaments. In the last instance, Wilhelm II must bear a large share of the blame for the deterioration in Anglo-German relations prior to 1914. For it was the Kaiser's steadfast support for Tirpitz which led to Berlin's failure to abandon *Flottenpolitik* before it was too late, and it was the threat posed by the High Seas Fleet to Britain's long-term security which played a major role in Britain's decision to enter the First World War on the side of Germany's enemies.

The Origins of the First World War

More ink has been spilt on the subject of Germany's role in the origins of the war than on any other single topic. Initially the debate was conducted in partisan terms, connected to Article 231 of the Treaty of

Versailles, which emphasized the responsibility of Germany and her allies for starting the war. The so-called 'War Guilt' clause led to what one scholar has termed 'patriotic self-censorship' in Germany in the inter-war years. German historians suppressed material which showed German actions prior to 1914 in a poor light, and claimed that Germany had been forced into war by the threat of aggression on the part of France and Russia.[52] It was only in the 1960s that a more realistic picture of Germany's role in the origins of the First World War began to emerge among German scholars. This was primarily the result of two major works by the Hamburg historian, Fritz Fischer, *Germany's Aims in the First World War* and *War of Illusions*, in which he argued that the German civil and military leadership had actively planned for war, and had escalated the July crisis in 1914 in the expectation that this would lead to a European war which Germany and her allies could win. Although some of Fischer's views remain controversial, few historians would dispute the fact that Germany was more willing than virtually any other power to risk war in 1914. An attempt by neo-conservative German historians to revive the idea that German policy was essentially defensive[53] has failed to undermine the new orthodoxy.

However, there remains disagreement about which factors were compelling the German leadership towards war prior to 1914. Volker Berghahn remains the champion of the view that it was domestic crises and pressures which were driving Berlin to think about a diversionary external adventure.[54] By contrast historians such as David Kaiser and Niall Ferguson have recently argued that Berlin's perception that geopolitical and military trends were beginning to work against German interests were of much greater importance than domestic factors in pushing the Reich towards war.[55] A further controversy concerns the issue of when the German decision for war was taken. Fischer, himself, and John Röhl both believe that it was made in advance of the July crisis. They have argued that steps to prepare the nation for war were taken from December 1912 onwards. However, Fischer and Röhl have both stepped back from arguing that the decision to start a war in the summer of 1914 had been made 18 months earlier.[56] The main critic of the view that the German decision for war was premeditated has been Wolfgang Mommsen, who has argued that there is no compelling evidence for the thesis that preparations were actively being made for war from late 1912 onwards.[57]

In the 1970s, largely thanks to the work of Fritz Fischer and Volker Berghahn, the view that Germany went to war in 1914 for domestic reasons gained currency. The thesis which they advanced postulated that by

1914 Wilhelm II's semi-absolutist regime had been driven into a 'cul-de-sac' as the result of a series of disasters in domestic and foreign policy. The Kaiser's attempt to use patriotism to kill off socialism had manifestly failed, most notably as a result of gains by the SPD in the Reichstag elections of January 1912. The election results, according to this thesis, created a situation in which Chancellor Bethmann Hollweg was unable to get measures passed through the Reichstag. The atmosphere of political stalemate made war attractive. This domestic encirclement of the Prussian ruling class was coupled with a sharp deterioration in Germany's international position. By 1911 at the latest *Weltpolitik* was universally considered to have failed. Naval competition with Britain had simply led to a permanent estrangement between London and Berlin. Additionally, Germany's attempt to gain concessions from France by challenging her position in Morocco had ended in diplomatic humiliation in the autumn of 1911 when the British threatened Germany with war if she did not back down. The German leadership came to see their country's future in apocalyptic terms, encapsulated in General von Bernhardi's view that the Reich's choice was between 'world power or downfall'.[58]

However, the view that Germany went to war in 1914 for domestic reasons no longer seems persuasive. More recent research has undermined Berghahn's gloomy picture of domestic encirclement, and questioned how far one should rely on the views of militarists such as Bernhardi to provide an insight into the workings of the German 'official mind'. It is clear for example that Bethmann saw the Conservative Party rather than the SPD as the main threat to the effective governance of the Reich. He accused them of wishing to destroy him. Thus, in one sense, the Reichstag election results of 1912 were not the disaster for the Chancellor depicted by Berghahn and Fischer. For the results weakened the Conservatives who had undermined Bülow's chancellorship in 1909 by voting against a Reich finance reform, and who had humiliated Bethmann during the Reichstag debate on the Franco-German agreement which ended the Moroccan crisis in the autumn of 1911. By contrast major pieces of legislation were passed on the eve of the war, such as the Army Bill of 1913 and the imperial tax credit of the same year. Thus the argument that a domestic political stalemate caused the Reich's leadership to launch a war of aggression begins to look threadbare.

The second question which needs to be answered is as follows: even if there had been a domestic crisis would it have compelled the German government to risk a European war? Again, the evidence on this point suggests that a domestic crisis would have been a reason to avoid such a conflict rather than to initiate one. Bülow, the Chancellor between 1900 and 1909, had pointed out in the 1890s that no state should enter into a war without thinking through the consequences. He wrote: 'Precipitance and lack of care are far more dangerous in foreign than in domestic policy ... great, serious mistakes in foreign policy can often never be put right.'[59] Bülow's successor, Bethmann, took a similar view. He told the Bavarian envoy at Berlin, in June 1914, that the moment for Germany to launch a 'preventive war' had passed, and revealed that he saw a war launched for domestic reasons as the height of folly:

> There are ... circles in the Reich which expect a war to effect a turnabout favorable to the conservative cause in Germany's domestic conditions. He, the Chancellor, thought that on the contrary a world war with unpredictable consequences would increase the power of the Social Democrats ... and would topple many a throne.[60]

Those who did believe that a war could have beneficial repercussions were concentrated in military circles, and included figures such as Bernhardi and General von Gelbsattel. It would be wrong to see their views as representative of the Reich's leadership as a whole. They were simply the spokesmen for an extremist faction within the Prussian establishment. By contrast even Wilhelm II himself seemed, at least in his more lucid moments, to concede that it would be a grave error to enter into a war if this could not be justified to the German people. For example in February 1913 the Kaiser sought to restrain the Austrians from going to war to prevent Serbia and Montenegro from gaining a port on the Adriatic. His reasoning revealed doubts about his ability to secure the backing of the German people for a war over the issue. 'The present situation means a true calamity for the vast majority of people in Europe and environs ... and I ask myself whether the issues at stake here ... are really important enough to justify you and Russia facing each other half mobilized.'[61]

If explanations which emphasize the role of domestic factors must now be treated with extreme caution, other pressures must have been pushing the German leadership to consider resorting to war. These can be found in two areas: perceptions of Germany's place within the international system, and assessments of her military strength relative to other powers. In other words, the roots of the German decision for war are to be located in considerations about the balance of power and the arms race. Berghahn and Fischer are correct to argue that it was the failure of *Weltpolitik* as manifested in Berlin's humiliation in the Agadir crisis, and the impossibility of reaching a naval agreement with London which would reconcile both German and British interests, which led to a reorientation in German foreign policy from 1911/12 onwards. This reorientation involved the revival of the old Bismarckian impulse towards a German hegemony in Europe. However, there was one crucial difference. Bismarck had been content to accept a latent German hegemony in Europe, whereas Kaiser Wilhelm II and his entourage wished to turn it into an actual position of territorial and economic dominance. Wilhelm II wished to bring about the creation of a United States of Europe under German leadership and control. The Social Darwinist impulse which had been at the heart of German foreign policy since the 1890s remained. However, with expansion blocked outside Europe, it was now redirected towards the continent itself, with disastrous consequences. When one accepts that the aim was European dominance, the trend of policy-making becomes explicable. Germany felt herself to be encircled by enemies. Her only reliable ally was the ailing Austro-Hungarian Empire. Although on paper Italy remained a member of the Triple Alliance, the Germans had given up on the Italians as early as 1908. At that time, Bülow had commented:

> In the event of a Franco-German war there is a 9 to 1 chance that the Italians would do as they did in 1870, when despite their alliance with France they waited to see how the hare would run and eventually remained neutral.[62]

In addition to this, nations which had been friends were becoming enemies. This was most obvious in the case of Russia. Germany and Russia had been bound together by dynastic ties and a shared political conservatism. By 1913, the Kaiser himself was prepared to concede that these links no longer counted for much in view of the rise of Pan-Slavism in the Tsarist Empire which was directed against Germany as well as Austria. Wilhelm declared to the Austrian Foreign Minister, Count Berchtold, that there could be no question of a return to the Holy Alliance between Germany, Austria and Russia. Russia, he observed, had changed since the time of Tsar Alexander III and one now had to deal with 'another Russia, which is hostile towards us, working towards our destruction, and in which elements other than the Emperor govern'.[63] This context of a growing awareness of Germany's diplomatic isolation should perhaps have led the Germans to shy away from war. Instead, it had the opposite effect. This is only explicable with reference with Berlin's perceptions of Germany's military position relative to other powers.

Perceptions of the military balance played a crucial role in pushing Germany towards war. Germany was the pre-eminent military power in Europe. However, the German military, and a vociferous section of German public opinion, did not believe that this situation could last. Helmuth von Moltke, the Chief of the Prussian General Staff, and his Austrian opposite number, Conrad von Hötzendorff, were convinced that the future would be bleak for the Central Powers as the countries of the *Entente*, notably France and Russia, expanded their own armaments.[64] The Germans were also aware of the need to compensate for the deficiencies of their Austrian allies. These two pressures, the need to counteract the military build-up of the *Entente*, and to bolster Austria-Hungary, combined to lead to a clamour from the German military establishment for armaments increases in the last years of peace. The Germans wanted to achieve supremacy in Europe, but believed that opportunities to achieve this ambition were running out. There was particular fear of the growth of Russian military power, which received a fillip as a result of the Great Programme of 1913. It was predicted that by 1916/17 Russia would be able to put hundreds of thousands of extra men into battle. This, coupled with the expansion of Russia's railway network in its western provinces, would render obsolete the calculations of the Schlieffen–Moltke plan which depended on Germany's ability to defeat France before Russia was able to mobilize her forces. The military's fear of Russia's latent power was matched by that of the civilians. Bethmann believed that: 'The future belongs to Russia which grows and grows and weighs upon us like a nightmare.'[65] Wilhelm shared his Chancellor's fears about the growth of Russian military power, and mused to his friend Max Warburg in June 1914 as to 'whether it would not be better to strike now rather than to wait'.[66] Others were more explicit. In July 1914 the German diplomat Kanitz informed the American ambassador in Constantinople that 'Germany should go to war when they are prepared and not wait until Russia has completed her plan to have a peace footing of 2 400 000 men. ... '[67]

The irony of this is striking: firstly because historians of Russia have found no evidence that Russia was intending to attack Germany, and secondly, because analyses of geopolitical trends have discovered that German power may actually have been increasing relative to Russia on the eve of the war. Hence, German policy on the eve of the war was based to a considerable extent on misperceptions. However, there were grounds for believing that Germany was destined to lose the arms race against the *Entente* powers. A special levy for the army was secured with great difficulty in 1913 after complicated and protracted negotiations between the federal states. At the time it was made clear that this was the last time that the states would agree to such a measure. In other words, the Army Bill of 1913 was a last throw of the dice on the part of the German military. They were unlikely to secure any further concessions. Future expansion of the army could only come as a consequence of a complete transformation in the financial and constitutional structure of the Reich. This was something which was not contemplated. Thus the years between 1914 and 1916 gave the German military a last window of opportunity to launch a pre-emptive strike against the *Entente* designed to secure German hegemony in Europe. This was not in any sense defensive, but decidedly aggressive. The culpability of the German military has been underlined by recent research which indicates that they did not even believe that a future war would be short. They expected a protracted struggle.[68] This underlines the criminal irresponsibility of their conduct.

If it can now be established that geopolitical and military considerations were more important than domestic ones in pushing the German leadership towards war, this still leaves open the question of when Berlin's decision for war was taken. This has been a subject of heated dispute among historians. Both Fischer and Röhl have isolated 8 December 1912 as a crucial date on the German road to war. On that day, the Kaiser convened a 'War Council' made up of leading army and navy personnel, including Moltke and Tirpitz. He did so in the context of the escalation of conflict in the Balkans which looked likely to lead to a European war, and shortly after learning, via his brother Prince Heinrich and the ambassador in London, Lichnowsky, that British neutrality in such a conflict could not be guaranteed. Although a decision was taken at the conference to postpone a war, there do seem to be strong grounds for arguing that the conference was of great significance. The conference agreed, for example, at Tirpitz's behest, that no war should be contemplated before the Kiel Canal had been widened. This work was to last until the summer of 1914: the exact moment when the Great War broke out. Wilhelm's utterances in December 1912 and in the subsequent 12 months, to individuals as diverse as the Swiss ambassador, George V's private secretary, and King Albert of the Belgians that a war would soon occur also lend credence to the view that the 'War Council' did make decisions of a decisive character. Nor can it be denied that the conference did take steps which heightened German military preparedness. It decided to increase the size of the Army Bill scheduled to be introduced into the Reichstag in 1913. Steps were taken to prepare the German people for war against Russia via a press campaign, gold reserves were built up after the conference, and courses at the Prussian military academy were shortened, suggesting that war was now seen as inevitable.[69] All this suggests that the 'War Council' should not be dismissed as insignificant.

The counter-argument has been advanced most forcefully by Wolfgang Mommsen. He believes that the 'War Council' did not make any decisions of note other than to agree to naval and military increases which had already been contemplated. He argues that the anti-Russian press campaign quickly fizzled out, and he claims that the Chancellor was not informed of the decisions taken until much later. All this, he suggests, indicates that it does not deserve the attention of the serious scholar of the origins of the war.[70] However, Mommsen is wrong on virtually every count. Bethmann was informed of the outcome immediately afterwards and agreed to implement the decisions made there. Additionally Röhl's more recent research has made it impossible for anyone to maintain that the decisions made in December 1912 were insignificant and not followed through. More doubt must be attached to Röhl and Fischer's inference that the decision to begin a war was taken prior to the assassination of Franz Ferdinand on 28 June 1914. Röhl has argued that the destruction of much of the documentation which would have allowed historians to piece together German decision-making during the July crisis amounts to a cover-up. He suggests that the decision to launch a war in the summer of 1914 had been taken in May of the same year.[71] This must remain a hypothesis. Evidence on German intelligence operations in July 1914 does not seem to indicate that the Germans were working to a pre-ordained plan.[72] The 'War Council' itself is best seen not in terms of a German decision for war, but in terms of a decision against long-term peace. The Kaiser and his military entourage resolved not to preserve peace at any price. If war broke out in favourable circumstances, this would be welcomed. Given the heightened tensions in Europe after 1911 such a scenario could be expected to present itself in the short to medium term. Wilhelm II's warnings about imminent war in 1912 and 1913 should be analysed against this context.

We can never establish with certainty when the German decision for war was taken because so much of the documentation which would have helped to establish the answer has been destroyed. However, it seems most likely that the decision was taken in response to the assassination of Franz Ferdinand. The Kaiser interpreted his friend's murder as 'a dreadful blow'[73] and he, Moltke, Bethmann and the Prussian War Minister Falkenhayn were all resolved to back Austrian demands for retribution from Serbia, even at the risk of a European war. Konrad

Jarausch has argued that the Germans were pursuing a policy of calculated risk in 1914, designed to secure a massive diplomatic victory over the *Entente* powers, while avoiding war.[74] However, this position is no longer tenable given the evidence which has recently emerged indicating that even the allegedly peace-loving Bethmann was working for war during the crisis. He warned the Crown Prince on 17 July not to undermine the government's strategy of working for war, while pretending to favour peace, by publicly advocating war.[75] Berlin's diplomatic actions in the crisis all indicate a preference for war. They co-operated with the British Foreign Secretary's mediation proposals, while advising the Austrians to reject them. The military also made no secret of their preference for war. The only point which can be made in mitigation is that when it became evident in the final days of the crisis that the British would intervene in support of France and Russia, the Kaiser and Bethmann wished to draw back. However, by that stage the Schlieffen–Moltke plan had already been implemented, and Moltke informed the Kaiser that the order could not be rescinded. Thus, in the final instance, it was German military planning which led to war in 1914, for their only available plan involved a two-front war and thus necessitated the escalation of what was essentially a Balkan crisis involving Austria and Serbia.

Germany was the only power which was actively working for a European war in 1914. She was doing so because the *Reichsleitung*, and particularly the military component within it, believed that the international balance of power was shifting inexorably against Germany. This was compounded by their fear of Russia and a perception that Germany was destined to lose the arms race against the *Entente*. Domestic factors were only peripherally involved. The July crisis was regarded as offering Germany a last chance to achieve a European hegemony. The fact that this view was based on misperception makes German decision-making in 1914 all the more catastrophic for Europe and tragic for Germany.

7

WILHELMINE GERMANY AT WAR

The Schlieffen Plan and its Failure

The very instant that Germany's political leadership committed itself irreversibly in favour of war in August 1914, the army high command embarked upon their long-prepared campaign strategy, the Schlieffen plan. In essence, this detailed military programme, the initial aim of which was the outflanking and subsequent encirclement of the French forces, consisted of an immediate offensive by the bulk of the German army against the weakest sector in France's defensive frontier, namely the country's northern region. To achieve the necessary concentration of German military power against this specific point and to ensure that the German armies were able to fight a rapid war of manoeuvre against their opponents, the Schlieffen plan directed its main offensive blow not across the narrow and heavily defended Franco-German border, which was guarded by a chain of strong fixed emplacements from Toul all the way to Verdun, but instead through the flat and largely unfortified terrain of neutral Belgium. From there, the plan envisaged that German forces would descend on Flanders, sweep through the industrial heart of France, and swing round Paris from the west and south. The French armies, encircled by this manoeuvre and with all avenues of retreat thereby severed, would then be annihilated against the Swiss and German frontiers. In six weeks, it was believed, French resistance and military power would be utterly crushed. With this goal achieved, German forces would then be free to redeploy by rail to fight the slowly assembling Russian armies in the east, against whom a decisive victory could be achieved at leisure.

The origins of this remarkable war plan – so detailed that it mapped out the expected battles on a day-to-day basis – are to be found in Germany's principal geopolitical dilemma: namely the country's intermediate location directly between the two major military powers, France and Russia. This predicament, which rendered both Germany's eastern and western borders vulnerable to outside attack, raised the distinct possibility, especially after France and Russia had become allies in 1894, that the Reich might one day have to fight a war on two fronts. With German military doctrine emphasizing offensive action, but with the country possessing insufficient military strength to launch attacks on two powerful adversaries simultaneously, it was clear that, were such a war to occur, the German General Staff would be required to concentrate initially on only one of their opponents and divide the country's armed forces accordingly. Two choices existed in relation to the disposition of German military strength in such a situation: the Reich could either go on the defensive in the west and the offensive in the east or it could go on the defensive in the east and the offensive in the west.

Both Moltke the Elder, Chief of the General Staff from 1857 to 1888, and his successor Alfred von Waldersee, who held the post from 1888 to 1891, had favoured the former option. This was, in part, a legacy of the geo-strategic advantage that had been bestowed upon Germany by the victory of 1871 and the capture of Alsace-Lorraine. The annexation of the Reichsland, as this province became known, had derived from neither territorial avarice nor from nationalist sentiment. Bismarck, as he had demonstrated in 1866 with his moderate demands towards Austria, did not believe that irredentist aspirations, even when inflamed by the euphoria of victory, should be allowed to influence foreign policy decisions. He was still in possession of this view when he insisted upon the cession of Alsace-Lorraine by France to Germany five years later. His sole motive for this demand was the province's strategic value: it served to make the border between Germany and France a naturally strong one by virtue of the Vosges mountains and the fortress city of Metz. Germany's military leaders, aware of Bismarck's reasoning – which they had done much to influence – lost no opportunity to utilize this situation to their advantage.[1] Given the defensible character of the short border with France and the contrast between this and the long open frontier with Russia, Moltke concluded, and Waldersee concurred, that strategic considerations made it sensible, in the event of a two-front war, for Germany to conduct a holding operation in the west and seek a decision in the east.

Alfred von Schlieffen, Chief of the General Staff from 1891 to 1906, and his successor Moltke the Younger, who held the post till September 1914, disagreed with this assessment. Despite all the evidence to the contrary, both of them were terrified by the prospect of 'vast Slavic hordes' and thus tended greatly to overestimate Russia's long-term military capability. As a result, they saw in Germany's existing plans for an offensive against Russia, the blueprint for a protracted war of attrition. According to their analysis of the situation, in the event of a German attack in the east, the Tsar's armies would simply retreat into the vast interior of the country until they were fully mobilized. Then, with sheer weight of numbers, they would overwhelm the German invaders.

On the basis of this assessment, Schlieffen and Moltke reversed Germany's strategy. Between 1892 and 1905 the emphasis formerly accorded to an attack upon Russia was gradually, but inexorably, shifted to an offensive against France. So great was the momentum in favour of this transformation that by the eve of the First World War, the German General Staff had even abandoned consideration of alternative approaches: all work on the *Grosse Ostaufmarschplan*, the scheme for an initial offensive against Russia, which had been regularly updated as a contingency measure even after the decision had been taken to concentrate Germany's efforts against France, was finally halted in April 1913. The necessary preparations for its implementation were then scrapped. The consequences of this decision – in particular, the extent to which it restricted Germany's options and predetermined the future direction of her military behaviour – is a much debated matter. The American military historian Dennis Showalter, for example, has attempted to downplay its significance. As he observes: '…the absence of an up-to-date version of the *Grosse Ostaufmarsch* [need not] be taken too seriously. This contingency plan, after all had only been abandoned in 1913; its revival would hardly have meant the removal of a generation of cobwebs.'[2] This view is supported by Marc Trachtenberg. He notes that in 1914, even without there being a current plan for an eastern offensive, Wilhelm II at one point still ordered a deployment against Russia. From this he concludes that Germany continued to possess choices despite having only one campaign plan.[3]

While there is some truth in both these judgements, the most recent examination of the issue, undertaken by Annika Mombauer, has decisively demonstrated that the scrapping of the eastern war plan did, notwithstanding the above, mark an 'important juncture' in German military policy. Instigated by the leading generals specifically to ensure that no alternative to the offensive against France existed, it deprived the Reich of military options irrespective of any contrary orders the Kaiser might give on the spur of the moment.[4] Hence, from this decision Germany's leaders would discover that there was no turning back. Thereafter, their army possessed only one plan of action for dealing with a war in Europe: the Schlieffen plan. It was this campaign strategy, finalized by Schlieffen in his great memorandum of December 1905 and thereafter progressively modified by Moltke the Younger, that led to German armies sweeping through Belgium and northern France following the German declaration of war in August 1914.

The initial results of Germany's military deployment appeared to vindicate the faith that the country's leaders and people had always placed in their army and its General Staff, as successes were achieved from the outset all along the front. To begin with, in the battle of the Frontiers, a series of French assaults against German positions in Lorraine were soundly beaten, forcing the French to retreat with their formations and morale severely dented. Meanwhile, the great German offensive drive through the north was exceeding even the most optimistic expectations. French armies, initially notable for their absence, were eventually engaged at Charleroi, where they were thrown back in considerable disarray. The massed German forces, enjoying a significant numerical advantage owing to Schlieffen's careful planning, then began a relentless pursuit of their tired and apparently beaten opponents. As August turned into September, they found themselves close to Paris. With both the battle and the war apparently won, German Chancellor Bethmann Hollweg chose this moment to record his country's war aims. His so-called 'September Programme', a scheme of annexations and indemnities so severe that it has drawn comparison with the settlements imposed by the Nazis, would never, however, be put into effect.[5] On 5 September, an Anglo-French counter-attack was launched on the Marne. Within a week German forces had been compelled to abandon their offensive and begin a withdrawal to the river Aisne. With this manoeuvre, Schlieffen's plan for a six-week victory was effectively in ruins.

The reason for the failure of the Schlieffen plan is a matter that has long fascinated historians, with the result that numerous hypotheses have been advanced to explain why this occurred. Broadly speaking, these explanations can be divided into two categories: those that blame the plan itself and consider that it was fundamentally flawed and those that hold that the plan was a good one and blame instead the younger Moltke's faulty execution of it.

Beginning with the criticisms of the plan itself, these have been levelled against several supposed defects. One of these is the way in which the plan was formulated. In drawing up his operational strategy, Schlieffen created a scheme of *manoeuvre a priori* that mapped out the entire course of the prospective campaign on a day-to-day basis: every aspect of the German army's behaviour from mobilization to final victory was, notionally at least, decided in advance. In undertaking to create so meticulous and predetermined a plan, Schlieffen was flying in the face of the received wisdom of the time concerning the role and limitations of staff work. Most of Schlieffen's predecessors and many of his contemporaries believed it to be impossible to plan much further than the initial mobilization and deployment. As Colmar von der Goltz had put it in 1883: 'no plan of operation can with any safety include more than the first collision with the enemy's main forces'.[6] The idea of actually planning a whole campaign in advance was, as a result of the widespread acceptance of this belief, actively ridiculed. The distinguished general and one-time Chief of the General Staff, Karl Wilhelm von Grolmann, for example, had once observed that 'to design a plan of operation for years from the office-table is nonsense and belongs to the sphere of the military novel',[7] a view that was echoed by the elder Moltke who adhered to the notion that 'only the layman believes he can see in the course of a campaign the carrying through of an initial idea, thought out in advance, considered in every detail, and adhered to right to the end'.[8] Schlieffen thought otherwise and, disregarding all advice to the contrary, planned his campaign strategy in great detail. While this meant that every German formation had clear and unambiguous orders for the first six weeks of the expected operation, the price of this precision was an almost total absence of flexibility to deal with those unexpected and inevitable 'frictions' that occur in every human enterprise including, as Clausewitz rightly observed, war.[9] The Schlieffen plan, possessing almost no margin for error, required everything to unfold as predicted. To count on this actually happening was, as the historian Gerhard Ritter has noted, 'an over-daring gamble'.[10] In consequence, Schlieffen has been accused of creating a strategic programme that was too rigid and unwieldy to succeed: unanticipated actions by the enemy could and did throw it into confusion.

Another criticism that has been levelled against the Schlieffen plan concerns the ideas that motivated it. At the heart of the plan, acting as the very *raison d'être* for the scheme, was the belief, known to historians as 'the short war illusion', that for Germany to stand any chance of winning a future war in Europe that war would have to be of strictly limited duration.[11] A long war, one that pitted the economic and human resources of the Reich against its opponents, Schlieffen regarded as disastrous for a modern, mass industrialized state like Germany. In his mind, the dislocation to, and disruption of, economic life caused by a long and drawn-out war of attrition would make it unfightable. As he put it, a protracted conflict could not be contemplated 'in an age in which the existence of nations is based on the uninterrupted progress of trade and commerce. ... A strategy of exhaustion is impossible when the maintenance of millions necessitates the expenditure of milliards.'[12] This being the case, a short war resulting in a rapid victory over the country's enemies was considered essential and the achievement of such an outcome had, therefore, to be the basis for German planning. Schlieffen made his calculations accordingly. Yet, that a war of this nature was actually attainable was considered extremely doubtful even at the time and many notable commentators put forward strong arguments against it.[13] Not the least of these was Helmuth von Moltke the Elder who, in his final address to the Reichstag in 1890 made the following observation:

> Gentlemen, if the war which has hung over our heads for more than ten years like a sword of Damocles – if this war were to break out, no one could foresee how long it would last nor how it would end. The greatest powers in Europe, armed as never before, would confront each other in battle. None of them could be thrown down so completely, in one or two campaigns, that they would have to admit defeat and be compelled to accept hard conditions for peace without any chance, even after a year's time, of renewing the fight. Gentlemen, it could be a Seven Years' War; it could be a Thirty Years' War; and woe to the man who sets Europe ablaze, who first throws the match into the powder barrel![14]

This warning that future European wars would, by definition, be lengthy was ignored by Schlieffen. Certain that a short war was essential for German success, he was unwilling to contemplate the idea that it could not be achieved. As a result, he staked everything on securing such an outcome, even to the extent of refusing to plan for a longer war or laying down the requisite stocks of ammunition and supplies to fight one. This presented a problem for Schlieffen's successor, the younger Moltke. Unlike his predecessor, he did not believe that a short war was possible and predicted that any future conflict would last, at the very least, one and a half to two years. Yet, despite this, he did nothing to alter the basic conception of the plan that he had inherited.[15] The illusion of a short war, even though few soldiers other than Schlieffen actually believed in it, was, in this fashion, allowed to remain in place as a core determinant of German operational thinking. Ironically, it is doubtful that such a war was actually necessary. Convinced by the argument that a protracted war was unfeasible for a large and advanced economy such as Germany's, no detailed consideration was undertaken to determine whether or not this was actually true. Yet, as actual experience was to show, it was the very strength of the German economy that made Germany ideally suited for a long war of attrition. Pitted against the weaker and less adaptable and dynamic economies of Russia and France, the German military machine and industrial complex was to prove by far the stronger and more successful, fighting her numerous enemies to a stalemate for over three years.[16] That Germany was eventually to lose the war was due to another fault of the plan, namely its ability to increase the number of Germany's enemies.

Of all the criticisms levelled against the Schlieffen plan probably the most significant is that it showed an almost cavalier disregard for the adverse political consequences that derived from its required actions. Particularly significant in this respect was the plan's demand for the invasion of Belgium. The violation of the territory of this particular state, the neutrality of which was guaranteed by treaty, was one of the few issues likely to produce unity among the diverse factions of Britain's ruling Liberal government in favour of a military response. As a consequence, the Schlieffen plan ensured that in the very first week of the war the number of Germany's enemies grew rapidly: as if having to contend with Russia and France was not enough, the plan also brought about the added encumbrance of fighting Belgium and Britain as well. Inadequate study had been devoted to the implications of these various additional opponents. The General Staff had rather complacently assumed that Belgium would offer no serious resistance to the German advance and that Britain, if it fought at all, would be unable to make a meaningful contribution to the course of battle with its 'contemptible' expeditionary force of a mere 100 000 men. Neither of these assumptions proved valid. Belgian opposition to the German invasion – epitomized by King Albert's assertion that Belgium was a nation, not a highway – proved uncommonly robust, delaying the German advance at Liège by four vital days; while the British army, arriving on the continent with unexpected rapidity, was in the right place at the right time to temper the progress of the German right at Mons. Neither of these outcomes was incapable of anticipation. That they were eventualities largely uncatered for in the Schlieffen plan can only be described as a serious deficiency.

In contrast to these criticisms of the fundamental nature of the Schlieffen plan, there exists a body of opinion that holds that the plan was essentially a sound one and that it only broke down because it was imperfectly executed by a new Chief of the General Staff, the Younger

Moltke, who failed to grasp its finer points and who made unnecessary and damaging alterations to its core strategic stipulations. Typifying such a position is the view, expressed by Gordon Craig, that 'if this plan had been carried out in 1914 in its original form and under the direction of an energetic and stubborn commander-in-chief, it would have achieved an overwhelming initial success'.[17] Several of Moltke's contemporaries thought likewise; they claimed that Germany had not achieved victory in 1914 because the plan had been 'watered down'.[18] At the heart of this argument lie three major accusations. The first of these is that Moltke altered the balance between the German right and left wings, thus ensuring that the armies entrusted with wheeling through northern France to the west of Paris were unable to fulfil their mission. Secondly, it is said that he destroyed the German army's room for manoeuvre by recasting the Schlieffen plan so as to respect the neutrality of Holland. This decision to avoid the Maastricht Appendix, a wedge of Dutch territory that separated northern Belgium from Germany, required that the entire German first army of 320 000 men pass through the six miles of the Liège bottleneck and thus created, in addition to enormous logistical problems, the necessity of capturing the city's fortresses and four railway lines in a *coup de main* at the very start of the conflict.[19] This was an outcome that even the most careful planning could hardly guarantee.[20] Finally, it is pointed out that, owing to a loss of nerve resulting from a setback in the struggle against Russia, he moved forces from the western front to the eastern front at a crucial moment, again undermining the strength of the armies on the right wing.

The justice and accuracy of these charges against Moltke have been called into question by several historians. To begin with, it has been pointed out that while Moltke did, indeed, alter the ratio between the German right and left wings, he did so by adding newly created formations to the left, not by subtracting forces from the right. The German armies on the right wing were, therefore, just as strong in 1914 as they had been in Schlieffen's memorandum of 1905. The often quoted ratio between right and left of 7 : 1 in Schlieffen's plan being changed to 3 : 1 by Moltke is thus misleading in that it implies a diminution in the forces of the right wing in favour of the left. As this did not happen, the figures presented should instead read as 7 : 1 becoming 7 : 2 or, as the eminent military historian J. F. C. Fuller represented it, 100 : 15 being replaced by 100 : 42.[21]

In a similar fashion, Moltke's decision not to march through Holland can also be defended. While it undoubtedly created logistical difficulties, this amendment to the Schlieffen plan relieved Germany of the problem of yet another opponent – Germany had too many foes already – and ensured against the threat of a strike into the Reich from across the Dutch frontier, which would, if the Netherlands were hostile, have to be garrisoned, thus drawing further forces away from France. In addition, Dutch neutrality had economic implications: a non-belligerent Holland could act as a 'windpipe' through which Germany could attempt to ameliorate the effects of a British naval blockade. This was to prove of considerable value in the years ahead.

Moltke's critics appear to be on firmer ground when they question his decision to send to the Russian front the two corps that had hitherto been engaged in the siege of Namur. These forces arrived too late to influence the fight there, but would undoubtedly have been very useful to the Germans on the Marne. Just how useful is, of course, a matter of conjecture. Although some claim that they could have swung the tide of battle, this is counterbalanced by those who suggested that a mere two corps were insufficient to make a significant difference.[22]

Whatever the reason for the Schlieffen plan's failure – and flaws in the plan itself appear the most likely answer – one thing is clear: its premature undoing was a disaster for Germany. With its breakdown, the German high command was left fighting precisely the sort of war for which they were least prepared, namely a war of attrition spread across two fronts. Moreover, because of the German advance into France, this was no longer a two-front war in which one front lay along a short and easily defensible frontier, but a two-front war in which both fronts exceeded 400 miles in length and required enormous reserves of manpower to maintain. In short, the failure of the Schlieffen plan extended rather than reduced Germany's military commitments, exacerbated the problem of Germany's numerical inferiority to the *Entente*, and left Germany overextended and fighting a war of attrition without any plan for dealing with such an eventuality. The ramifications of this unfortunate situation were to be experienced at all levels of German national life.

War of Attrition and Domestic Change

In accordance with the provisions of article 68 of the Reich constitution, the outbreak of war in 1914 was followed by the suspension of the civil penal code and the imposition of military regulations. The mechanism used to effect this transformation was the Prussian Siege Law of 1851. Under the remit of this archaic measure, local civilian administrations were made subordinate to the authority of the deputy commanding generals of the country's 24 military districts, who were empowered to take all action necessary to ensure that the harmony of the domestic front was maintained and that nothing happened inside the Reich to undermine the national war effort. So extensive and all-embracing was this task that, in effect, German government and society experienced a sudden and immediate militarization. As Friedrich Wilhelm von Loebell, the Prussian Minister of the Interior, put it: Germany was taking on 'the character of a military dictatorship'.[23]

Among certain circles, this institutionalizing of military patterns of authority throughout the Reich was a welcome development. German conservatives, for example, who had long been engaged in a fruitless struggle to ward off the spread of democratic and egalitarian ideas among the masses, had always felt that such measures would aid them in their battle. Being prevented by constitutional practice from achieving them during peacetime, they had looked to war with all its possibilities for emergency executive action as their tool for imposing military discipline on the populous and thereby reinstilling traditional modes of thought, behaviour and deference into German society. As Ernst von Heydebrand und der Lasa, the leader of the Conservative Party, explained it: 'a war will lead to a strengthening of the patriarchal order and mentality'.[24]

This assumption was, however, centred on the premise of a short and successful war and was based on a logic applicable only to a situation in which such an outcome was achieved. It hypothesized that, during the brief period before the army and its aristocratic leaders basked in the glory of victory and utilized their enhanced prestige for domestic political gain, the strict military penal code would permit an attack on their enemies, the Social Democrats. Their leaders would be arrested, their party organizations suppressed and their newspapers closed. Enhanced patriotic feeling, military discipline and the euphoria of victory would make these actions tolerable to the masses and restore the place of traditional hierarchies in German national life.

Two developments upset these calculations. First, the Social Democrats, contrary to their revolutionary and internationalist doctrines, demonstrated a clear willingness to support the government in a time of national emergency and voted unanimously in favour of war credits. Even the most reactionary of conservatives could find nothing to criticize in this behaviour, which provided no grounds at all for acts of repression against the so-called 'red menace'. Secondly, the war, contrary to expectations, turned out to be neither short nor victorious, but developed instead into a protracted war of attrition in which reserves of manpower and quantities of munitions were deciding factors. In such circumstances, obtaining further recruits for the army and an increase in the production of war materials became a matter of the most vital significance. As a result, instead of possessing the luxury of being able to use the war for domestic political purposes, those in charge of the German state machinery found themselves preoccupied with the essential task of preparing the nation for the unexpected rigours of the world's 'first technical–industrial war'.[25] It quickly transpired that this mammoth undertaking would require from them a completely new outlook on the role and boundaries of government in German national life.

Foremost among the required changes was the need to temper the traditional exclusiveness of the state in order to gain the co-operation of all sections of German society for the war effort. At the start of the conflict, at the moment when Reichstag deputies of all political complexions had patriotically and unanimously voted war credits, the Kaiser had symbolically announced: 'I recognize no more parties; I know only Germans.' This presumption of national unity had led to the political truce of the *Burgfrieden*. Initially conceived of only as a temporary suspension of party wrangling pending the quick conclusion of the war, the failure of the Schlieffen plan had not only required an indefinite prolongation of its duration, it had also necessitated a deepening of its application beyond the confines of the Reichstag building and out into the rest of society. The reason for this was the nature of the war. The First World War was a total war, the successful prosecution of which depended upon the maximizing of industrial production. This was an outcome that could only be achieved by the willing co-operation of a workforce persuaded to labour to their utmost. Unfortunately for the government, given that in several peacetime labour disputes they had created a legacy of mistrust and alienation by conspicuously siding with the employers, they were among the very last people capable of motivating the workers to further exertions. Consequently, to achieve this outcome, the government needed the support of various bodies with which it had previously spurned close contact. Of particular importance in this respect were the representatives of the urban industrial masses, namely the Social Democrats and the trade unions. Only they were close enough to the aspirations of the workers and familiar enough with their conditions to undertake this task. Only they could achieve the requisite industrial harmony by pacifying fraught industrial relations and persuading the workers to ever greater efforts under the difficult conditions of wartime. However, their willingness to fulfil this necessary role was contingent upon the government offering them something in return. Reluctantly, the government had to comply. To begin with, the Imperial Associations Law of 1909, a measure which disadvantaged unions by subjecting them to the stringent rules applied to political parties, was abolished. Subsequent to this, the unions were able to achieve an informal system of wage bargaining and also secure the presence of union representatives on official bodies, such as the War Boards that regulated certain aspects of wartime employment in crucial industries. Progressively, the war was enabling the unions to gain that measure of official recognition that the employers had always striven to deny them in peacetime.

Another necessary change in government practice brought about by the need to fight a war of attrition was the institution of state intervention in industry as part of a broader effort to create and manage a war economy. This imposition of official regulation was particularly apparent in matters concerning raw materials. Prior to the outbreak of war, the German Empire had been dependent on imports for many of the ingredients essential to its industrial output. Particular dependence on overseas supplies existed in respect to manganese, nitrates, cotton, copper, rubber and iron ore. Although this fact had been recognized prior to the war, no worthwhile countermeasures, such as stockpiling, had taken place because of the expectation held by those in charge of the economy that the war would be over sufficiently quickly for this dependency not to be an issue. This assumption was, of course, wrong. Not only did the war prove lengthy, but it also transpired that wartime rates of consumption of military supplies were much greater than had been anticipated: the enormous demand for munitions by the German armies, for example, outran even the wildest pre-war estimates of likely expenditure. If German industry was to meet this demand it would require an uninterrupted flow of raw materials. Herein lay a problem. The Allied naval blockade, implemented at the start of the war, was gradually severing the link between German industry and world markets for natural resources. Although this was partly overcome by an expansion of commerce with neutral countries such as Holland, Norway and Sweden as well as by the exploitation of occupied territories, this in itself was not adequate to make up the shortfall. It was clear, therefore, that without concerted action the German war effort would grind to a halt for want of the necessary supplies. In response to this situation, the government established a War Raw Materials Department (*Kriegsrohstoffabteilung*) responsible for the central procurement and distribution of those natural resources vital to war production. Headed in the first instance by the successful Jewish industrialist Walther Rathenau and subsequently by the very able technocrat Major Josef Koeth, in the opinion of one historian, this was 'an organisation which saved the German war effort from disaster ... '.[26]

Wartime regulation of industry was complemented by the government's involvement in the realm of agriculture, where the necessities of total war likewise promoted intervention. The reason for this was much the same in both cases: just as Germany was dependent on outside supplies of raw materials, so, too, a full third of her food supplies had traditionally been imported. Making good any deficiencies caused by the loss of imports was a crucial undertaking: only a properly nourished population would have the strength to fight and work. Accordingly, some measures were taken. Inside the Reich, the apparatus of government intervention was slowly introduced. In February 1915 wheat production was placed under government control and rationing of bread and flour was introduced. This was followed in May 1916 by the establishment of a War Food Office (*Kriegsernährungsamt*), a body analogous to, but weaker than, the War Raw Materials Department.

Complementing these domestic undertakings were several external measures. To start with, efforts were made to augment German food production by supplementary purchases from overseas suppliers. Until pressure from Allied countries prevented it, this meant a substantial increase in imports from neighbouring nations like Denmark and the Netherlands. On top of this, Germany was also in a position to obtain extra resources from those territories occupied by her armies. This took many forms. Not only were food products consistently requisitioned, but so too was labour. Nearly 500 000 civilian workers were brought to Germany to make good the shortfall in farmhands caused by the conscription of Germans to the front. The contribution of such exactions imposed on defeated adversaries was considerable. To give but one example, between occupation in late 1916 and the end of the war, Romania alone was compelled to surrender over 1.8 million tons of food to the German authorities.[27]

Notwithstanding the unprecedented actions taken by the government to regulate the war economy, Germany was badly affected by the strains of total war, with the result that conditions inside the Reich deteriorated rapidly. Most people experienced a significant decline in their standard of living. Industrial workers, for example, though the beneficiaries of a sharp rise in wages, witnessed an even sharper rise in the price of essential goods;[28] and that was when they were available at all. By the so-called 'turnip winter' (*Kohlrübenwinter*) of 1916 many types of food and fuel were only to be found on the black market. As this source was out of the reach of the majority of German citizens, the consequence was that disorders and ultimately deaths stemming from malnutrition and exposure to severe cold became widespread.

It is hardly surprising, under conditions of growing domestic deprivation coupled with a war whose end seemed to be nowhere in sight, that morale on the home front began to falter. By the middle of 1916 the sense of war-weariness had reached sufficient levels to have major internal repercussions. Industrial disputes and food strikes began to occur in increasing numbers; calls for democratic reform of the political system began to grow louder; most ominously of all, the elusiveness of victory and the plight of the people, began to elicit a search for scapegoats. The group nominated for this dubious distinction were the Jews. So intense and extreme was the upsurge in anti-Semitism at this time that it even attracted the notice of outsiders, one of whom, the American ambassador, James Watson Gerard, made reference in his letters to the danger of Jews being 'pogrommed'.[29] Taken together, these phenomena, symptomatic of the growing internal malaise, sha2red one important attribute: they demonstrated the desperation of the German public for a solution to their problems. It was unfortunate that in 1916 a miraculous panacea seemed to be at hand in the person of two strong military leaders, Field Marshal Paul von Hindenburg and General Erich Ludendorff, whose appointment to high office promised to deliver Germany from all its ills, a situation epitomized by Bethmann Hollweg's dictum: 'The Name Hindenburg puts terror into our enemies, electrifies our army and people, who have complete confidence in him.'[30] Sadly, the overriding faith in these two men and the general willingness to place matters into their hands would ultimately lead down the road to dictatorship.

The Rise of the Military Dictatorship and the Collapse of 1918

It was on 29 August 1916 that Wilhelm II finally gave in to pressure from his military entourage, his Chancellor and his generals, by dismissing General Erich von Falkenhayn as Chief of the General Staff. Falkenhayn's successor was Field Marshal Hindenburg, who was supported and some would say dominated by the new Quartermaster General, Ludendorff. The date of the appointment of the new leadership of the *Oberste Heeresleitung* (OHL – supreme command) was not without symbolism, for it was the second anniversary of the great victory which a German army, led by Hindenburg and Ludendorff, had achieved over the Russians at Tannenberg, East Prussia, in 1914. The war had been going badly for Germany during the course of 1916, and it was hoped that the appointment of Hindenburg and Ludendorff to the OHL would provide a fillip to the Reich's war effort.

This did indeed prove to be the case, but only in a manner which was ultimately counterproductive to German interests. Hindenburg and Ludendorff escalated the war by championing the introduction of unrestricted U-boat warfare against Britain and neutral shipping in British waters, while undertaking massive offensives on the eastern front in 1917, and the western front in 1918. Under their auspices, the OHL worked for the German right and heavy industry's objective of an annexationist *Siegfrieden* (victorious peace), despite the fact that this so clearly stood in the way of a negotiated and honourable peace settlement with the *Entente* powers. Hindenburg and Ludendorff also placed the domestic truce within Germany under strain as a result of their policy of the militarization of civilian life, via the regimentation of labour, and their tolerance of war profiteers and the indulgences of the rich. Additionally, the OHL stood out against domestic political reform, and thus exacerbated the class tensions which led to the revolution and the collapse of the Hohenzollern monarchy at war's end in the autumn of 1918. Hindenburg and Ludendorff's 'silent dictatorship'[31] was exercised behind the façade of constitutionalism. However, from August 1916, and particularly after July 1917, when Chancellor Bethmann Hollweg was dismissed at their instigation, until October 1918, when Wilhelm II forced Ludendorff to resign, no one doubted that the OHL determined Germany's political as well as its military course, unchallenged by either civilian politicians or the Kaiser himself. Walther Rathenau noted this subservience to the military leadership as early as February 1917, when he observed 'that whenever a bill is submitted to the Reichstag, the first question asked is whether or not the official moving the bill has the backing of the Supreme Command'.[32]

A major reason for the emergence of the dictatorship of Hindenburg and Ludendorff was the total lack of leadership offered by Wilhelm II. While notionally 'Supreme War Lord', Wilhelm did not have the strength of character to arbitrate effectively between the civilian and military strands of government. Rather, put under the pressures of total war, he was prone to nervous collapse. This lack of clear leadership from the top created a vacuum that others sought to fill. The first conspiracy to deprive the Kaiser of authority occurred as early as April 1915 when Admiral Tirpitz worked for Wilhelm II's abdication and replacement by the more hawkish Crown Prince. This came to nought, but the appointment of Hindenburg and Ludendorff gave the militarists their chance to reduce Wilhelm's role to that of figurehead. Colonel Max Bauer, Ludendorff's chief political adviser, set out their objective: 'the Kaiser must be almost completely shut out…, because his wavering weakness would ruin everything in all the major decisive questions'.[33] Even the Kaiser's role as a figurehead was increasingly in doubt as the war progressed, for Hindenburg, the victor of Tannenberg, gradually replaced Wilhelm II as the symbol of national unity.

Wilhelm II had become a pathetic figure even before 1914 was out. He depicted his life in melancholy colours. 'The General Staff tells me nothing and never ask my advice. If people in Germany think that I am the Supreme Commander they are grossly mistaken. I drink tea, saw wood and go for walks, which pleases the gentlemen.' The Chief of the Kaiser's Naval Cabinet, Admiral von Müller, who recorded these remarks, noted poignantly, 'This was of course said as a joke, but it was none the less tragically true.'[34] Spending most of his time at, or near, military Headquarters, the Kaiser grew increasingly out of touch with the mood in the country and even with civilian politicians such as his Chancellor Bethmann Hollweg.

However, the process through which Wilhelm II became a *Schattenkaiser* (shadow emperor) during the war was more gradual than some of the older literature has a tendency to suggest.[35] On questions of strategy, for example, at least in the first two years of the war, the decisions he took when faced with conflicting viewpoints could still sometimes prove decisive. In January 1916, he successfully resisted pressure from his generals and admirals for the escalation of the U-boat war against Britain because he believed that 'to torpedo big passenger liners full of women and children is an act of incomparable barbarian brutality with which we will bring ourselves the hatred and poisonous rage of the whole world'.[36]

Additionally, the 'kingship mechanism', which underpinned Wilhelm II's power in peacetime, continued to function in the early years of the war, for he was still able to choose his own advisers. Thus in January 1915, the Kaiser was still strong enough to resist a concerted effort on the part of Ludendorff, Moltke, Bethmann, Tirpitz, General von Plessen and the Crown Prince, to dismiss Falkenhayn and adopt the massive gamble of trying to win the war against Russia while leaving the western front much weakened. Wilhelm held on to Falkenhayn for as long as he possibly could, despite continuing attempts, even after the debacle of January 1915, by the latter's numerous opponents to have him dismissed. Bethmann's assistant, Kurt Riezler, who disliked Falkenhayn, commented with frustration in the summer of 1915 on: 'The enormous position of Falkenhayn, who can do everything he wants as far as the Kaiser is concerned.' Riezler believed that Wilhelm had a 'mystical relationship with his Chief of General Staff'.[37] Wilhelm only dismissed Falkenhayn in August 1916 because Falkenhayn's confident prediction that the French army would 'bleed to death'[38] at Verdun, thus allowing Germany to win the war with only limited casualties, proved to be a catastrophic error of judgement. In the same manner, Wilhelm II resisted pressure from the German right and the OHL to dismiss Bethmann and the Chief of his Civil Cabinet, Rudolf von Valentini, until July 1917 and January 1918 respectively.

Although the traditional picture of Wilhelm II as a shadow emperor throughout the war years requires some modification, it does hold up well as a description of his position in 1916–18, the years of the dictatorship of the OHL. The aggressive meritocrat Ludendorff who was a nationalist, but not a monarchist, treated the Kaiser with particular disrespect. Under Hindenburg and Ludendorff, Wilhelm II's marginalization within the decision-making process became complete. They used threats of resignation, and their prestige, to force the Kaiser to dismiss trusted advisers whom they disliked, such as Bethmann and Valentini, and to replace them with nonentities who would be subservient to the OHL, such as Michaelis and Berg. Berg, who became Chief of the Kaiser's Civil Cabinet in January 1918, was scathingly referred to by one member of Wilhelm II's entourage as an 'effective representative of the H-L company'.[39] Riezler observed accurately within two months of the appointment of Hindenburg and Ludendorff to OHL: 'The Kaiser has fled into the shadows of the two soldiers – swims in their water without an independent will.'[40]

If the Kaiser's inability to play his assigned constitutional role, and his marginalization within the decision-making process, were a cause of the emergence of the military dictatorship, so too were divisions in the *Reichsleitung* over strategy and war aims, together with personality clashes. The failure of the German armies to break through against the French lines at Verdun underlined the bankruptcy of Falkenhayn's strategy of seeking to bring victory through a war of attrition. Only two alternatives were left: to make peace or to escalate the war in the hope of outright victory. Hindenburg and Ludendorff preferred escalation to a negotiated and modest peace settlement. The desperate military position in which Germany found itself made the nationalist elements within German society cling ever more tenaciously to the chimera of military triumph. Bethmann, an opponent of the most extreme annexationists, noted this perversity: 'the less the hopes for a quick and decisive victory were fulfilled, the more our chauvinists believed they had to prove their bravery and loyalty by proposing the most power-hungry war aims and smearing everybody who refused to follow their lead as subversive weaklings'.[41]

Ironically Bethmann himself had worked for the appointment of Hindenburg and Ludendorff to the OHL in 1916 because he feared Falkenhayn's political aspirations, and believed that the new leadership at OHL would allow him to continue his policy of limited annexations, diplomatic overtures to the *Entente*, and liberal conservatism at home, free from military interference. Instead Hindenburg and Ludendorff proved to be consistent champions of a *Siegfrieden*, and drew up ever more ambitious plans for the expansion of Germany in Europe even as the military tide turned against Berlin. Their appointment to OHL witnessed not the triumph of the civil over the military leadership, as sought by Bethmann, but the progressive subordination of the civil government to the military and the pursuit of policies such as unrestricted U-boat warfare, and political reaction at home, which were vehemently opposed by the increasingly powerless Chancellor.

Hindenburg and Ludendorff were extremely fortunate in that their first months at the OHL coincided with two events which seemed to turn the tide of the war in Germany's favour. Romania was defeated by a joint German and Austrian force in December 1916, and in March 1917 the Russian Revolution broke out, forcing Tsar Nicholas II to abdicate and raising doubts as to the ability of Russia to continue her struggle against the Central Powers. Such good fortune ought to have created the conditions for an honourable peace settlement between Germany and the *Entente*. However, the OHL's overweening ambition and lack of understanding of geopolitical realities prevented this outcome. Success against Romania and Russia simply made the OHL and its allies in heavy industry dream of the creation of a great empire in eastern Europe. The lack of willingness of the OHL to agree to a moderate peace settlement with the Provisional government and the Bolshevik regime in Russia resulted in the prolongation of the war in the east. Even when that war was concluded as a result of the harsh peace dictated by the OHL to the Bolsheviks at Brest-Litovsk in March 1918, a large German army of occupation had to be left in the east in order to enforce the settlement, thus reducing the chances of a military breakthrough on the western front. Concurrently, the OHL's willingness to escalate the submarine war against Britain in early 1917 also proved a disastrous error. The 'miracle weapon' of the U-boat failed to starve the British into submission, and the torpedoing of neutral vessels turned

American public opinion against Germany and brought the United States into the war on the side of the *Entente*, again with grave consequences for the Reich. The OHL's championing of an annexationist *Siegfrieden* was inextricably bound up with domestic political objectives. The High Command, together with its allies in heavy industry and on the German right, intended to use the legitimacy which a victorious peace would confer to ensure that the class-based political order which had characterized Germany before 1914 would not succumb to the tide of democracy and revolution, but instead would be secured for the future. Some individuals, such as Colonel Max Bauer, the chief political strategist at the OHL, were already looking beyond Kaiserdom and thinking in proto-Fascist terms. He speculated: 'Perhaps a strong man can save us, a man who can enflame the people, by the trust they have in him, and who knows how to make an audacious decision and carry it out.'[42] The OHL mobilized radical nationalist elements within German society in support of the twin aims of an annexationist peace and the preservation of an authoritarian political system. Hindenburg gave his blessing to the creation of the *Vaterlands-Partei* on 2 September 1916, the anniversary of Prussia's victory over France at Sedan in 1870. Led by arch reactionaries, Admiral Tirpitz and the civil servant Wolfgang Kapp, and funded by heavy industry, the organization campaigned tirelessly in favour of a *Siegfrieden*, and boasted 1.25 million members by the spring of 1917.[43]

There was a contradiction at the heart of the OHL's strategy. Securing victory against the *Entente* would necessitate mobilizing all the resources of the German economy and society, yet refusing the working class political reform would make it impossible to do this without straining the *Burgfrieden*, the domestic truce of 1914, to breaking point. By January 1917, the privations on the home front had grown so extreme that the German people sought a way out of the conflict and food in their bellies, not more bloodshed. As one contemporary observer noted, a dangerous gulf had developed between the rhetoric of Germany's political leaders and the aspirations of their subjects:

> The truth is, the soul of the people is sick unto death of the useless carnage and hateful sinfulness of it all. In the Reichstag the same old bombastic phrases still bring a volley of applause, so that the quiet observer is astonished by the childishness of these representatives of the nation; but the man who would bring peace and not war would be hailed as a real leader and king.[44]

Instead of addressing this war-weariness with new peace feelers and political concessions, the OHL called for yet further sacrifices on the part of the working class. The High Command rejected the previous policy of seeking to increase production through co-operation between industry and labour as inadequate. A series of measures were introduced in the autumn of 1916 under the name of the 'Hindenburg Programme', designed to boost production in the interests of the war effort. One such measure was the *Hilfsdienstgesetz* (Patriotic Auxiliary Service Law) passed by the Reichstag in December 1916. It introduced labour service for all men aged 17–60, and restricted the rights of workers to move to a better job. Such repressive legislation failed to increase the output of war materials to the levels anticipated, and only produced 60 000 new civilians for service by April 1917, not the 200 000 predicted by the General Staff.[45] The combination of the repression of the working class, hostility to political reform, and the turning of a blind eye to the activities of war profiteers and those who benefited from the black market, meant that the policies of the OHL seemed to be driving Germany towards a domestic catastrophe as well as an external one. The representative of the army's Regional Command in Münster noted that it was the lack of fairness in the distribution of scarce commodities which caused most resentment. 'It is strange that the people will put up with any privation, but that they cannot stand it if others have a bit more than themselves', he wrote. 'If one would be able to reassure everyone that inconveniences resulting from food shortages were evenly distributed, dissatisfaction would disappear at once.'[46] His recommendation was not implemented.

The High Command under Hindenburg and Ludendorff relentlessly pursued the disastrous course of military escalation and domestic repression. Those who appreciated the folly of the OHL's policies saw their positions undermined. The most prominent victim of the military dictatorship was Bethmann Hollweg. The Chancellor believed that the political system would have to be reformed after the war if its core elements were going to be saved. By early 1917 Bethmann was determined to abolish the three-class voting system in Prussia with immediate effect, as he believed that only a major concession of this type could appease the increasingly militant labour movement and reward the working class for the sacrifices they had endured during the war. Riezler, his assistant, noted in respect of reform of the Prussian franchise: 'whether there is war or peace, it is absolutely clear that it must be implemented by autumn at the latest ... if a full blown coup caused by increasing hunger is to be avoided'.[47] Bethmann actually succeeded in persuading Wilhelm II to deliver a message to the German people at Easter in 1917 in which the Kaiser promised that the three-class franchise in Prussia would be abandoned, but failed to secure a guarantee that this would occur before the end of the war.

However, Wilhelm's 'Easter egg to the German people'[48] failed to satisfy the working class who wanted immediate electoral reform and a commitment to an equal suffrage. Nor, more importantly, did it please the OHL which had not been consulted about the proclamation beforehand. Ludendorff, in particular, showed the level of insight which had led Treasury Secretary, Karl Hellferich, to describe him as 'in military affairs a genius, politically a child, as a character a rascal'.[49] Failing to understand the gravity of the domestic situation, which had been underlined by the outbreak of strikes of a political character, Ludendorff described the Easter message as a 'kowtow to the Russian revolution' and the result of 'a policy dictated by fear'.[50] The OHL conspired to have Bethmann removed from office in the weeks that followed as his political objectives were so obviously at variance with the reactionary course which it was determined to follow. The matter became more pressing when the Reichstag passed a Peace Resolution in July 1917, in the light of which the Chancellor was able to secure a commitment from the Kaiser to the introduction of equal suffrage in Prussia and the appointment of parliamentary leaders in government. This was too much for Hindenburg and Ludendorff, who secured the support of the Reichstag in their campaign against Bethmann by posing, duplicitously, as supporters of reform and peace. Their tactics, as one observer pointed out, involved mobilizing the deputies against the Crown, thus 'forcing the Kaiser against all Prussian traditions'[51] to dismiss an adviser in whom he still retained confidence. The event represented a symbolic abdication on the part of Wilhelm II, for his right to control appointments had been the key to his authority since his accession in 1888.

The OHL's victory over the Chancellor and the Kaiser in the July crisis of 1917 embodied the victory of nationalism over monarchism, and of the advocates of *Siegfrieden* and domestic reaction over those who wished to preserve the *Burgfrieden* through political concessions at home, and an honourable peace settlement with the *Entente*. Neither of Bethmann's immediate successors, Michaelis and Hertling, was strong enough to challenge the military dictatorship, because neither had an independent basis for their political authority, and both owed their elevation to the Reich's highest civilian office to the OHL. As a result, between July 1917 and the autumn of 1918, the OHL had free rein to pursue the policies which led inexorably towards Germany's defeat and domestic revolution. The only mystery is why the High Command did not dispense with the façade of constitutional government altogether. The most plausible explanation was advanced at the time in a perceptive analysis by Riezler, who believed that the OHL needed to hide the true nature of its power from the German people for political reasons: 'If the OHL becomes identified by the people with the Pan-Germans, it will be discovered that the Chancellor has been robbed of all freedom of manoeuvre both abroad and at home by the Generals, then resistance to the system of militarism will commence and the beginning of the collapse.'[52]

As 1918 opened, Germany had achieved victory on the eastern front against Russia, but such an outcome was still not in sight on the western front. Two factors made the German army's position increasingly precarious, and dictated that a decision had to come soon: collapsing morale on the home front, and American intervention on the side of Britain and France. The British blockade, which deprived Germany of imported foodstuffs and raw materials, coupled with spiralling inflation, rendered the plight of ordinary Germans ever more desperate as the war progressed. By 1918 industrial workers were subsisting on the number of calories more appropriate for young children. The fact that the privations were not shared equally caused continuing resentment towards war profiteers, and led to the outbreak of widespread strikes in January 1918 in Berlin and other cities. The Austrian ambassador was convinced that these constituted a 'pure political demonstration of the working classes', and exhibited the 'development of class warfare as a result of the social upheavals of this war'.[53] By the early summer of 1918 even the German army's Home Front Regional Command was prepared to concede that the Reich stood on the brink of revolution. Its representative in the central German city of Magdeburg conceded that the *Burgfrieden* of 1914 had collapsed:

> The previous large gulf between rich and poor, which had largely been closed in the early days of enthusiasm for the War, now continues to widen, the more the longer. Among the poorer sections of the population a pernicious hatred against the rich and the so-called war profiteers has built up, which one can only hope will not lead to a terrible explosion.[54]

The OHL's response to the threat of domestic collapse and to the strategic dilemma caused by American intervention was to launch Operation *Michael*, a last-ditch attempt to win the war through a massive offensive on the western front. The future of the military dictatorship and of the Reich depended on a successful outcome. As Riezler observed: 'Everything depends on the offensive – if it succeeds fully, then will come the military dictatorship which the people will cheerfully tolerate – if it does not succeed, a severe moral crisis which probably none of the present government leaders has the talent to master peacefully.'[55] The offensive was launched on 21 March 1918. Its military aim was to defeat the Western Allies before the American presence on the side of the *Entente* could make itself felt. Politically, *Michael* would provide the basis for the *Siegfrieden* which would quell the growing demands in Germany for wide-ranging political reform. Initially the offensive went well. Even Wilhelm II temporarily recovered from the lethargy and despondency into which he had previously fallen. Admiral von Müller recorded in his diary on 26 March 1918: 'Spirits were so high that His Majesty declared that if an English delegation came to sue for peace it must kneel before the German standard for it was a question here of a victory of the monarchy over democracy.'[56]

Yet a number of factors rendered such victory celebrations premature. The advance was uneven, with some parts of the front giving way to the German attacks to a greater extent than others. Resistance in all sectors proved more robust than the Germans had anticipated, partly because the Allies had been forewarned of the offensive. German troops proved too weak and too war-weary to capitalize on the initial advance, and the discovery of comparatively lavish provisions in the Allied trenches demoralized them still further. Additionally the Germans lacked the tanks and rubber-wheeled trucks which would have facilitated a speedier advance. Finally, and of great significance, was the fact that Ludendorff, who masterminded Operation *Michael*, did so brilliantly at the tactical level, but never developed clear strategic goals for his offensive. His plan was simply to break a hole in the Allied lines and see what happened. While it is doubtful in view of the superiority of the Allies in men and materials, and the swift addition of American forces, that the German offensive could ever have succeeded, Ludendorff's lack of strategic direction ensured that, despite numerous local successes, it would ultimately fail. As a result, by July 1918, the German offensive had ground to a halt, and in the following month the Allied armies began the sustained counter-attack which was to bring them victory.

The failure of Operation *Michael* removed the last support of the military dictatorship: the popular belief that it might yet secure victory against all the odds. The OHL's attempts to cover up the scale of the military disaster simply caused added resentment. In September 1918 one observer noted: 'The news from the front is more and more depressing, there is nothing to eat, and the methods employed to prevent the depression from gaining ground goad the people to fury.'[57] A 'gallows humour' developed among the bourgeoisie who could see their world collapsing in the impending defeat and revolution. The last two months of the German Empire's existence saw military leaders and the civilians quarrelling over who was to blame for the defeat. In October 1918, the German Empire was finally transformed into a parliamentary monarchy. However, this came too late to save either Wilhelm II or the Hohenzollern dynasty, for simultaneously the *Burgfrieden* had finally given way as soldiers and sailors deserted and mutinied and strikes broke out calling for the end of the monarchy, and in some cases for a revolution on the Bolshevik model.

The conversion of the OHL to the cause of political reform was utterly cynical and extricated only on the deathbed. Ludendorff, and those who shared his outlook, were already looking to the future. The OHL was determined that civilian politicians, particularly from the hated SPD, would shoulder the blame for Germany's defeat and the armistice. In engineering a 'revolution from above' the military leaders were therefore deliberately laying the ground for the *Dolchstoss* (stab-in-the-back) legend which would plague the Weimar Republic, Germany's first democracy, between 1919 and its collapse in 1933. This was the myth that the German army had not lost the war, but had instead been undermined by sedition on the home front, from unpatriotic workers and democratic politicians. The Bavarian military plenipotentiary at the OHL correctly pointed out that the High Command was preparing for the return of an authoritarian regime at a later date:

> one often hears the opinion expressed that it is a good thing that the left-wing parties will have to incur the odium of the peace. The storm of indignation of the people will fall on them. One hopes then that one [the old order] can get back in the saddle and continue to govern according to the old recipe.[58]

The attempt by the military leadership to manage the process of political change and defeat was thrown off course by the outbreak of the long anticipated domestic revolution. Germany in the autumn of 1918 reminded many observers of Tsarist Russia in its last days. The people simply could not tolerate their conditions any longer. On 29 October a mutiny began among the sailors of the German High Seas Fleet at Kiel, who refused an order from their commanding officers to undertake a suicide mission against the Royal Navy because they no longer wanted to risk their lives uselessly. Within days the revolution had spread to Germany's major cities, including Berlin. On 9 November 1918 two rival republics were proclaimed in the German capital, one democratic and one communist, and an eyewitness recorded that 'sinister-looking red flags' were 'waving where so short a time ago the black, white and red were hanging'.[59] On the same day, Wilhelm II had finally abdicated as Emperor, and crossed the frontier into Holland.

Two days after the Kaiser's abdication, the armistice came into effect. The war which had begun in August 1914 with such high hopes of German victory thus ended in defeat and the collapse of the political order which the initiators of the conflict had hoped to preserve. A few weeks before the defeat, in reply to Wilhelm II's assertion that the civilian politicians were to blame, Admiral von Müller left a damning assessment of the OHL's responsibility for the catastrophe. It serves as a fitting judgement on the corrupting effect of militarism on the German body politic:

> But who were our politicians during the war? Hindenburg, Ludendorff and the political branch of the Great General Staff. . . . Mistake after mistake had been made, above all the casual handling of the peace with Russia, whose collapse had been a boon of immeasurable value to us and should have been exploited to release troops for the West. But instead of this we conquered Latvia and Estonia and became involved with Finland – the result of an excess of megalomania.[60]

The German military bore the responsibility for initiating the First World War. Similarly it is to the military leaders, rather than to the civilians, that blame for Germany's defeat should be attributed. They refused to sanction peace negotiations, they escalated a war which could not be won, and they held out for so long against domestic concessions that a revolution became inevitable. Yet their success in convincing the German people that the army had been defeated by treachery on the home front, rather than by the Allies in battle, created the environment in which Nazism could emerge to challenge German democracy less than 15 years after the fall of the *Kaiserreich*.

CONCLUSION

After the collapse of the *Kaiserreich* in 1918 there was a tendency among historians, as well as among those who had been diplomats and politicians during the period, to identify Bismarck's dismissal in 1890 as the point from which things started to go wrong. The Iron Chancellor's successors failed to maintain the diplomatic link with Russia, embarked upon an ambitious and disastrous navalist *Weltpolitik* and ultimately stumbled into a war which could not be won. There is some justice in this interpretation, although rather less than those who advanced it in the 1920s would have accepted. However, it ignores domestic developments entirely and does not take into account that the constitutional and political structure of the Empire was a significant factor in the Reich's eventual decay and collapse. Max Weber, commenting on the *Daily Telegraph* affair in the autumn of 1908, argued that the Reich's flawed political structure was a greater problem than Wilhelm II's personality. He wrote with reference to the constitutional crisis: 'There is far too much talk about the "impulsiveness"... of the Kaiser as an *individual*. The political *structure* is the cause of it.'[1] Weber, like the modern scholars of the *Gesellschaftsgeschichte* school, went too far in emphasizing the importance of structures, and in minimizing the role of individuals. In reality both structures and personalities are important, and both contributed to the political malaise of the German Empire.

The constitution of 1871 gave Prussia a dominant position within Germany. As a result Prussian traditions were carried over into the new Reich. These included militarism, a political system where the legislature had no control over the executive, and the right of the King of Prussia to appoint his own ministers, which as German Kaiser he was also given at the Imperial level. The exalted status of the military in the Second Reich had a damaging impact in a number of ways. The armed forces were not subject to effective political or legal control, as was made clear by the Zabern Incident of 1913. Additionally the military's success against France in the war of 1870–71 resulted in an unhealthy admiration for the officer corps among the German population. The officer corps' special position within the state meant that it had more autonomy than in other countries, which it could exploit in order to press for the implementation of particular policies. Its narrow view of German society and reactionary political outlook made this extremely dangerous. This was most evident between 1912 and 1914, when the military argued successfully for the unleashing of a European war, and during the First World War itself, when the High Command was able to continue a struggle which could not be won by resisting the demand of the civilians for a negotiated peace.

The fact that the Reichstag had no control over the executive also had a damaging effect on the Reich's political development. Political parties were reduced to the role of pressure groups. They had no incentive to represent anything other than the narrow self-interest of their core constituencies, as they had no prospect of real power. Additionally the absence of representative government created a climate where extra-parliamentary organizations were able to flourish, many of which, such as the Pan-German League and the Navy League, urged the government to implement the aggressive and expansionist policies which alienated Germany's neighbours. Additionally, the gulf between the Reichstag and the executive widened over time, as social and economic change altered the Imperial legislature's composition, notably to the advantage of the working-class SPD, at a time when government leaders were still drawn from the same narrow aristocratic clique. The failure of the political structure to evolve over time in order to accommodate social and economic change contributed to the polarization of German politics in the last years of the Empire's existence, between those who wished to destroy the class-based political system and those, notably in the Conservative Party, who wished to maintain it at all costs. The failure of the constitutional and political structure of the Reich to evolve can also be seen as a factor in Germany's defeat in the First World War, for there were limits as to how far the *Burgfrieden* of 1914 could be placed under strain by a political leadership whose legitimacy was contested by a sizeable minority of the population. When the sacrifices demanded did become too great, notably after 1916, the population responded with strikes and revolt.

However, Max Weber was wrong to argue that personalities did not play a prominent role in the Reich's political malaise. The constitutional and political structure of 1871 set down the parameters within which Germany's decision-makers would operate, but it did not remove their freedom of action. When we bear this in mind, Bismarck cannot escape responsibility for the political disasters which occurred after his dismissal.

Although fairly successful in the sphere of foreign policy and diplomacy, Bismarck's legacy in domestic politics was largely a negative one. He encouraged a pattern of politics where entire groups were branded 'enemies of the Reich', thus contributing to the atomization of German society and the polarization of party politics. Bismarck failed to take steps to bring the military under closer political control, and he defended the constitution of 1871, despite economic and social change. The measures which he initiated in order to appease those classes in German society who were disenchanted with the system, such as the social welfare programme of the 1880s, were no substitute for political reform.

Yet, it is Bismarck's successors who must shoulder most of the blame for the disastrous course of German domestic and foreign policy after 1890. In the domestic sphere, the Iron Chancellor's hostility to internal reform was carried over into an era where such reform was becoming ever more pressing, thus exacerbating the tensions in German society. Yet the most significant mistakes made by Bismarck's successors lay in the spheres of foreign and military policy. They failed to appreciate, as Bismarck had done, that Germany's geographical position in the centre of Europe obliged her leaders to pursue a skilful foreign policy, so as to avoid the danger of a war on two fronts. The *Reichsleitung* after 1890, and particularly after 1897, implemented a diplomatic strategy which seemed incoherent, seeking to win over Russia one moment, and to appease Britain another. The failure of Germany's leaders to make a clear choice between Britain and Russia meant that in the end they antagonized both these powers, and thus went to war in 1914 in the most unfavourable circumstances imaginable.

The same muddled thinking is evident in the military sphere. The decision to build a large battlefleet against Britain, before Germany's position on the European continent had been secured, was an enormous strategic blunder. As a result Germany antagonized the British Empire, while neglecting her armed forces on land. Again, the First World War exposed the folly of trying to pursue *Weltpolitik* and the objective of a German hegemony in Europe simultaneously. The fact that this disastrous political course was embarked upon under Kaiser Wilhelm II is of some significance, for it is in the character of the last Kaiser that we can see that both structures and personalities matter. The constitution of 1871 left considerable powers over appointments and foreign and military policy in the hands of the Emperor, a fact that was masked, but not addressed, by Bismarck's political dominance prior to 1890. Both *Weltpolitik* and *Flottenpolitik* bore the imprint of Kaiser Wilhelm II, and together they symbolized his 'personal regime'. The pursuit of the two policies proved disastrous and placed Germany in the position of diplomatic isolation which made the *Reichsleitung* willing to launch a war, in a desperate last attempt to achieve true world power status for Germany, in 1914. The collapse of the regime followed on as an inevitable consequence of defeat in that war.

NOTES

Introduction

1. T. C. W. Blanning and David Cannadine (eds), *History and Biography: Essays in Honour of Derek Beales* (Cambridge, 1996), p. 282.

1 The New Empire

1. V. R. Berghahn, *Imperial Germany 1871–1914* (Providence, RI, and Oxford, 1994), p. 310.
2. David Blackbourn, *The Fontana History of Germany 1780–1918* (London, 1997), p. 261.
3. William Carr, *The Origins of the Wars of German Unification* (London, 1991), p. 32.
4. David Blackbourn, *Populists and Patricians. Essays in Modern German History* (London, 1987), p. 155.
5. Philipp zu Eulenburg to Bernhard von Bülow, 8 June 1896. *EK*, III, p.1696.
6. Berghahn, *Imperial Germany*, p. 102.
7. Daniel J. Goldhagen, *Hitler's Willing Executioners. Ordinary Germans and the Holocaust* (London, 1996), p. 73.
8. F. L. Carsten, *A History of the Prussian Junkers* (Aldershot, 1989); Hanna Schissler, 'The Social and Political Power of the Prussian Junkers', in Ralph Gibson and Martin Blinkhorn (eds), *Landownership and Power in Modern Europe* (London, 1991).
9. Otto Büsch, *Militärsystem und Sozialleben im alten Preussen, 1713–1807* (Berlin, 1962).
10. Gordon A. Craig, *The Politics of the Prussian Army 1640–1945* (Oxford, 1964), p. 117.
11. Theodore S. Hamerow, *The Social Foundations of German Unification 1858–1871* (2 vols, Princeton, 1969–72), II, pp. 174–5.
12. The best recent evaluation of the differing portrayals of Bismarck is Karina Urbach, 'Between Saviour and Villain: 100 Years of Bismarck Biographies', *Historical Journal*, XLI (1998), 1141–60.
13. Edward Crankshaw, *Bismarck* (London, 1981), p. 53.
14. Henry Kissinger, 'The White Revolutionary', *Daedalus*, XCVII (1968), 888–924.
15. Hans Rosenberg, 'The Pseudo-Democratisation of the Junker Class', in Georg Iggers (ed.), *The Social History of Politics* (Leamington Spa, 1985), p. 102.
16. Gerhard Ritter, *The Sword and the Sceptre: The Problem of Militarism in Germany* (4 vols, Coral Gables, Fla, 1969–73), I, p. 139.

17. Prince Wilhelm to General von Hake, 9 April 1832. Klaus-Jürgen Müller (ed.), *The Military in Politics and Society in France and Germany in the Twentieth Century* (Oxford, 1995), p. 47.
18. David Stevenson, *The Outbreak of the First World War: 1914 in Perspective* (Basingstoke, 1997), p. 12.
19. Lothar Gall, *Bismarck: The White Revolutionary* (2 vols, London, 1986), II, p. 9.
20. David Blackbourn, 'Economy and Society: A Silent Bourgeois Revolution', in David Blackbourn and Geoff Eley, *The Peculiarities of German History: Bourgeois Society and Politics in Nineteenth-Century Germany* (Oxford, 1984).
21. Michael Stürmer, 'Staatsstreichgedanken im Bismarckreich', *Historische Zeitschrift*, CCIX (1969), 584ff.
22. Hans-Ulrich Wehler, *The German Empire 1871–1918* (Leamington Spa, 1985), p. 53.
23. Wolfgang Mommsen, *Imperial Germany 1867–1918: Politics, Culture and Society in an Authoritarian State* (London, 1995), p. 5.

2　Bismarck's Domestic Policies

1. Wehler, *German Empire*, p. 91.
2. Erich Eyck, *Bismarck and the German Empire* (London, 1950), pp. 206–7.
3. Ronald J. Ross, 'Enforcing the Kulturkampf in the Bismarckian State and the Limits of Coercion in Imperial Germany', *Journal of Modern History*, LVI (1984), 467.
4. Bismarck, speech of 28 January 1886. Richard Blanke, *Prussian Poland in the German Empire (1871–1900)* (New York, 1981), p. 60.
5. Bülow to Holstein, 10 December 1887. *HP*, III, p. 237.
6. Herbert von Bismarck to Holstein. Ibid., p. 141.
7. Fritz Stern, *Gold and Iron* (London, 1977), p. 202.
8. Gall, *Bismarck*, II, p. 88.
9. James C. Hunt, 'Peasants, Grain Tariffs, and Meat Quotas: Imperial German Protectionism Reexamined', *Central European History*, VII (1974), 318.
10. Helmut Böhme, *Deutschlands Weg zur Grossmacht* (Cologne, 1966), pp. 419ff.
11. Margaret Lavinia Anderson and Kenneth Barkin, 'The Myth of the Puttkamer Purge and the Reality of the *Kulturkampf*: Some Reflections on the Historiography of Imperial Germany', *Journal of Modern History*, LIV (1982), 647–86.
12. Wehler, *German Empire*, p. 132.
13. Philip Paur, 'The Corporatist Character of Bismarck's Social Policy', *European History Review*, XI (1981), 445.
14. Gall, *Bismarck*, II, p. 129.
15. Paur, 'Corporatist Character', p. 454.
16. Bismarck in the Reichstag, 2 April 1881. W. M. Simon, *Germany in the Age of Bismarck* (London, 1967), p. 201.
17. Wehler, *German Empire*, pp. 133–4.
18. Gall, *Bismarck*, II, p. 130.
19. Ibid., p. 135.

3 Bismarck's External Policies

1. A. J. P. Taylor cited in Urbach, 'Between Saviour and Villain', p. 1154.
2. Gordon A. Craig and Alexander L. George, *Force and Statecraft: Diplomatic Problems of Our Time* (Oxford, 1990), p. 39.
3. Michael Stürmer, 'A Nation State against History and Geography: The German Dilemma', in Gregor Schöllgen (ed.), *Escape into War? The Foreign Policy of Imperial Germany* (Oxford, 1990), pp. 63–72.
4. Prince Bismarck, Memorandum dictated at Kissingen, 15 June 1877. E. T. S. Dugdale (ed.), *German Diplomatic Documents, 1871–1914* (4 vols, London, 1928–31), I, p. 54.
5. Klaus Hildebrand, 'Opportunities and Limits of German Foreign Policy in the Bismarckian Era, 1871–1890: A System of Stopgaps?', in Schöllgen, *Escape into War*, p. 85.
6. A. J. P. Taylor, *Bismarck. The Man and the Statesman* (London, 1955), p. 140.
7. Bismarck in the Reichstag, 5 December 1876. Ibid., p. 185.
8. Bismarck to Wilhelm I, 24 August 1879. Imanuel Geiss, *German Foreign Policy, 1871–1914* (London, 1976), p. 36.
9. Holstein, diary entry, 6 December 1886. *HP*, II, p. 323.
10. V. N. Lamsdorf, diary entry, 17 January 1887. George F. Kennan, *The Decline of Bismarck's European Order. Franco-Russian Relations, 1875–1890* (Princeton, NJ, 1979), p. 262.
11. Holstein, diary entry, 18 November 1886. *HP*, II, p. 313.
12. Werner Conze, *The Shaping of the German Nation: A Historical Analysis* (London, 1979), p. 63.
13. Peter Winzen, 'Treitschke's Influence on the Rise of Imperialist and Anti-British Nationalism in Germany', in Paul Kennedy and Anthony Nicholls (eds), *Nationalist and Racialist Movements in Germany before 1914* (London, 1981), p. 159.
14. Eugen Wolf, *Vom Fürsten Bismarck* (Leipzig, 1904), p. 16.
15. Ernst von Weber, *Die Erweiterung des deutschen Wirtschaftsgebiets und die Grundlegung zu überseeischen Staaten* (Leipzig, 1878).
16. A. J. P. Taylor, *Germany's First Bid for Colonies, 1884–1885* (London, 1938), p. 6; Wolfgang J. Mommsen, 'Bismarck, the Concert of Europe, and the Future of West Africa, 1883–1885', in Stig Förster, Wolfgang J. Mommsen and Ronald Robinson (eds), *Bismarck, Europe and Africa: The Berlin Africa Conference 1884–1885 and the Onset of Partition* (Oxford, 1988), pp. 152–3.
17. Ibid., p. 169.
18. H. Pogge von Strandmann, 'Domestic Origins of Germany's Colonial Expansion under Bismarck', *Past and Present*, XLII (1969), 140–59.
19. Holstein, diary entry, 13 December 1884. *HP*, II, p. 169.
20. Axel T. Riehl, *Der 'Tanz um der Äquator'. Bismarcks anti-englische Kolonialpolitik und die Erwartung des Thronwechsels in Deutschland 1883–1885* (Berlin, 1993).
21. Holstein, diary entry, 19 September 1884. *HP*, II, p. 161.
22. Eyck, *Bismarck*, p. 275.
23. Hans-Ulrich Wehler, 'Bismarck's Imperialism, 1862–1890', in James J. Sheehan (ed.), *Imperial Germany* (New York, 1976), pp. 180–222.
24. Ibid., p. 212.
25. Wehler, *German Empire*, pp. 171–6.

26. Mary E. Townsend, *Origins of Modern German Colonialism, 1871–1885* (New York, 1921).
27. Bismarck's speech to the Reichstag, 28 November 1885. Otto Pflanze, *Bismarck and the Development of Germany* (Princeton, 1990), III, p. 133.

4 The Change of Regime

1. Holstein, diary entry, 27 March 1888. *HP*, II, pp. 365–6.
2. Crown Princess Victoria to Queen Victoria, 11 December 1880. Roger Fulford (ed.), *Beloved Mama. Private Corrrespondence of Queen Victoria and the German Crown Princess 1878–1885* (London, 1981), p. 94.
3. Holstein, diary entry, 16 April 1885. *HP*, II, pp. 190–1.
4. Bismarck to Wilhelm I, 30 September 1886. Ibid., p. 388.
5. Thomas A. Kohut, *Wilhelm II and the Germans. A Study in Leadership* (New York and Oxford, 1991), p. 28.
6. Holstein, diary entry, 6 May 1885. *HP*, II, p. 195.
7. Hugo Baron von Reischach, *Under Three Emperors* (London, 1927), p. 91.
8. Holstein, diary entry, 5 July 1885. *HP*, II, p. 212.
9. Holstein, diary entry, 12 April 1885. Ibid., p. 190.
10. Crown Princess Victoria to Queen Victoria, 5 August 1880. Fulford, *Beloved Mama*, p. 85.
11. Crown Princess Victoria to Queen Victoria, 7 March 1887. Agatha Ramm (ed.), *Beloved and Darling Child. Last Letters of Queen Victoria and her Eldest Daughter 1886–1901* (Stroud, 1990), pp. 45–6.
12. *EK*, I, p. 225.
13. Alexander III cited in letter of Otto von Bismarck to Prince Wilhelm of Prussia, 23 May 1884. GStA Berlin BPH Rep. 53/133.
14. Prince Wilhelm to Tsar Alexander III, 25 May 1884. GStA Berlin BPH Rep. 53/11.
15. John C. G. Röhl, *Young Wilhelm: The Kaiser's Early Life, 1859–1888* (Cambridge, 1998), p. 541.
16. Prince Wilhelm to Tsar Alexander III, 19 June 1884 and 13 March 1885. GStA Berlin BPH Rep. 53/12–13.
17. Tsar Alexander III to Prince Wilhelm, 7/19 May 1885. GStA Berlin HA Rep. 53 J Lit. R Nr. 6.
18. Holstein, diary entry, 17 August 1886. *HP*, II, pp. 296–7.
19. Herbert von Bismarck to Rosebery, 28 March 1888. Rosebery Papers, National Library of Scotland, Edinburgh, MS 10004.
20. Holstein, diary entry, 15 May 1888. *HP*, II, p. 376.
21. The Empress Frederick to Queen Victoria, 12 May 1888. Ramm, *Beloved and Darling Child*, p. 70.
22. Kaiserin Friedrich to Wilhelm II, 7 November 1888. GStA Berlin HA Rep. 52 T Nr. 13.
23. Holstein, diary entry, 9 November 1887. *HP*, II, p. 356.
24. Holstein, diary entry, 15 May 1888. Ibid., p. 377.
25. Michael Balfour, *The Kaiser and his Times* (London, 1964), p. 146.
26. Sir John Wheeler-Bennett, *Three Episodes in the Life of Kaiser Wilhelm II* (Cambridge, 1956), p. 19.

27. Alan Clark (ed.), *'A Good Innings'. The Private Papers of Viscount Lee of Fareham* (London, 1974), p. 116.

28. Wilfrid Scawen Blunt, diary entry, 9 February 1911, in his *My Diaries. Being a Personal Narrative of Events 1888–1914* (2 vols, London, 1919–20), II, p. 352.

29. Aufzeichnungen Seiner Majestät Kaiser Wilhelms II, Haus Doorn, 28 March 1927. GStA Berlin BPH 53/165.

30. John C. G. Röhl, 'The Emperor's New Clothes: a Character Sketch of Kaiser Wilhelm II', in John C. G. Röhl and Nicolaus Sombart (eds), *Kaiser Wilhelm II. New Interpretations* (Cambridge, 1982), p. 33.

31. Wilhelm II's marginalia on Monts to Bülow, 20 October 1903. PA Russland Nr. 82 Nr. 1 Bd. 50.

32. King Albert of Saxony quoted in letter of Holstein to Hatzfeldt, 14 April 1897. *HP*, IV, p. 28.

33. Holstein, diary entry, 11 November 1888. *HP*, II, p. 382.

34. John C. G. Röhl, 'A Document of 1892 on Germany, Prussia and Poland', *Historical Journal*, VII (1964), 144.

35. Wilhelm II to Alfred Niemann, 24 December 1940. Willibald Gutsche, 'Illusionen des ExKaisers: Dokumente aus dem letzten Lebensjahr Kaiser Wilhelms II. 1940/41', *Zeitschrift für Geschichtswissenschaft*, X (1991), 1032–4.

36. Bülow to Wilhelm II, 19 August 1898. GStA Berlin HA Rep. 53 J. Lit. B. Nr. 16a Vol. I.

37. Stern, *Gold and Iron*, p. 11.

38. Gall, *Bismarck*, II, p. 196.

39. John C. G. Röhl, 'The Disintegration of the Kartell and the Politics of Bismarck's Fall from Power, 1887–90', *Historical Journal*, IX (1966), 73, 76–7.

40. Balfour, *The Kaiser and his Times*, p. 130.

41. Gall, *Bismarck*, II, p. 207.

42. Robert Lucius quoted in Norman Rich, *Friedrich von Holstein* (2 vols, Cambridge, 1965), I, p. 268.

43. Anton Graf von Monts, *Erinnerungen und Gedanken des Botschafters Anton Graf Monts*, edited by K. Nowak and F. Thimme (Berlin, 1932), p. 287.

44. H. W. Koch, *A Constitutional History of Germany in the Nineteenth and Twentieth Centuries* (London, 1984), p. 123.

45. Blackbourn and Eley, *Peculiarities*, p. 276.

46. Gordon A. Craig, *Germany 1866–1945* (Oxford, 1981), pp. 178–9.

47. John C. G. Röhl, *Germany without Bismarck* (London, 1967), p. 17.

48. Gall, *Bismarck*, II, p. 233.

49. Stern, *Gold and Iron*, p. 437.

50. Wehler, *German Empire*, p. 25.

51. Mommsen, *Imperial Germany*, p. 143.

52. Helmut Böhme, *An Introduction to the Social and Economic History of Germany: Political and Economic Change in the 19th and 20th Centuries* (New York and Oxford, 1978), p. 83.

53. Mommsen, *Imperial Germany*, p. 147.

54. Koch, *Constitutional History*, p. 123.

55. Golo Mann, *A History of Germany since 1789* (London, 1968), p. 219.

56. Blackbourn, *The Fontana History of Germany*, p. 401.

57. Arthur Rosenberg, *The Birth of the German Republic* (Oxford, 1931), p. 3.

5 Domestic Politics under Wilhelm II

1. J. Alden Nichols, *Germany after Bismarck: The Caprivi Era 1890–1894* (Cambridge, Mass., 1958), pp. 43 and 46.
2. Ibid., p. 68.
3. Röhl, *Germany without Bismarck*, pp. 57–9.
4. Nichols, *Germany*, p. 44.
5. Alexander Gerschenkron, *Bread and Democracy in Germany* (Berkeley, 1943); Hans-Jürgen Puhle, *Agrarische Interessenpolitik und preußischer Konservatismus im wilhelminischen Reich 1893–1914* (Hanover, 1967).
6. Ian Farr, 'Populism in the Countryside: The Peasant Leagues in Bavaria in the 1890s', in Richard J. Evans (ed.), *Society and Politics in Wilhelmine Germany* (London and New York, 1978).
7. James N. Retallack, *Notables of the Right: The Conservative Party and Political Mobilization in Germany 1876–1918* (London, 1988), p. 102.
8. Geoff Eley, 'Anti-Semitism, Agrarian Mobilization, and the Conservative Party: Radicalism and Containment in the Founding of the Agrarian League, 1890–93', in Larry Eugene Jones and James N. Retallack (eds), *Between Reform, Reaction and Resistance: Studies in the History of German Conservatism from 1789 to 1945* (Oxford, 1993).
9. David Blackbourn, 'The Politics of Demagogy in Imperial Germany', *Past and Present*, CXIII (1986), 153.
10. Eley, 'Anti-Semitism', p. 217.
11. Röhl, *Germany without Bismarck*, pp. 57–8.
12. Roger Chickering, *We Men Who Feel Most German: A Cultural Study of the Pan-German League, 1886–1914* (London, 1984), p. 74.
13. Konrad H. Jarausch, 'The Illusion of Limited War: Chancellor Bethmann Hollweg's Calculated Risk, July 1914', *Central European History*, II (1969), 53.
14. Sir Edward Goschen to Sir Edward Grey, 21 January 1910. PRO: FO 371/900, f261.
15. B. Sösemann (ed.), *Theodor Wolff: Tagebücher 1914–1919* (Boppard am Rhein, 1984), I, p. 156.
16. Geoff Eley, 'The Wilhelmine Right: How it Changed', in Evans, *Society and Politics*, p. 124.
17. John C. G. Röhl, *The Kaiser and his Court. Wilhelm II and the Government of Germany* (Cambridge, 1994), pp. 107–30.
18. Holstein to Eulenburg, 17 February 1895. *EK*, III, p. 1472.
19. Anton Count Monts to Eulenburg, 20/21 March 1897. Ibid., III, p.1805.
20. Eulenburg to Holstein, 2 December 1894. Isabel V. Hull, *The Entourage of Kaiser Wilhelm II 1888–1918* (Cambridge, 1982), p. 83.
21. Holstein to Eulenburg, 21 December 1895. *HP*, III, p. 578.
22. Holstein to Bülow, 30 July 1900. *HP*, IV, p. 190.
23. Wilhelm II to Eulenburg, 25 December 1895. Röhl, *Germany without Bismarck*, p. 158.
24. Bülow to Eulenburg, 23 July 1896. *EK*, III, p. 1714.
25. Bülow to Eulenburg, 15 February 1898. Ibid., p. 1885.
26. Eulenburg to Bülow, 24 July 1901. Katharine A. Lerman, 'The Decisive Relationship: Kaiser Wilhelm II and Chancellor Bernhard von Bülow, 1900–1905', in Röhl and Sombart, *Kaiser Wilhelm II*, p. 241.

27. Katharine A. Lerman, *The Chancellor as Courtier. Bernhard von Bülow and the Governance of Germany 1900–1909* (Cambridge, 1990), p. 77.
28. Zedlitz, diary entry, 29 November 1903.
    Robert von Zedlitz-Trützschler, *Twelve Years at the Imperial German Court* (London, 1924), pp. 50–1.
29. Spitzemberg, diary entry, 15 April 1904. R. Vierhaus (ed.), *Das Tagebuch der Baronin von Spitzemberg 1859–1914* (Göttingen, 1960), p. 439.
30. Holstein to Eulenburg, 27 November 1894. *EK*, II, p. 1414.
31. Sir Frank Lascelles, General Report on Germany for 1906. *BD*, II, p. 433.
32. Harden to Holstein, 20 June 1907. *HP*, IV, p. 485.
33. Harden to Holstein, 7 May 1907. Ibid., p. 470.
34. Holstein to Eulenburg, 1 May 1906. Ibid., p. 419.
35. Walther Rathenau, diary entry, 20 October 1911. Hartmut Pogge von Strandmann (ed.), *Walther Rathenau. Industrialist, Banker, Intellectual, and Politician. Notes and Diaries 1907–1922* (Oxford, 1985), p. 135.
36. Princess Radziwill to General di Robilant, 20 July 1908. Cyril Spencer Fox (ed.), *This was Germany. An Observer at the Court of Berlin. Letters of Princess Marie Radziwill to General di Robilant 1908–1915* (London, 1937), p. 37.
37. Lucanus to Wilhelm II, 6 February 1907. GStA Berlin HA Rep. 53 J Lit. L Nr. 12.
38. Zedlitz, diary entry, 18 December 1907. Zedlitz, *Twelve Years*, p. 211.
39. Sir Edward Goschen to Sir Charles Hardinge, 26 February 1909. Hardinge Papers, University Library, Cambridge, Vol. 15.
40. Wilhelm II to Colonel Stuart-Wortley, 15 October 1908. Lamar Cecil, *Wilhelm II. Emperor and Exile, 1900–1941* (Chapel Hill, NC, and London, 1996), pp. 134–5.
41. *HP*, I, p. 207.
42. Jenisch to Wilhelm II, 15 October 1908. GStA Berlin BPH Rep. 53/231.
43. Findlay to Hardinge, 11 November 1908. Hardinge Papers, Vol. 11.
44. Findlay to Hardinge, 8 December 1908. Ibid.
45. Wilhelm II to Bülow, 19 November 1908. GStA Berlin Bestand 2.2.1. Geheimes Zivilkabinett Nr. 685.
46. Bülow to Wilhelm II, 20 November 1908. Ibid.
47. Report of Bavarian envoy in Berlin, Hugo von Lerchenfeld-Köfering, 19 November 1908. Lerman, *The Chancellor as Courtier*, p. 225.
48. Goschen to Hardinge, 3 February 1909. Hardinge Papers, Vol. 15.
49. Zedlitz, diary entry, 30 November 1908. Zedlitz, *Twelve Years*, p. 228.
50. Zedlitz, diary entry, 4 March 1910. Ibid., p. 280.
51. Rathenau, diary entry, 2 June 1911. Pogge, *Rathenau: Notes and Diaries*, p. 127.
52. Bethmann Hollweg quoted in Konrad H. Jarausch, *The Enigmatic Chancellor. Bethmann Hollweg and the Hubris of Imperial Germany* (New Haven, Conn., and London, 1973), p. 85.
53. Sir Maurice de Bunsen to Sir Arthur Nicolson, 19 December 1913. *BD*, XII, pp. 728–9.
54. Crown Prince Wilhelm of Prussia to Wilhelm II, 1 January 1912. GStA Berlin HA Rep. 54/57.
55. Goschen to Nicolson, 15 May 1914. *BD*, XII, p. 744.
56. Spitzemberg, diary entry, 6 December 1913. Vierhaus, *Das Tagebuch der Baronin von Spitzemberg*, p. 564.
57. Müller, diary entry, 8 December 1912. Röhl, *The Kaiser and his Court*, p. 162.

6　External Policies under Wilhelm II

1. Röhl, *Germany without Bismarck*, p. 64.
2. Nichols, *Germany after Bismarck*, p. 54.
3. Lamar Cecil, *The German Diplomatic Service* (Princeton, 1976), p. 259.
4. Baron von Eckardstein, *Ten Years at the Court of St. James' 1895–1905* (London, 1921), p. 162.
5. Martin Gosselin to the Earl of Kimberley, 25 November 1894. PRO: FO 244/512.
6. Sir Edward Malet to Lord Rosebery, 9 December 1893. Malet Papers, PRO: FO 343/13.
7. Pauline R. Anderson, *The Background to Anti-English Feeling in Germany, 1890–1902* (New York, 1969), p. 228.
8. The argument here closely follows Matthew S. Seligmann, *Rivalry in Southern Africa 1893–99: The Transformation of German Colonial Policy* (Basingstoke, 1998).
9. Johann von Bernstorff, *Erinnerungen und Briefe* (Zurich, 1936), p. 30.
10. Graf von Hatzfeldt to Friedrich von Holstein, 21 January 1896. *GP*, XI, p. 53.
11. Graf von Hatzfeldt to Fürst zu Hohenlohe, 22 April 1897. *GP*, XIII, p. 16.
12. Graf von Hatzfeldt to Friedrich von Holstein, 22 April 1897. *HP*, IV, p. 29.
13. Röhl, *Germany without Bismarck*, p. 166.
14. Graf von Dönhoff to Fürst zu Hohenlohe, 6 January 1896. PA Afrika Generalia Nr. 13 Bd.1.
15. Volker Berghahn, 'On the Societal Function of Wilhelmine Armaments Policy', in Iggers, *Social History of Politics*, p. 163.
16. W. G. Runciman (ed.), *Max Weber: Selections in Translation* (Cambridge, 1978), p. 266.
17. J. C. G. Röhl, *From Bismarck to Hitler: The Problem of Continuity in German History* (London, 1970), p. 59.
18. Paul M. Kennedy, *The Rise of the Anglo-German Antagonism* (London, 1980), p. 311.
19. Spitzemberg, diary entry, 15 January 1896. Vierhaus, *Spitzemberg: Tagebuch*, p. 341.
20. Kaiserin Friedrich to Wilhelm II, 29 May 1898. GStA Berlin HA Rep. 52 T Nr. 13.
21. Wilhelm II to Kaiserin Friedrich, 1 June 1898. *HP*, IV, p. 83.
22. Wilhelm II to Nicholas II, 2 January 1896. W. Goetz (ed.), *Briefe Kaiser Wilhelms II. an den Zaren 1894–1914* (Berlin, 1920), p. 301.
23. Holstein to Hatzfeldt, 22 January 1896. Gerhard Ebel (ed.), *Botschafter Paul Graf von Hatzfeldt: Nachgelassene Papiere 1838–1901* (2 vols, Boppard am Rhein, 1976), II, p. 1069.
24. Holstein to Hatzfeldt, 14 April 1897. *HP*, IV, pp. 27, 28.
25. Alfred von Tirpitz, *My Memoirs* (2 vols, London, 1920), I, p. 156.
26. V. R. Berghahn, *Germany and the Approach of War in 1914* (2nd edn, London, 1993), p. 42.
27. Geoff Eley, *From Unification to Nazism. Reinterpreting the German Past* (Boston, 1986), p. 121.
28. Max Weber. Ibid., p. 127.
29. Wilhelm II quoted in Metternich to the German Foreign Office, 9 November 1902. PA, Deutschland Nr.138 Geheim Bd. 5.
30. Tirpitz to Grand Duke Friedrich I of Baden, 31 March 1903. Walther P. Fuchs (ed.), *Grossherzog Friedrich I. von Baden und die Reichspolitik 1871–1907* (4 vols, Stuttgart, 1968–80), IV, p. 499.
31. Wilhelm II to Excellenz von Budde, 15 August 1905. PA, England No. 78 Bd. 31.

32. Bülow to Wilhelm II, 6 August 1900. GStA Berlin HA Rep. 53 J Lit. B Nr. 16a. Bd. 1.
33. Spitzemberg, diary entry, 14 March 1903. Vierhaus, *Spitzemberg: Tagebuch*, p. 428.
34. Holstein, diary entry, 14 December 1907. *HP*, IV, p. 509.
35. Wilhelm II to Bülow, 12 November 1902. *GP*, XVII, p. 117.
36. Wilhelm II's comment on report of Metternich to Bülow, 3 March 1909. *GP*, XXVIII, p. 99.
37. Alfred von Kiderlen-Wächter to Hedwig Kypke, 31 January 1911. Ernst Jäckh (ed.), *Kiderlen-Wächter der Staatsmann und Mensch. Briefwechsel und Nachlass* (2 vols, Stuttgart, Berlin and Leipzig, 1924), I, p. 79.
38. Spitzemberg, diary entry, 29 September 1912. Vierhaus, *Spitzemberg. Tagebuch*, p. 548.
39. Haldane to Elizabeth Haldane, 8 March 1912. Haldane Papers, National Library of Scotland, Edinburgh. MS. 6011.
40. Bülow to Wilhelm II, 8 November 1899. GStA Berlin HA Rep. 53 J Lit. B Nr. 16a Bd. 1.
41. Prince Lichnowsky to Kaiser Wilhelm II, 11 August 1914. GStA Berlin HA Rep. 53 J Lit. L Nr. 5.
42. Lamar Cecil, 'History as Family Chronicle: Kaiser Wilhelm II and the Dynastic Roots of the Anglo-German Antagonism', in Röhl and Sombart, *Kaiser Wilhelm*, pp. 101–4.
43. Roger Chickering, 'Patriotic Societies and German Foreign Policy, 1890–1914', *International History Review*, I (1979), 470–89.
44. Winzen, 'Treitschke's Influence', pp. 154–70.
45. Tirpitz, *My Memoirs*, I, pp. 189–91, 200–2, 204–6.
46. Aaron Friedberg, *The Weary Titan. Britain and the Experience of Relative Decline, 1895–1905* (Princeton, NJ, 1988).
47. Viscount Esher to Maurice Brett, 6 September 1906 in Maurice V. Brett (ed.), *The Journals and Letters of Reginald, Viscount Esher* (4 vols, London, 1934–38), II, p. 183.
48. Stumm to Bülow, 8 September 1908. PA England Nr. 87 Bd. 66.
49. Metternich to Bülow, 21 February 1902. *HP*, IV, pp. 253–4.
50. Roderick R. McLean, 'Monarchy and Diplomacy in Europe, 1900–1910' (D.Phil dissertation, University of Sussex, 1996), Chs 1 and 2.
51. Wilhelm II's comment on Lichnowsky to the German Foreign Office, 29 July 1914. Max Montgelas and Walther Schücking (eds), *Outbreak of the World War. German Documents Collected by Karl Kautsky* (New York, 1924), p. 322.
52. Holger H. Herwig, 'Clio Deceived. Patriotic Self-Censorship in Germany after the Great War', *International Security*, XII, 2 (1987), 5–44.
53. Schöllgen, *Escape into War?*
54. Berghahn, *Germany and the Approach of War.*
55. David Kaiser, 'Germany and the Origins of the First World War', *Journal of Modern History*, LV (1983), 442–74; Niall Ferguson, 'Public Finance and National Security: The Domestic Origins of the First World War Revisited', *Past and Present*, CXLII (1994), 725–52.
56. Fritz Fischer, 'Twenty-Five Years Later: Looking Back at the "Fischer Controversy" and Its Consequences', *Central European History*, XXI (1988), 207–23; Röhl, *The Kaiser and his Court*, pp. 162–89; John C. G. Röhl, 'Germany', in Keith M. Wilson (ed.), *Decisions for War 1914* (London, 1995), pp. 27–54.

57. Wolfgang Mommsen, 'The Topos of Inevitable War in Germany in the Decade before 1914', in V. R. Berghahn and Martin Kitchen (eds), *Germany in the Age of Total War* (London, 1981), pp. 23–45.

58. Friedrich von Bernhardi, *Germany and the Next War* (London, 1914), esp. pp. 103–6.

59. Bernhard von Bülow to Philipp Eulenburg, 7 February 1895. *EK*, II, pp. 1454–5.

60. Lerchenfeld to Hertling, 4 June 1914. Ernst Deuerlein (ed.), *Briefwechsel Hertling–Lerchenfeld* (2 vols, Boppard am Rhein, 1973), I, p. 297.

61. Wilhelm II to Archduke Franz Ferdinand of Austria-Hungary, 26 February 1913. Robert Kann, 'Emperor William II and Archduke Francis Ferdinand in Their Correspondence', *American Historical Review*, LVII (1952), 345–6.

62. Bülow to Wilhelm II, 19 April 1908. GStaA Berlin HA Rep. 53 J Lit. B Nr. 16a Bd. IV.

63. Berchtold's report on an audience with Wilhelm II, 28 October 1913. Ludwig Bittner and Hans Uebersberger (eds), *Österreich-Ungarns Aussenpolitik von der Bosnischen Krise 1908 bis zum Kriegsausbruch 1918* (8 vols, Vienna and Leipzig, 1930), VII, p. 515.

64. Norman Stone, 'Moltke-Conrad: Relations between the Austro-Hungarian and German General Staffs 1909–14', *Historical Journal*, IX (1966), 201–28.

65. Riezler, diary entry, 7 July 1914. Quoted in Karl Dietrich Erdmann (ed.), *Kurt Riezler. Tagebücher-Aufsätze-Dokumente* (Göttingen, 1972), p.183.

66. Fritz Fischer, *War of Illusions. German Policies from 1911 to 1914* (London, 1975), p. 471.

67. Matthew S. Seligmann, 'Germany and the Origins of the First World War in the Eyes of the American Diplomatic Establishment', *German History*, XV (1997), 320.

68. Stig Förster, 'Der deutsche Generalstab und die Illusion des kurzen Krieges, 1871–1914. Metakritik eines Mythos', *Militärgeschichtliche Mitteilungen*, LIV (1995), 61–95.

69. Röhl, *The Kaiser and his Court*, pp. 162–89.

70. Mommsen, 'Topos of Inevitable War', esp. pp. 33–4.

71. Röhl, 'Germany', pp. 44–6.

72. Ulrich Trumpener, 'War Premeditated? German Intelligence Operations in July 1914', *Central European History*, IX (1976), 58–85.

73. Goschen diary, 29 June 1914. C. H. D. Howard (ed.), *The Diary of Edward Goschen 1900–1914* (London, 1980), p. 289.

74. Konrad Jarausch, 'The Illusion of Limited War: Chancellor Bethmann Hollweg's Calculated Risk, July 1914', *Central European History*, II (1969), 48–76.

75. Bethmann Hollweg to Crown Prince Wilhelm of Prussia, 17 July 1914. Röhl, 'Germany', pp. 37–8.

7 Wilhelmine Germany at War

1. Graydon A. Turnstall, Jr, *Planning for War against Russia and Serbia: Austro-Hungarian Military Strategies, 1871–1914* (New York, 1993), p. 11.

2. Dennis E. Showalter, 'The Eastern Front and German Military Planning, 1871–1914 – Some Observations', *East European Quarterly*, XV (1981), 175.

3. Marc Trachtenberg, 'The Meaning of Mobilization in 1914', in Steven E. Miller, Sean M. Lynn-Jones and Steven Van Evera (eds), *Military Strategy and the Origins of the First World War* (Princeton, 1991), pp. 215ff.

4. Annika Mombauer, 'Helmuth von Moltke and the German General Staff – Military and Political Decision-Making in Imperial Germany, 1906-1916' (Doctoral Dissertation, University of Sussex, 1997), pp. 137–40, 202.

5. Fritz Fischer, *From Kaiserreich to Third Reich: Elements of Continuity in German History 1871–1945* (London and New York, 1986), pp. 56–60.

6. Colmar von der Goltz, *The Nation in Arms* (London, 1906), p. 187.

7. Quoted in Jehuda L. Wallach, *The Dogma of the Battle of Annihilation: The Theories of Clausewitz and Schlieffen and Their Impact on the German Conduct of Two World Wars* (Westport, 1986), p. 54.

8. Gerhard Ritter, *The Schlieffen Plan: Critique of a Myth* (London, 1958), p. 49.

9. Carl von Clausewitz, *On War* (London, 1968), pp. 164–7.

10. Ibid., p. 66.

11. L. L. Farrar, Jr, *The Short War Illusion: German Policy, Strategy and Domestic Affairs August–December 1914* (Oxford, 1973).

12. Craig, *Politics of the Prussian Army*, p. 281.

13. Stig Förster, 'Der deutsche Generalstab und die Illusion des kurzen Krieges', pp. 61–95.

14. Ibid.,p. 66.

15. Ibid., pp 83–90.

16. Jack Snyder, 'Civil–Military Relations and the Cult of the Offensive, 1914 and 1984', in Miller, Lynn-Jones and Van Evera, *Military Strategy*, p. 29.

17. Craig, *Politics of the Prussian Army*, p. 280.

18. Wallach, *Dogma of the Battle of Annihilation*, p. 89.

19. Arden Bucholz, *Moltke, Schlieffen and Prussian War Planning* (Oxford, 1991), pp. 266–7.

20. L. C. F. Turner, 'The Significance of the Schlieffen Plan', in Paul M. Kennedy (ed.), *The War Plans of the Great Powers, 1880–1914* (London, 1979), pp. 212–13.

21. Wallach, *The Dogma of the Battle of Annihilation*, p. 93; J. F. C. Fuller, *The Decisive Battles of the Western World* (London, 1956), III, p. 195.

22. For the former view, see Turner, 'The Significance', pp. 212–13; for the latter view, see Farrar, *Short War Illusion*, pp. 13–14.

23. Holger H. Herwig, *The First World War: Germany and Austria-Hungary 1914–1918* (London, 1997), p. 27.

24. Wehler, *German Empire*, p. 199.

25. Gerald. D. Feldman, *Army, Industry and Labor in Germany 1914–1918* (Leamington Spa, 1992), p. 135.

26. Ibid., p. 45.

27. Lothar Burchardt, 'The Impact of the War Economy of the Civilian Population of Germany during the First and Second World Wars', in Wilhelm Deist (ed.), *The German Military in the Age of Total War* (Leamington Spa, 1985), p. 45.

28. Jürgen Kocka, *Facing Total War: German Society 1914–1918* (Leamington Spa, 1984), pp. 16–26.

29. Matthew Seligmann, 'World War One and the Undermining of the German–Jewish Identity as Seen through American Diplomatic Documents', in Bertrand Taithe and Tim Thornton (eds), *War: Identities in Conflict 1300–2000* (Stroud, 1998), p. 199.

30. Herwig, *First World War*, p. 196.

31. Martin Kitchen, *The Silent Dictatorship. The Politics of the German High Command under Hindenburg and Ludendorff, 1916–18* (London, 1976).

32. Rathenau's notes on his First Talk with General Ludendorff, 16 February 1917. Pogge, *Walther Rathenau*, p. 218.
33. Colonel Bauer in December 1916. Hull, *Entourage of Kaiser Wilhelm*, p. 269.
34. Müller, diary entry, 6 November 1914. Walther Görlitz (ed.), *The Kaiser and his Court. The Diaries, Note Books and Letters of Admiral Georg Alexander von Müller Chief of the Naval Cabinet, 1914–1918* (New York, 1964), p. 42.
35. Holger Afflerbach, 'Wilhelm II as Supreme Warlord in the First World War', *War in History*, V (1998), 427–49.
36. Diary of Imperial adjutant general Hans von Plessen, 10 January 1916. Ibid., p. 439.
37. Kurt Riezler, diary entry, 11 July 1915. Erdmann, *Riezler: Tagebücher*, p. 283.
38. Wild von Hohenborn, diary entry, 11 December 1915. Herwig, *First World War*, p. 182.
39. Müller to Valentini, 30 March 1918. Kitchen, *Silent Dictatorship*, p. 174.
40. Riezler, diary entry, 22 November 1916. Erdmann, *Riezler: Tagebücher*, p. 383.
41. Bethmann Hollweg to Valentini, 9 December 1915. Jarausch, *Enigmatic Chancellor*, p. 213.
42. Bauer quoted by Kitchen, *Silent Dictatorship*, p. 38.
43. Herwig, *First World War*, p. 378.
44. Princess Blücher, diary entry, January 1917. Evelyn Princess Blücher, *An English Wife at Berlin. A Private Memoir of Events, Politics, and Daily Life in Germany throughout the War and Social Revolution of 1918* (London, 1920), p. 159.
45. Herwig, *First World War*, p. 264.
46. Monthly Report, 17 January 1917. Kocka, *Facing Total War*, p. 41.
47. Riezler, diary entry, 25 March 1917. Erdmann, *Riezler: Tagebücher*, p. 420.
48. Müller, diary entry, 5 April 1917. Görlitz, *The Kaiser*, p. 254.
49. Riezler, diary entry, 14 July 1917. Erdmann, *Riezler: Tagebücher*, p. 444.
50. Kitchen, *Silent Dictatorship*, p. 130.
51. Riezler, diary entry, 14 July 1917. Erdmann, *Riezler: Tagebücher*, p. 444.
52. Riezler, diary entry, 9 June 1917. Ibid., p. 436.
53. Ambassador zu Hohenlohe to Foreign Minister Czernin, 4 February 1918. Herwig, *First World War*, p. 379.
54. Monthly Bulletin, 3 August 1918. Kocka, *Facing Total War*, p. 53.
55. Riezler, diary entry, 15 April 1918. Erdmann, *Riezler: Tagebücher*, p. 460.
56. Müller, diary entry, 26 March 1918. Görlitz, *The Kaiser*, p. 345.
57. Princess Blücher, diary entry, September 1918. Blücher, *An English Wife*, p. 245.
58. Bavarian military plenipotentiary's report, 7 October 1918. Kitchen, *Silent Dictatorship*, p. 259.
59. Princess Blücher, diary entry, 9 November 1918. Blücher, *An English Wife*, p. 279.
60. Müller, diary entry, 29 September 1918. Görlitz, *The Kaiser*, p. 398.

SUGGESTED READING

Details of the books and articles which are most useful for individual chapters can be found in the notes; however, good general books on the history of modern Germany include: David Blackbourn, *The Fontana History of Germany. The Long Nineteenth Century* (London, 1997), William Carr, *A History of Germany 1815–1945*, 3rd edn (London, 1987), Gordon A. Craig, *Germany 1866–1945* (Oxford, 1981), David Blackbourn and Geoff Eley, *The Peculiarities of German History* (Oxford, 1984), and Gordon Martel (ed.), *Modern Germany Reconsidered 1870–1945* (London, 1992). On the Imperial era as a whole, there are: Hans-Ulrich Wehler, *The German Empire, 1871–1918* (Leamington Spa, 1985) and V. R. Berghahn, *Imperial Germany 1871–1914* (Providence, RI, and Oxford, 1994). Useful essay collections include: David Blackbourn, *Populists and Patricians* (London, 1987), Geoff Eley, *From Unification to Nazism* (Boston, Mass., 1986), Wolfgang J. Mommsen, *Imperial Germany 1867–1918* (London, 1995) and James J. Sheehan (ed.), *Imperial Germany* (New York, 1976).

On Bismarckian Germany, some of the main works in English are: Theodor S. Hamerow, *The Social Foundations of German Unification*, 2 vols (Princeton, 1969–72), Otto Pflanze, *Bismarck and the Development of Germany*, 3 vols (Princeton, NJ, 1990), Fritz Stern, *Gold and Iron* (London, 1977), Lothar Gall, *Bismarck. The White Revolutionary*, 2 vols (London, 1986), Erich Eyck, *Bismarck and the German Empire* (London, 1950), A. J. P. Taylor, *Bismarck. The Man and the Statesman* (London, 1955) and W. M. Simon, *Germany in the Age of Bismarck* (London, 1967). Interesting new insights into Bismarck's diplomacy can be found in Karina Urbach, *Bismarck's Favourite Englishman. Lord Odo Russell's Mission to Berlin* (London and New York, 1999).

On Wilhelmine Germany, useful books include: Richard Evans (ed.), *Society and Politics in Wilhelmine Germany* (London, 1978), James Retallack, *Germany in the Age of Kaiser Wilhelm II* (Basingstoke, 1996) and John C. G. Röhl, *The Kaiser and his Court* (Cambridge, 1994). On the Caprivi era, there is J. Alden Nichols, *Germany after Bismarck* (Cambridge, Mass., 1958), and on politics in general the following are indispensable: John C. G. Röhl, *Germany without Bismarck* (London, 1967), Isabel V. Hull, *The Entourage of Kaiser Wilhelm II, 1888–1918* (Cambridge, 1982), Katherine A. Lerman, *The Chancellor as Courtier* (Cambridge, 1990), Geoff Eley, *Reshaping the German Right* (New Haven, Conn., 1980) and Konrad Jarausch, *The Enigmatic Chancellor. Bethmann Hollweg and the Hubris of Imperial Germany* (New Haven, Conn., 1973). On Wilhelm II himself, see: John C. G. Röhl, *Young Wilhelm. The Kaiser's Early Life, 1859–1888* (Cambridge, 1998), John C. G. Röhl and Nicolaus Sombart (eds), *Kaiser Wilhelm II. New Interpretations* (Cambridge, 1982), Lamar J. R. Cecil, *Wilhelm II*, 2 vols (Chapel Hill, NC, 1989–96) and Michael Balfour, *The Kaiser and his Times* (London, 1964).

Developments in foreign policy can be followed in: Imanuel Geiss, *German Foreign Policy 1871–1914* (London, 1976), Gregor Schöllgen (ed.), *Escape into War? The Foreign*

Policy of Imperial Germany (Oxford, 1990) and Norman Rich, *Friedrich von Holstein*, 2 vols (Cambridge, 1965). Germany's relations with Britain are covered in Paul M. Kennedy, *The Rise of the Anglo-German Antagonism* (London, 1980). On military affairs, see: L. L. Farrar, *The Short War Illusion* (Santa Barbara, Calif., 1973), Gordon A. Craig, *The Politics of the Prussian Army* (New York, 1964), Gerhard Ritter, *The Sword and the Sceptre* (London, 1971–74), Gerhard Ritter, *The Schlieffen Plan* (London, 1958) and Arden Bucholz, *Moltke, Schlieffen and Prussian War Planning* (Leamington Spa, 1990). Interesting material can also be found in David Stevenson, *Armaments and the Coming of War: Europe 1904–1914* (Oxford, 1996).

On Germany's role in the origins of the First World War, the key works are: V. R. Berghahn, *Germany and the Approach of War in 1914*, 2nd edn (London, 1993), Fritz Fischer, *War of Illusions. German Policies from 1911 to 1914* (London, 1975), John C. G. Röhl's essay on Germany in *Decisions for War 1914*, Keith M. Wilson (ed.), (London, 1995), and Imanuel Geiss (ed.), *July 1914* (London, 1967). Good books on the war itself include: Holger Herwig, *The First World War. Germany and Austria-Hungary* (London, 1997), Roger Chickering, *Imperial Germany and the Great War, 1914–1918* (Cambridge, 1998), Fritz Fischer, *Germany's Aims in the First World War* (London, 1967), Martin Kitchen, *The Silent Dictatorship* (London, 1976), G.ʹ D. Feldman, *Army, Industry and Labor in Germany, 1914–1918* (Princeton, NJ, 1966) and Jürgen Kocka, *Facing Total War. German Society 1914–1918* (Leamington Spa, 1984).

INDEX